Post-Shoah Dialogues

Re-Thinking Our Texts Together

Edited by

James F. Moore

Studies in the Shoah

Volume XXV

D1292255

University Press of America,® Inc.
Dallas · Lanham · Boulder · New York · Oxford

Library of Congress Control Number: 2003117055
ISBN 0-7618-2837-0 (paperback : alk. ppr.)

BT 93
.P677
2004

i 076182s 370

Table of Contents

Preface

The idea for a dialogue was already present in the earliest of my essays through my acknowledgement that no Christian theology after the Shoah could be authentic unless it is done in the context of dialogue. Of course, a presumed dialogue would be better than the assumptions of much previous Christian theologizing as the beginning and ending point for such theologies was the church and its traditions (particularly its sacred texts). Now this sort of theology would not do. But the actual inception of a dialogue occurred as a result of a conversation one evening in Seattle, Washington, after an event at the Annual Scholars' Conference on the Holocaust and the Churches in 1992. Henry Knight and Steven Jacobs and myself were walking and talking about the need to move the discussions of this important conference toward a future which gave up most commitment to the very principles that founders of the conference continually espoused. We would shape a dialogue which was inter-faith which attempted to make reflection on future theologies for both Christians and Jews truly post-Shoah. That is, we would assure that theologies would be a pathway for Christians as well as Jews to incorporate the effects of the Shoah as an historically important shaping event for Jews **and** for Christians. We also decided that this conversation would begin with our sacred texts, taking on one of the most difficult challenges that faces us in our post-Shoah religious world.

So we planned for an initial event and invited our friend Zev Garber to join us so that we balanced the dialogues partners, Christians and Jews. And we began with Jacob, a figure so clearly central to religious identity, and Jesus as a focus for our first discussion so that we began at a point most difficult yet potentially most fruitful. We also decided that each dialogue would couple texts from Hebrew scriptures and from Christian scriptures so that we would challenge ourselves to talk across traditions taking the textual histories of our two communities seriously. For our Jewish colleagues, this became one of the first opportunities to openly discuss Christian texts with Christians that led to thinking together about doing Christian theology. That is, this dialogue became a constructive engagement in which Jewish scholars could be instrumental in deciding what might be adequate Christian theology. This may be one of the few such interactions, at least in the United States.

The dialogue in the other direction is more complicated since what are Jewish sacred texts are also incorporated by Christians into their independent sacred tradition. Thus, both Hank and I agreed from the outset that we would make this discussion of Christian texts by Christians into an effort inviting our Jewish colleagues in on equal ground. The maneuver that makes that possible is a principle that I first addressed in a paper at the international Holocaust conference, "Remembering for the Future," in Oxford in 1988, a midrashic approach. Simply put, this way of thinking about Christian texts is to assume that they function like a set of Midrash on the Torah (an idea first suggested to me by Jacobus Schooneveld at the same conference) which shifts any reading of Christian texts back into a discussion of the Torah tradition. This means not only that texts from Christian scriptures will be linked to an interpretive tradition initiated by Rabbinic Judaism but also that we were required to understand that tradition on its own terms, thus our reading of Hebrew scriptures. Furthermore, not only does this create a level playing field for our Jewish colleagues but their willingness to follow us in this path also means that Christians are invited to participate with Jewish thinkers in a process of re-thinking Jewish thought bringing Christian sources to bear as one more interpretation of that tradition along side of others.

Thus, the process of the dialogue began at Tulsa's Annual Scholars' Conference on the Holocaust in March 1993 and this dialogue continues annually at the conference, wherever it is located. That annual conversation is the context for the essays that appear in this volume. The ongoing annual discussion has now found such a home that the group has a label, at least among our colleagues. We are "The Midrash Group." Among other things that could be said about the scholarly contributions of our discussions, we must also agree that our annual face-to-face discussions have now produced a communal collegiality among us that is quite remarkable. Thus this is a group not only in an academic sense but also in the developing personal relations between us. I am certainly grateful for this experience and thank my dialogue partners especially for their commitment to a process that I conceived but they have given life to.

Of course, we are also grateful to the many other friends who have been instrumental in supporting us through the years. Among those is surely Franklin Littell, who has been a constant supporter of our work. We also are grateful the other co-founder of the Scholars' Conference, Hubert Locke, who has consistently championed our cause personally and publicly. Other friends like Burton Nelson, Richard Libowitz, Leonard Grob, Pat Kelley, Audrey Doetzel, Peter Haas and too many others too numerous to mention have been actively involved over the years in our annual discussions. Of course, we would not have had the annual opportunity to hold a place at the Scholars' Conference without the support of the leadership of the Scholars' Conference, notably Marci Littell. I am grateful to Rabbi Dr. Joseph Edelheit who was the first to push me both to greater commitment to dialogue and to take seriously the Shoah as a vital element for doing Christian theology. His friendship remains one of my most important assets and his ongoing dialogue with me is a model upon which the Midrash Group was shaped. Above all, I think for me, especially, and for my dialogue partners as well, we are indebted to the support and critical advice from Dr. Barbara Strassberg, who aside from being an outstanding scholar and writer in her own right is my wife.

The essays in this volume are representative of the conversation over the years starting with the very first set of essays from the inaugural meeting in 1993. The other three sets are from more recent conversations and show clearly the way that both the substance of our dialogues and the focus our joint efforts has shifted as we have grown toward a greater and greater sense of mutual respect and common passion. In fact, what may merge from this ongoing work is a theology that is neither purely Christian or Jewish but is dialogical having trajectories that reach back into our respective religious communities but move forward together toward commonly held goals. The model also may be a pathway for any future projects on the Shoah no matter what the discipline. Whatever the future may hold for us, our hope is that publication of this set of essays will be an inspiration for additional creative work along these lines. The essays are presented essentially as they were presented in order to maintain the progressive sense of a dialogue over the years. Some of the essays have appeared in edited form over the years but this is the first occasion for their being together in a single volume. We are appreciative to University Press of America and its Studies in the Shoah series for making this possible.

James F. Moore, Valparaiso University, October 2003

Acknowledgements

All Biblical texts quoted in this documented are taken from the *New Revised Standard Version Bible*, copyright 1989 by the Division of Christian Education of the National Council of Churches of Christ.

The essays in part one of the text are a version of essays that were printed earlier in *SHOFAR*, volume 15:1, Fall 1996, pp. 3-94. They appear in this volume by permission of the publisher

The essays in part two of this volume are expanded versions of essays previously printed in *SIDIC*, Volume XXXV:1, Winter 2002, pp. 29-43. They appear in this volume by permission of the publisher

The essay in part four written by Zev Garber is a version of the text printed in his *Shoah: The Paradigmatic Genocide*. Lanham, MD: The University Press of America, 1994, pp. 119-136.

The essay written by Steven Jacobs in part three is a version of an article printed in ZYGON, volume 38:3, September 2003, pp. 735-742. It appears in this volume by permission of the publisher

Chapter 1: Introducing the Dialogue
James F. Moore

Those of us who live in the second generation after Auschwitz have for some time sensed that we are now faced with a transition stage in our thinking about the Shoah. The first generation, the generation of eyewitnesses, is still with us but in another decade or two will be gone. We also face the same dangers that all historical events and their memory face, the loss of centrality and intensity of the event. Thus, with the gradual loss of the eyewitness account and with the natural tendency for new generations to lose sight of the importance of historical events, this generation, our generation feels the heightened call to be a new generation of witnesses. We have heard the appeal that Elie Wiesel makes:

> "We all stood at Sinai; we all shared the same vision there; we all heard the *Anochi*. 'I am the Lord...' If this is true, then we are also linked to Auschwitz. Those who were not there then can discover it now. How? I don't know. But I do know it is possible."[1]

Of course, these words were written with specific intent to address a Jewish audience whose own communal memory could join Wiesel at least in the first part -- "We all stood at Sinai" -- even if some would be searching for the "How?" of the second part of Wiesel's appeal. We can only speculate about what Wiesel would say if the audience were not merely the contemporary Jewish community but the Jewish-Christian dialogue community instead. If we who are in dialogue hear Wiesel's appeal, what does it mean for us. Can we share standing at Sinai? Do we hear the same words or see the same vision? And even if we could answer confidently these questions, we must ask whether being linked to Auschwitz is

---

[1] Elie Wiesel, "Jewish Values in the Post-Holocaust Future: A Symposium," *Judaism* 16:3 (Summer 1967), 281.

connected to standing together at Sinai. This is a more complex question than at first seems since we often debate whether the two are closer and, thus, more sinister in this relationship than we are willing to grant, at first.

What then, do we say if this community of dialogue is also one in which all who talk with one another cannot share being at Auschwitz with Elie Wiesel. Again the question is complex and has met with stormy conversation over the years. There are those who listen to the second generation and their thoughts about Auschwitz with great cynicism. They are not so optimistic as Wiesel who may not know how our generation can stand with the eyewitnesses but nevertheless believes that we can. Surely, Wiesel has briefly pinpointed a central feeling that we do share, that we struggle to discover, to stand with in our own way. And this struggle is partly our response to the need, that soon the ones who were at Auschwitz can no longer bear witness. But that is not all. We also struggle because this is now our work, shaped as we shape the story and attempt to preserve the memory.

There is yet another powerful even if subtle word that springs from Wiesel's appeal. He has linked our standing at Sinai with our standing at Auschwitz. Even if Wiesel has not always thought the same thing nor stood in the same place on this matter, he is consistent in this word. Theology, namely the passing on of our religious traditions for a new generation, is now done in this terribly frightful crucible, the unthinkable juxtaposition of Sinai and Auschwitz. Thus, we who are theologians of this second generation know that our story will be ours, forged from our struggle with standing at Auschwitz as Christian or Jew who was not there, but it will continue to be set into this explosive and potentially destructive interaction that threatens to undo our witness and our souls. Still, this must be done. We must think on Sinai, and Zion, and Calvary and we must think of Auschwitz and Treblinka and Warsaw. But we cannot do this in separated worlds but rather together. This is how theology is done for us in this second generation. Those of us who dialogue in this volume of essays are among those who have heard and now respond to the appeal of Elie Wiesel.

Our Dialogue As Model

The discussion that produced the essays in this book is a possible model for the theological framework I have just described. The format I have imposed brings with it several features that make it ideal for the difficult work that post-Shoah theology requires. The make-up of the group of scholars, for example, was specifically chosen to present a balanced perspective between Christians and Jews.   The particular individuals involved also represent distinct perspectives that enrich the conversation between us. The discussion is also well suited to our purpose since it is both possible to give definite shape to our mutual thinking while assuring at the same time a sense of both openness to surprise and creative and productive interaction. Thus the format also implies a sort of openness to the future that the difficult and ever changing discussion in dialogue requires. Indeed, if we could manage such discussions regularly in busy schedules, the conversation format would be an especially inviting model for post-Shoah dialogue.

Of course, other factors must also work together to make the discussion itself function as post-Shoah dialogue. A key is obviously the particular participants who generate the initial discussion. A dialogue cannot work well unless there is a mix of people willing to risk dialogue, that is to say, with the openness to whatever a dialogue might produce. This dialogue cannot work without a mix of contributors who bring a particular faith commitment to the conversation. The scholars I invited to join me in this discussion meet both of these criteria and offer the additional advantage of working in both the academic world and in the world of the faith community. The dialogue has a built-in check in that way that can measure whether our conversation has any viability in both academic and faith circles. Given the goals of our approach to post-Shoah theology, this basic practical test is especially valuable.

The partners in dialogue should also be familiar with the scholarship on the Shoah so that whatever arises from the conversation can be immediately tested in the context of post-Shoah reflections on religious belief and life. Judging whether a theological idea can have legitimacy after the Shoah is basic to our common agreement as scholars; yet having the wisdom to make such a judgment comes from the experience of working among those who have done the groundwork thinking on the Shoah. Thus, our group not only contributes to the success of this model for post-Shoah theology by bringing that experience but our shared involvement in the Scholars' Conference on the Holocaust and the German Church Struggle, which has both a significant history and a recognized credibility, assures us of a larger circle of participants who can lend wisdom in making these judgments.

Therefore, we offer this discussion as a paradigm for post-Shoah theology, especially as that now must be done in the second generation of scholars. It is this kind of setting that, we contend, provides the optimum context for both generating dialogue and testing our conclusions, for creating a viable post-Shoah theology. In addition, the nature of such a discussion suggests that the circle of contributors can and probably must expand. That is, the nature of this dialogue implies that this may also be a model for interaction that involves anyone who is studying seriously the relationship between Christianity and Judaism in this post-Shoah world.   Thus, the discussion here can become an example of this interaction applicable to any class on contemporary Judaism and the dialogue itself may well suggest a model for creating this interaction in the classroom. Surely, then the results apply to more than just the shaping of theology but have to do with the nature of and the future shape of contemporary Judaism and Christianity.

The Criteria

There is much about our conversation that requires a certain sense of openness in conversation, readiness, even eagerness to allow for surprises and variety of approach and perspective. We do not want to discourage the flexibility nor the creativity of discussion that a panel represents. Still, there are certain beginning criteria that function as necessary boundaries for our discussion, agreements or ground rules that help provide a framework for beginning our conversation. These rules are fairly self-evident given the goals of our discussion, a post-Shoah theology. They are: (1) that our theology be self-consciously dialogical; (2) that our theology be sensitive to the issues that emerge for religious thought out of the Shoah; (3) that our discussion be theological, that is attending to theological concerns and not primarily other certainly important concerns.

Our theology must be dialogical. Those of us who are practiced in dialogue may find this criterion fairly self-evident, but it is nevertheless vital to this approach to post-Shoah theology. That is to say, the point of our work is not merely to settle the parochial questions interesting to our particular group but rather to engage in those questions that have the potential to affect us both and to form some potential common ground. This is a mutual conversation and what we say or choose for our focus requires this ongoing sense of mutuality. On that level dialogue includes at least four critical features: (1) a willingness to listen to the other as other; (2) a willingness to accept as valid the truth commitments of the other; (3) a willingness to explore anew and bring to the conversation the particular perspective that is our own (our own faith perspective); and (4) a willingness to risk change.[2] Many have suggested to me that the last of these components of dialogue is

---

[2] I originally proposed this model for understanding dialogue in:
James Moore, "Team-Taught, In-Class Dialogue: A Limited But Promising Method For Teaching Judaism," in *Methodology in the Academic Teaching of Judaism*, Zev Garber, ed., (Lanham, MD: University Press of America, 1986), p. 202ff.

really the first, the main commitment. Since there is likely to be a changed viewpoint in some way produced by the conversation (indeed, this may even be the goal of dialogue), a willingness to risk change is required before we begin and not as a potential by-product of the conversation. If this is so, then points 3 and 2 are filled with more than what is at first implied. Our willingness to bring to the conversation our own faith perspective (and we are talking here of religious dialogue, dialogue on and about the sacred as we experience and come to know and make real in our lives the sacred) already presumes the limits of our personal or communal view. We engage in conversation with the desire to re-think what is our own perspective even if we also come to dialogue with a firm commitment to that perspective and to that faith community. And we must say that the dialogue will produce change but change that is itself both a unique experience to each participant, not to be superficially assumed as the same as one's own, but is also already in the conversation a part of the dialogue. This bringing to the conversation one's own perspective with the willingness to risk change is that which drives the conversation forward toward legitimate surprise. But this means that point two is also deeper than seems at first. We come to the dialogue already prepared to grant the legitimacy of the other's claims. That does not mean mere tolerance as not every claim may in the end be acceptable. Indeed, we expect that our post-Shoah reflections will call some views into question. Even so, our willingness to risk change means that our willingness reaches to the core of our own belief. Now this is risk since we our led to that precarious level of thinking that sees competing claims for truth to be the only viable vehicle by which our dialogue can proceed, either in acceptable directions or in honest acceptance, indeed, inclusion of the other. Once again, we enter with a new level of naivete, a commitment to start again in our thinking about the other. We discard prejudice that is born by our own traditions and begin with this exciting and threatening commitment to accept the other fully. We know that this expanded sense of our willingness to accept the other's views as true gives a richer meaning to the first point as well. We know that our intent in actually listening to the views of another is changed, or at least directed in particular ways. We listen with intent and that intent is shaped by respect and a desire to re-think what we claim is true or believe might be true about ourselves, our world, our God and with that about the other. Whatever we might have thought is true about the other is always open to a new listening, to surprises because we assume that we might be wrong, we might not really have heard before, we might honestly hear something so new and vital that we truly have not considered before. This is what we mean by saying from the outset that our theology must be dialogical.

Our theology must also be post-Shoah. Now there is a way in which our conversation will be necessarily post-Shoah, that is, we are necessarily products of cultures that are sustained in a world that has suffered the impact of the Shoah. We cannot detail here all that might be meant by that statement, but we cannot escape the reality of the Shoah as an historical event which has had enormous impact especially on our two faith communities. But we argue that our conversation must be self-consciously post-Shoah. Johannes Metz has said that no theology can be done now without considering what that theology means in the light of Auschwitz.[3] Irving Greenberg has said that nothing can be said theologically today unless it could be said in the presence of the one million children who died.[4] That is to say, our commitment is not merely the recognition that the historical fact of the Shoah cannot be denied (it is at least that) but means also that our theologies cannot be the same anymore. Our language cannot be naively offered as if Auschwitz had not been. Now we are returned to where we began, to Elie Wiesel. We attempt the impossible in this dialogue since we try through the vehicle of dialogue, through whatever wisdom we can muster, to stand at Auschwitz, to ask the impossible question, "What does it mean that there is a connection between standing at Sinai and standing at Auschwitz, knowing, of course, that none of us stood at Auschwitz?"

This impossible but necessary task will mean something different to every contributor to this conversation. We know that to listen to one another with all eagerness to hear will mean that we discard assumptions about what it means for any of us to think as if we were there, to speak as if those who were already dying could hear us. We do know that we cannot waste this moment with meaningless chatter even if we fear always that what we say will sound like meaningless chatter. This surely also means that when we speak theologically we will speak with certain questions always in mind. We will ask whether this particular way of talking, of thinking of conceiving ourselves and the other makes sense inside of the Shoah story. And we will know the words well from Wiesel or from Fackenheim that such an effort is hopeless.[5] Nothing makes sense inside of the Shoah story. Even so, we still ask and realize that there is a way to do this. We keep

---

[3] Johannes Baptist Metz, *The Emergent Church* (New York: Crossroad, 1981), p. 28.

[4] Irving Greenberg, "Cloud of Smoke, Pillar of Fire: Judaism, Christianity, and Modernity after the Holocaust," in *Auschwitz: Beginning of a New Era?*, Eva Fleischner, ed. (New York: KTAV Publishing House, 1977), p. 13.

[5] cf., Emil Fackenheim, *To Mend the World* (New York: Schocken Books, 1982), p. 230ff.

asking always fearful that our theologies will be ruined on the rocks of this task but still knowing that our basic trust, our faith commitment is perhaps the only hope that we will not be broken on the rocks of this task. This is the shape of the bold confidence that mixes with the possibility of utter despair that comes forth with the complete humility that we must surely fail and finishes with the realization that we must succeed and can only in this way succeed. We will know some questions that we share and others that perhaps only we have come to ask. All of these questions, perhaps especially the questions, become our theology. This is what we mean when we say that our theology must be post-Shoah.

Finally, our dialogue must be theological. Of course, there are other disciplines that demand attention in post-Shoah thinking. In fact, our ability to consider a post-Shoah theology now is dependent on much work that has already been done by historians, social scientists, philosophers, and literary critics and creative writers. But, our dialogue must be theological. This means that our conversation will focus on theological themes. The earlier dialogues of our era did not do this in the interest of building a level of trust and mutual concern. Many feared that discussions on theology would threaten dialogue itself and ruin efforts for mutual cooperation. Theological themes are also the most problematic after the Shoah. Fackenheim's question, "Why did they do it?," is at first a moral question but is also the deep theological question, an ultimate question.[6] This question is one that eludes our answers. Thus, early partners in dialogue avoided these questions many times. And these questions, ultimate questions, may be the most troubling for those of us who were not there. Eliezer Berkovitz implies that such questions of morality and religion cannot be answered fully except by those who were there.[7] Can we judge whether such answers worked or work even now unless we were there?

But theological matters are now the critical arena for our dialogue. If we are to heed Wiesel and connect Sinai with Auschwitz, we cannot do this in any other way except by asking the theological questions. But this means, of course, that our theology must connect Sinai with Auschwitz. Thus, pre-Shoah theologies cannot be our theologies until they have been

---

[6] Emil Fackenheim, "Holocaust and Weltanschauung: Philosophical Reflections as to Why They Did It," in *Remembering for the Future*, Yehuda Bauer, ed., (New York: Pergamon Press, 1988), volume 2, p. 1850ff.
[7] Eliezer Berkovitz, *With God in Hell* (New York: Sanhedrin Press, 1979), pp. viii-ix.

sifted through the sieve of the Shoah. This is all the more reason for saying that our dialogue must be theological. This connecting of basic tradition with current questions is what we have always meant by theology. This hermeneutical task is the theological task. This search for meaning between text and context, between Sinai and Auschwitz is the theological search. Anyone who seeks to ask such questions enters into this theological discussion whether they are theologians or not, but the quest is a theological quest that follows theological instincts. And the arena we have been describing is what we mean by a dialogue that is theological.

The Focus of Our Discussion

We must have a beginning point of course. Various kinds of entrees into reflection on the Shoah can take a beginning from a variety of different places -- the historical facts, the stories of survivors and victims, the case studies of sociologists or psychologists -- but a theology begins within our traditions. To ask the theological questions that we must ask requires that we ask them of our sacred texts. We begin with the sacred text as all theologies do. Of course, we begin with the sacred text inside the framework we have already described. We approach the sacred text in dialogue and all that we have agreed that means. We read the sacred texts from a post-Shoah perspective and all that this means. And we think together about these texts in the context of theological questions.

There is a great deal of flexibility in our discussion even so. The angles that can emerge in any of these three ways that shape our dialogue already produce a potential for alternative readings. But this is our hope. I have argued elsewhere that all theology after the Shoah is midrashic.[8] That is to say, this theology explores a plurality of possible readings of our traditions, our texts, which may give possible meaning for us in connecting Sinai with Auschwitz. To set these alternative side by side, we create both an obvious ambiguity of meaning and a creative tension between readings (what Paul Ricoeur calls a conflict of interpretations[9]). This creative tension is a natural part of any open hermeneutical process, but it is especially vital for post-Shoah dialogue. We must be careful that we do not close off this creative tension, this ambiguity too early. The tension is in fact the driving force of new insight and ongoing conversation.

---

[8] James F. Moore, *Christian Theology After the Shoah* (Lanham, MD: University Press of America, 1993), p. 21ff.

[9] Paul Ricoeur, *Le Conflit des Interpretations* (Paris: de Seuil, 1969).

But our conversation is truly midrashic in that we aim not to accept mere ambiguity as if all meanings, all interpretations can hold equal validity for us in our making the connection between Auschwitz and Sinai. The process may, in fact, be more concerned not so much with finding a best reading of any text than with uncovering rules for reading that are now essential for our generation. Exciting new ideas might emerge, but a foundation that guides all of our reading, all of our conversation on any text or set of texts may be even more fruitful for our future. This open process is a primary aim for us and will, of course, lead us to reject some readings that cannot stand the crucible of the connection.

In a sense, then, the choice of specific text is arbitrary. If rules for reading apply for any text then we are likely to discover these guiding principles in dialogue on whatever texts we would choose. Surely, some texts are more central and more obviously important for the shaping of our unique religious identities. They are undoubtedly prime candidates for conversation. Yet, we should expect that basic principles forged by dialogue would produce the opportunity for ever new always developing discussion on new texts. Our choice here in this discussion, by that measure, is only a beginning. Our discussion is by nature open-ended seeking to stay open to new possibilities and new texts.

Our conversation may lead us to see much more of a connection than might seem to us as we begin. We explore together because we have challenged ourselves to think through texts. Such a thinking puts some in unfamiliar territory and even challenges those of us who are Christian to enter into the Torah texts in a new way as if we tried to think our way into these texts as Jewish scripture and not merely as a piece of Christian scripture. Our searching also brings with it all the dynamics and difference that we represent as individuals and as members of our own traditions. We read and think and interpret differently with different keys and from different perspectives. We have decided that this is an exciting prospect, and we are prepared to begin with you in this dialogue. At any rate, we believe that it is the only productive direction for post-Shoah theology to take.

Chapter 2: Thinking the Tradition Anew: A New Reading of Genesis 32 and Matthew 26 in Light of the Shoah and Dialogue
James Moore

Christian theology must now be done in the light of two basic factors that make all theologies new for us. First, all Christian theologies are post-Shoah theologies and cannot proceed as if the events of the Shoah had not happened or have no impact upon how Christians think even about their basic faith commitments. Second, all Christian theology is dialogical taking account of a full generation of a new Jewish-Christian dialogue. This second factor is linked to the first as well since even in the solitude of thought of a single Christian thinker, their must always be the image, the presence of Jews in conversation. These two factors become for us two principal criteria for judging the adequacy of any view. It is for this reason that creative theology has a most appropriate place and role in the work of the Scholars' conference.

What better way to examine the impact of the two above criteria than to focus on scripture. Not only does scripture play an important role in the shaping of all Christian theology but scripture is also the center place of all Christian worship. Thinking about scripture is the linking point between doing theology, even in the academy, and doing theology in the midst of the church's life. Thus, all Christian theology is fundamentally hermeneutical and takes the form of midrashic interpretation, akin to the homiletical task of the preacher or the teacher. Even without the necessity of dialogue and the challenge of the Shoah, Christian theology would be midrashic, re-thinking together, with the intent of speaking to and for Christians. In so far as we also speak in dialogue, we deign to speak also to and with Jews.

To this latter point, I now add the last ingredient of our work together. If all Christian theology is dialogical, then the open interchange of public dialogue is the ideal forum for doing theology. Not only do we publicly acknowledge the partnership of peoples and thinkers which challenges every effort to drive a wedge between us again inside and outside of Christian communities, but we also make ourselves vulnerable to the surprises of dialogue, the creative flow and spirit of actual interchange. We make evident what we always take for granted, that our theologies are done in dialogue. Such public conversation, long the hallmark of the dialogue, now moves to this appropriate stage -- the community of scholars committed together to think about our traditions, our scriptures.

There is yet one more feature of this work we pursue today. Given the immediate challenge of the Shoah, all theology moves forward to acknowledge the relationship between Christian thinking and Christian acting. We cannot afford any longer a gap between our best thinking and actions of the communities we represent. All theology is praxis in this way, not only providing a challenge to moral action and conviction but also giving a foundation for thinking about the connection between thought and act, faith and morality. We cannot do this haphazardly expecting that such links will naturally arise, even though the remarkable insights that have emerged in dialogue do show how even accidental progress can happen in the context of open and earnest conversation. Still, we must proceed with a structure for seeing the link between thought and action, which surely was evident during the Shoah and must be considered as essential in post-Shoah Christian theology.

I have provided just such a model in my book on post-Shoah Christian theology, but that work is too complex to reproduce here. Besides, that would not be valuable for us now. Still, certain components of that approach will be valuable for my reflections on the texts we have selected. A spectrum of possibilities for action can be discovered by any critical analysis of the role of Christians in and during the Shoah. Four possible responses are potential symbols of present Christian response -- indifference, collaboration, resistance and rescue. Indeed, models for these responses can be easily seen through the narrative figures of Christian scripture. If we make clear how those models are conceived and reinforced by the narratives, we may gain a clue concerning the connection between thinking and acting. Surely, we aim to shape a Christian theology that reinforces resistance and rescue rather than indifference and collaboration even though the latter two are valuable insights into the complexities of Christian responses and any particular circumstance. We may see that more clearly by turning to the texts from Genesis 32 and Matthew 26.

GENESIS 32:22-32

This text from Genesis is a perfect example of ambiguity within scripture. The narrative of the story is fairly clear, but the meaning of the narrative either within the whole story of Jacob and Israel as well as for the reader and/or the community of believers is not so clear. Several points in the narrative make for several possible interpretations and conflicting readings. Rather than frustrating the interpreter, this plurality of meanings creates the opportunity for creative advance, ever new vision arising from the text. No single interpretation can grab center stage and claim absolute right. Instead, our reading of this text demands making the variety of possibilities known and setting them side by side. And now we can also bring our special perspective to bear on the text, a view that includes both Jewish-Christian dialogue and our awareness of the challenges, the negative hermeneutic of the Shoah. Thus, we proceed by tracing these options, re-telling the narrative in a number of ways, and we stand in good tradition as both the Midrash and Christian theological tradition have reproduced these differing versions of the story.

Jacob approaches the river Jabbok and a confrontation with his brother Esau. All of this scene is fully understandable if one has read the whole narrative. The narrative of Jacob, the cycle of stories, reads as if this approaching confrontation is the purpose of the whole narrative. We have been led purposely to this point by the flow of the narrative. Thus, what would we expect but that Jacob would approach his brother to face this confrontation. The whole morality of the story demands this end.

But Jacob spends the night at the Jabbok and sends the whole of his company and family away so that Jacob can be alone. This too is understandable in the flow of the narrative. Jacob uses this pause as a strategy to send a present ahead to Esau, to win favor before the confrontation. This is not a battle for final supremacy, but an effort at reconciliation. So Jacob spends the night on the Jabbok and sends his company and family away so that Jacob is left alone. So much for what is clear because we read this story now so much in the light of what we think of this Jacob who is now alone at the center of our attention.

This phrase, "And Jacob was left alone..." has intrigued many interpreters through time from both Jewish and Christian traditions. Indeed, from one perspective Jacob must be left alone. He alone has driven this story and brought on this confrontation through his plotting and scheming. Finally, all of this catches up with Jacob and only this solitary man can finally face the consequences. He must face the consequences since Jacob clearly has assumed the place of the one blessed at the expense of the brother. Indeed, one reading of this narrative is bound to be taken to mean this. Jacob, soon to be Israel, is blessed at the expense of the brother.

And this being set apart is not a pretty sight. Jacob schemes to steal the birthright from Esau. Now after plotting to take that blessing from Isaac and plotting to assume the wealth of Laban through marrying both daughters, Jacob is left alone with the wretchedness of his life. At least, that is the reading often found in Christian thinking. Jacob, for some of the early church leaders, was the symbol of wretchedness. Jacob lacked the enduring faithfulness of Abraham which would later make Abraham a model for Paul and others of the life of the disciple of Christ. Jacob lacks the innocent anguish of the survivor Isaac who bore the blessing of God even as he also lived with the scars of the planned sacrifice. Jacob was the symbol of wretchedness, the symbol that John Calvin lifted up to show the wretchedness of all humanity.[1]

It is also interesting that Karl Barth, following Calvin, writes of Jacob and this passage on wrestling with God as the symbol of human wretchedness. We are, in a sense, condemned to wrestle with God since only God can reveal God's self to us. Our humanity, in Barth's vision, struggles against this trying to trap God and box God in. Only when in humility we let go can we actually receive God's blessing.[2] Thus, Jacob, and Israel, are a symbol of this false wrestling with God that can produce nothing. Barth's vision is hardly fair to the text, but is consistent with his theology, a view of Judaism that he maintained throughout the second world war despite his indignation for Nazi mistreatment of the Jews. Left alone before God, the futility of our religious efforts to force a blessing from God is exposed, in Barth's view.

Luther, on the other hand, reads this text as a symbol of our humility before God, finally confronted by God we are subdued. Left alone, we, all humanity, struggle to find a merciful God only to find that God already present ready at our humility to bless us.[3] This, too, is consistent with Luther's theology that seems on the surface to be kinder to the Jew, Jacob, but this openness is merely an illusion. Luther reads the figure of Jacob as a symbol of humankind and not of Israel. This, too, is unfair to the text itself, but consistent with Luther's view.

In fact, this tendency in Christian theology to read the patriarchs as symbols of all humankind, or more narrowly as symbols of what was

---

[1] John Calvin, *Institutes of the Christian Religion*, translated by Henry Beveridge (Grand Rapids, Mi: Wm B. Eerdmans Publishing Company, 1962), p. 377.
[2] cf., Karl Barth, *Church Dogmatics* (Edinburgh: T. & T. Clark, 1975), volume I:1, p. 330 and volume I:2 p. 338.
[3] Martin Luther, *Luther' Works* (Philadelphia: Fortress Press, 1955), volume 12

to be Christianity, is obvious throughout the history of Christian thought. Jacob is a type of something, a lesson for the sake of the Christian believer. But, because of this typological reading, Jacob is never positively read as a type of Israel. If Jacob is representative of Israel (as with Calvin), Jacob and Israel are seen as the most wretched of all humanity, having the merciful God but conniving to force God's blessing. Of all the texts of the Hebrew scriptures, this text is an important test of Christian theological views of Judaism and Jews. It is a prime example of Christian teaching of contempt either explicit or implicit.

A fascinating counter-example can be found in the *De Principiis* of Origen. Origen also reads Jacob as a type but argues that this story shows that Jacob is a model of humanity aided by God to come to the truth. Again this is typology, robbing Jacob of historical place and religious identity, but this is also a view of Jacob that is cast as a positive type.[4] That is, Israel can be seen as a positive symbol for human relationship to God. Nevertheless, Origen is by no means especially philo-Judaic, and his view is rather a product of his theology (a kind of proto-pelagian view that eventuated in Origen being labelled a heretic).

Jacob is left alone and the first major question for Christians with regard to this text and most others in the Hebrew scriptures is how do we see Jacob when Jacob is isolated, set apart? How do we see Israel when Israel is left alone? The tradition has consistently seen Israel as a type of what was to come, and this way of reading the Torah is typical of Christian theologizing concerning much of the Hebrew scripture. Christians have tended to reduce Israel, Judaism, Jacob to a type and have failed to encounter Jacob, Judaism, or Israel as living, historical people. We have failed to read the texts in their own right.

Now this is a strong charge and certainly not entirely true for Christians, particularly after the Shoah. Even so, we should be careful of typological readings of texts from the Torah especially after the Shoah. The fact is that the Shoah is a prime example of how Israel was left alone, singled out and set apart. If Jacob is to remain a Jew for us, we must think about Jacob as person again in the text just as we aim to avoid thinking of Jews left alone in the Shoah as types of anything, especially of Judaism.

But the text invites us to a new theology just in this phrase, and Jacob was left alone. The phrase not only comes as part of a fuller narrative but also means that what we say about this text is first said about

---

[4] Origen, *On First Principles* (Glouchester, Mass: Peter Smith, 1973), p. 220.

Jacob alone. That is to say, this story is essentially about Jacob as a person and then about Israel (the text, itself, even suggests this sequence). Above all, we are concerned that this basic rule about Christian interpretation of texts from Hebrew scripture be fundamental for any Christian theology. This means, of course, that Jacob must be allowed to speak for himself. Israel must be allowed a voice in our theologies most particularly in speaking about how Jacob, Israel, and Judaism are to be viewed.

Returning to the Text

Presuming that our dialogue will satisfy this first judgment about Christian interpretations of this text about Jacob, we can return to the text once again and think about the narrative and Jacob's role in that narrative as individual. In fact, if we have eliminated the need to lift Jacob to a symbol for Christian theologizing, many of the judgments about Jacob that arise from the texts can be made. Jacob had deceptively obtained the blessing from Isaac robbing his brother of the birthright. Thus, this encounter with Esau has to be seen as a confrontation that Jacob had every reason to fear. His fear was not only a fear of the brother but also of the God who blesses and curses. This basic fear of brother and God has been a central theme for Rabbinic tradition as well sorting through the meaning of the text for the people of Israel.

Given the centrality of fear, then the phrase "And Jacob was left alone," takes on greater significance. Jacob's being alone is his choice, an effort to repent and seek mercy on his own before the confrontation. In fact, one thing we can say about Jacob from the start is that as manipulative as others were of and for him, Jacob shaped his own life with his choices. At least, this seems to be the case, as it is here in this text. Jacob sent the company away in order to be alone. Thus, we have to read this text as meaning that Jacob left himself alone, by his choice.

This fact makes Eli Wiesel's reading of Jacob as the child of a survivor quite curious.[5] Indeed, Jacob may not know what impact the scars of Isaac's memory had had on him and his life. Perhaps Isaac never spoke of the experience at Moriah, least of all to his children. Were there nightmares that could not or would not be explained? Who knows what inner world of Isaac the father might have been. We are not privy to those matters as Isaac never tells his story of that experience even for us to read. Thus, just as we see that Isaac the potential victim has no real choice in

---

[5] Eli Wiesel, *Messengers of God* (New York: Summit Books, 1976), pp. 103ff.

that narrative, Isaac the survivor has no story of that experience to pass on to his sons.

Jacob had no choice in that matter, of course. He neither had a role in living the original drama at Mount Moriah nor did he have a choice in hearing Isaac's narrative. We might wonder if Jacob ever knew of the traumatic event. As completely as Jacob seems to be in control of his life, making his own bed to sleep in, factors beyond our comprehension and perhaps his shaped Jacob's living in ways that are not and maybe cannot be told. This is a different story from the one we began with. This figure Jacob has no ordinary story that we can judge simply by thinking he was certainly a scoundrel. He is a child of a survivor and that generation has a tale to tell like no other and Jacob's is told only between the lines.

Thus, to see Jacob alone is to see into this man in a different way. His generation is like no other and cannot be judged and described like any other. The feelings that mixed with the fear of the pending confrontation with brother and God are now to be seen as something more. Jacob has a case to be made before this God whose command brought about the trauma at Mount Moriah and whose plan seemed to capture Jacob in a world he would not choose or even understand. Jacob is left alone because only he can bring this case against God. No friends or family can do this. Only Jacob has the right to approach (perhaps reproach) God for what God has done. Jacob is a child of a survivor.

For this reason, we who cannot know what it is to be a child of a survivor now must admit that in these ways Jacob is not a model for us. Perhaps we can gain much from reading this narrative, but we must not be quick to force Jacob into a mold, make this narrative fit a theological plan to fit our Christian message. We Christians stand outside of this narrative in two important ways. We are not direct heirs of the promise made to Jacob and we are not children of survivors. We hold back from making claims too quick about the man, Jacob.

But the story seems to open us to an immediate link to the stories of the Shoah. We can be tempted to say that the experience now so familiar to many in groups like ours is a window into Jacob's world. Eli Wiesel is a vehicle that allows us to do that. I suspect that we would say much that is helpful about this narrative if we follow Wiesel's lead. Still, we must argue that the narratives of so many children of survivors of the Shoah are not the same as Jacob's and vice versa.

The Centrality of the Divine Wrestler

Our re-thinking Genesis 32 has led to important basic criteria for reading any text of the Hebrew scriptures for the sake of shaping a

Christian theology. We have argued that Christians have failed to take this text on its own merits in the past because they have too quickly seen the text as type of Christian living or as the condition of "fallen humanity." Thus, we are challenged with this and other texts to read the text for its own sake, especially in allowing the figure Jacob to be our focus as he is put before us in this narrative. This encounter with Jacob allows us a chance once again to let our partners in dialogue define themselves before we impose a definition even if for the sake of sensitive interpretation. We are also challenged by this text to see that Jacob is a child of a survivor with experiences that we can only begin fathom. The text might help identify the dynamics of the experience of one who shares Jacob's life experience, but we are reluctant to draw any universal conclusions from this story. Every child of a survivor lives a different experience, but the text does open up for us the chance to begin to shape a theology that is truly post-Shoah -- a theology for the second generation.

In this effort to look at this text in that light, we are quickly led to the central action of this narrative -- Jacob wrestling with the stranger in the night. With all that Jacob brings to this moment alone, the image of wrestling seems most appropriate. Jacob is at this late point in his life wrestling, not settled. Especially, we see that Jacob wrestles with one who later Jacob takes to be the Lord. To understand the struggle that Jacob, the child of a survivor, undergoes, we must clarify who this stranger is in terms of Jacob's life narrative.

Again the options from Christian tradition are many. Some see the stranger as an angel who has come to assist Jacob through the night.[6] Some argue that the angel is God's representative sent to encounter and subdue this stubborn man.[7] Others even go on to say that the struggle was really with the evil one only to be at the end turned in favor of God's will.[8] These various images, and there must be greater variety than this, are intended to reflect and fit a variety of theological positions. In every case, the traditional Christian readings of this text fit the basic thematic of sin and grace, assuming that humanity has fallen in Adam's sin and all of humanity is in need of God's grace. Thus, the idea that Jacob could be wrestling with God to beat God, to subdue God, is quite anti-thetical to most Christian readings of this text.

---

[6] Ibid. Origen
[7] Ibid. Barth.
[8] Again Barth seems to make this argument in his second volume of the *Church Dogmatics*.

At best, we are confronted with a great deal of ambiguity on this matter if we look closely at the text. There is hardly a clear image presented concerning the intent of the "divine wrestler." We cannot tell if this vision comes with blessing or curse, with willingness or reluctance. Just as Jacob is surely a complex person, the divine combatant is pictured in complex ways. Therefore, the notion that we must read always a fallen humanity and a merciful God as the central thrust of this text seems dubious.

In fact, if we are to see Jacob as the child of a survivor, then the encounter between Jacob and the stranger must be seen differently. Jacob, indeed, has a challenge to present to the Lord. Jacob's place in the scheme of things is by no means clear and Jacob's inheritance is certainly a mixed bag. Abraham had his encounter with God that clearly marked Abraham and Isaac carried his encounter with the "tremendum" that gave Isaac assurance of God's blessing. Whatever we may say about Isaac, about the survivor, we surely can say that Isaac had the right to stand before God as no other could. But what of Jacob? Jacob only has Isaac's blessing, a mixed blessing at that. Jacob has only the knowledge that he is Isaac's son. And from that Jacob has inherited a legacy he may not completely know let alone understand.

If we look at Jacob as the child of a survivor, the whole structure of the text changes. Rather, our perspective is adjusted to accept the text as it is given. Jacob wrestles with the stranger, the divine wrestler, and subdues God. Jacob has a case before God that God cannot defeat. And Jacob hangs on until he knows God's name and receives a blessing. In this text, we are confronted not with a fallen humanity, but an unjustly victimized person (people?). In this text we have not the clearly merciful God but a God who is responsible for the trauma of Isaac and for the impact of that experience on the next generations. In Jacob's eyes, there is little reason to assume that God intends blessing. Thus, Jacob holds on to subdue God.

Having said this much, I must back away from the narrative to draw some links to the Shoah. What we have said thus far speaks about Jacob (and the people who would be Israel!), but can we say the same about the generation of and after the Shoah. We ask this not only to seek whether the text from Genesis may have a voice to speak to a post-Shoah people but also to inquire as to whether the meaning of the text can be the same now as it was originally (in so far as we can gauge that meaning). We must bring the challenge of the Shoah to this text. In so doing we might add yet more clues about the shape of a post-Shoah Christian theology (and Christian interpretations of Hebrew scriptures after the

Shoah).

Drawing Comparisons

We have already shown a reluctance to draw direct links between Jacob and children of Shoah survivors. Despite Wiesel's insightful midrash, we fear that such easy links will cloud important theological distinctions and, therefore, critical issues in our post-Shoah thinking. One of our reservations arises directly from this role of the divine wrestler. Of course, the survivors of the Shoah, together with their children, wrestle with God's role in the Shoah, and answers for them come in as much variety as for any other group of Jewish people. Jacob's response to the divine wrestler may not be sufficient for many who survived the Shoah. The idea that this dramatic encounter could create an equally dramatic turning point for Jacob, even a turning around, is not so obvious post-Shoah. I am not sure what visions or spiritual encounters might possibly fill in the gaps and salve the pain of experiences. It is surely too flippant to assume that the message of Jacob's narrative be that those angry with God will be able to be changed by a dramatic encounter with God. We are somewhat mistrustful of that message as we are with the conclusion of JOB. The encounter at the Jabbok does not remove the scar of Isaac's experience that is embedded in succeeding generations.

Just as we must be careful about being too glib about the possibility of salving wounds (even with dramatic spiritual experiences), we also should say that God surely has a different role in the two stories. There is a sense of the Genesis narrative that events, even the trauma of Moriah, are part of God's master plan. Even if Jacob has doubts about God's blessing of him, the reader is not in doubt. Jacob is fundamentally rooted in God's plan, whatever that is (we have the promise to Abraham). Even more, the trauma at Moriah is told as if all was part of God's command. God truly is guilty (responsible) for what happened to Isaac. The *Akeda* reads as if God intends that experience as a test of Abraham. Isaac is both an incidental pawn in that testing and an essential central figure in the strange plot-line of that narrative. The *Akeda* is also a challenging narrative to read after the Shoah.

So, if we are disinclined to read the *Akeda* as a text with direct meaning for the victims of the Shoah, we should be equally dubious about reading the story of the Jabbok encounter as having a direct meaning for children of survivors. There is no way that we can argue with obscenity that the Shoah was God's intended plan. The children of Shoah survivors, on this score, are not even conceivably like Jacob, the child of a survivor. To say that would be an abomination akin to arguing that Jesus can be seen as a model of suffering for those who suffered the atrocities of Auschwitz. It is this very distinction between Jacob and the children of Shoah survivors that makes the effort to read this text after the Shoah so difficult. The meaning of the text set into the pattern we have suggested appears quite obvious (despite the ambiguity of both Jacob's life story and the identity of the wrestler). That meaning cannot be appropriate for the children of Shoah survivors.

Offering a Possible Place for Jacob in our Theology

Then, what place can this narrative have for a post-Shoah Christian theology? The original meaning of the text continues to have potential for Jewish and Christian communities, but as a post-Shoah text, we must wonder if the text can be read with any clear meaning today. In the end, I believe, we have no choice but to struggle to find a way to read this text as a post-Shoah text both because the text continues to be read as part of the life of the worshipping communities of both Judaism and Christianity and because the narrative from Genesis finally provides a critical message that does fit our post-Shoah theologies.

Our dialogue can produce conversation about what place this narrative may have in Jewish thought after the Shoah; but we can offer here a framework for post-Shoah Christian theology that will help us to locate the narrative of Jacob in post-Shoah Christian theology. This theology must reflect a Christian response to the Shoah, that is, a way to account for the challenges that the Shoah presents.[9] I have argued elsewhere that such a response can take the shape of the Christian response within the Shoah[10] -- Christian theology tested by the critical crisis in Christianity that the Shoah produced. That response was, like the response of every group, ambiguous, characterized by at least for major

---

[9] I say this because my aim is to reflect on post-Shoah Christian theology. In fact, my colleagues will produce Jewish reflections on this text and with that perhaps a different framework for understanding. There are different agendas at work for each of us and maybe the bringing of these agendas to our conversation will work a creative merger of ideas or we may find the need to recognize with respect our clear differences. Even so, any Christian theology must be a theology of respect today.

[10] James F. Moore, "Resurrection as Rescue: Christian Theological Interpretation of Scripture after the Shoah", G. Jan Colijn and Marcia Littell, ed. *The Netherlands and Nazi Genocide* (Lewiston, NY: Edwin Mellen Press, 1992), pp. 431ff.

options -- (1) indifference, (2) collaboration, (3) resistance, (4) rescue. Whatever the Jacob story means for Christians now must give ways for understanding these various Christian responses to the Shoah.

If we can assume that these four ways of responding are clear and not in need of elaboration, then we can attempt to locate the Jacob narrative into this framework of Christian thinking. Our efforts must allow for the plurality of possibilities that enable continuing conversation rather than stereotypical rigidity of view. Above all, we attempt to avoid the two critical problems that have already surfaced -- the temptation to make Jacob a type of human and/or proto-Christian figure and the temptation to make direct links between the experience of Jacob and the experiences of those during the Shoah. If we can do this, then rather striking elements of this brief narrative strand from Genesis 32 begin to emerge.

We notice rather quickly the mysterious point about the stranger needing to flee at daybreak. This event of Jacob wrestling took place at night. Surely the night we speak of is not the blessing of restful sleep. Jacob's night is fraught with, even overwhelmed by, anxiety. This is the fearful darkness that holds who knows what in its shadows. Jacob wrestles through the night and is forced to do so until daybreak. It is also fascinating that the identity of the man who wrestles with Jacob is vague throughout this struggle and even seems unclear when Jacob hangs on at daybreak. Even as vague as Jacob is about his identity, he is more certain of that than of the identity of the one with whom he wrestles.

We can overplay metaphors to be sure, but the striking appearance of this phrase about daybreak at the end of the night leads us directly into the framework of post-Shoah Christian thought. Our problem remains our position in time. Are we still in darkness or have we seen a daybreak? This question posed to the Christian is different than one posed to the Jewish community and even more so than to survivors or children of survivors. Jacob's experience is not ours, but we share with Jacob the night fraught with anxiety. In that anxiety, choices are not made with certainty. We are less clear about whether we wrestle with God or evil. We have no absolute certainty that we are in the right not to mention that we are joined in the battle with good or evil. The night, the kingdom of the night, that we have passed through has attacked and destroyed our ability to be certain.

This is surely the impact of the Shoah on our theologies. If we could at any time have made judgments about Jacob (Israel) that derived from a certainty of our own position before God, that certainty evades us now. Our theologies retreat from such judgments now. Instead, our reading of the Jacob narrative carries with it our struggle through the night, one that saw many back away in fear to indifference as bystanders, others even out of spiritual tenacity join the enemy as collaborators. Our struggle through the night, quite different from Jacob's struggle is ambiguous, not very favorable. If we return to the night, before it is daybreak, we see that all our claims now about what we believe are set into this ambiguous picture of what happened during the night.

But this is hardly a message that is heard when this text is read liturgically for Christians in worship or when preachers preach or teach. When we turn to Jesus at night in the garden in the narrative from Matthew, this key link will be even more important, its significance more evident. If Jacob is left alone in his struggle through the night, then Christians must be ever vigilant of why Israel was left alone in so many ways by those who could have acted differently during the kingdom of the night. This portion of the Christian struggle with the Shoah is essential to our theologizing even into the second generation. Surely we are not privy to the experience of Moriah, but we have a different opportunity with those who are children of survivors. If Christian theology is to remain both dialogical and post-Shoah, we cannot afford to lose this element of humility in this new generation of thinking.

Emil Fackenheim's challenge to the Jewish community that they should return into history, the challenge to take up the mission of *Tikkun Olam*, becomes especially problematic for the second generation. The children of survivors are doubly troubled if they return into history, as important as that truly is. First, the night is murky. History gives no obvious clues of divine purpose. In fact, given history we are left fumbling around to determine if divine purpose is good or evil, blessing or curse. To return to history is to enter the problematic arena of life as we have it not as what might be the kingdom of God. Second, the children of survivors are faced with a blank in their own history (their personal narrative). To return into history is to enter again a world that produces more questions and potential pain than true healing, true *tikkun*. What assurance does Jacob receive as day breaks and he now faces confrontation with Esau? Little has changed except for Jacob's name. This little can be quite important, however.

Christians have had little reason to return to history since the illusion of Christendom has given Christians the belief that history was already in Christian hands (the hands of the Christian God, that is). But now the assurance is not so clear and Fackenheim's challenge can be posed equally to Christians as to Jews. If Christians return to history with its murkiness, then we return with less assurance that all is in the hands of

our God. In addition, we carry a hole in our story. The apostasy of the
Shoah is our legacy but cannot be the essence of Christianity. If we are
to join in *Tikkun Olam*, we must find healing ourselves first. We cannot
enter into the day without an essential transformation of Christianity, at
least as Christians have related to Jews.

Surely, we see in this text that in a name we are shown what that
means for us. If Jacob is the one who has striven with humanity and with
God (and in our striving we often cannot tell the difference), then our only
response is to join with Jacob in that struggle. We must resist every attack
on Jacob either from God or from humanity. We accept an identity that
also strives with God and humanity for the sake of *Tikkun*, and we
recognize that this struggle continues even into daybreak. Even if we
know what the stakes are now, we probably do not know what the result
may be. But we have no choice; we are challenged to join in this
wrestling, this resistance of all that would destroy Jacob. This is an
essential feature of our being Christian in this post-Shoah age.

And this joining in the struggle is all the more necessary for the
second generation, those who are literally post-Shoah. We join with the
generation of the children of the survivors who bear (and must bear) the
scars of their parents, but also carry their own scars quite unique to their
struggles (Jacob's limp). It is especially important that we see that
dialogue between those of this second generation has its own important
dynamic not to replace the conversation of the first generation but to take
up the challenges in a new way. And the age of this conversation is
dawning, is now upon us.

MATTHEW 26:36-46

There is much more that can be said about the Jacob narrative at
the Jabbok, but we have at least set some critical boundaries for that
reading as well as any other reading of Hebrew scriptures for the sake of
Christian theology. We also located the narrative in a framework that
allows us to read the text from both a dialogical and post-Shoah
perspective. That reading leaves us with a considerable challenge,
especially for the second generation after the Shoah.

In light of those reflections we can move to consideration of the
garden scene in the gospel of Matthew, a part of the extended narrative
complex often called by Christians the passion narrative. That this
passion narrative is a complex of narrative strands has already received
considerable treatment in my book.[11] Even so, this story of Jesus in

---

[11] James F. Moore, *Christian Theology after the Shoah: a Re-Interpretation of
the Passion Narratives* (Lanham, Md: University Press of America, 1993),

Gethsemane taken from the version in Matthew 26 stands out as a striking image especially in light of what we have said about Jacob at the Jabbok. There is much that is parallel between the texts, at least on the surface. Jesus, like Jacob, wrestles with God at night before his encounter with the ruling authorities. Much like Jacob, Jesus is filled with anxiety about what the morning would bring. Jesus takes disciples with him but still goes off alone to pray. Again, the issue of Jesus' identity is still in question in this text. The text is not clear exactly what it is that God intends. The ambiguity, so often dissolved by attempts to add a post-resurrection perspective, riddles the narrative. Taken as it is given to us, the ambiguity is especially unsettling.

It is this ambiguity that strikes us as an appropriate beginning point. Before we take up this central mood for the narrative we must, however, argue that the narrative (quite apart from the intent of the gospel writer) is fundamentally a Jewish story. Whatever Jesus may have thought his identity was, he was nevertheless quite clear that his work, his mission had to do with "the lost sheep of the house of Israel."[12] This point is especially important to say for the Matthean version since this gospel, alone among the gospels, emphasizes that the mission of the disciples of Jesus, distinct from Jesus' mission, was for the "nations," that is, the gentiles.[13] But Jesus remains a Jew both ethnically and in personal commitment. We see little to claim that Jesus understood his role as more than the basic role for his people as he and others understood that role in God's economy. Thus, we are looking at a Jewish Jesus in this narrative who struggles with his identity before a great confrontation prior to any clear resolution of either his identity or his fate. If this is true (and why not?), then we must ask first what this scene means in relation to Jesus' explicit work on behalf of his people. That is, what is the cup that Jesus is to drink if that is to be understood in connection with the specific identity and role of Israel? This question is probably not asked by many Christian preachers who use this text for homilies during holy week or any other time. In fact, the great tendency of the Christian teaching tradition has been to deny Jesus' specificity, Jesus' Jewishness, in this scene. Jesus' cup was his uniquely to drink. Jesus' role whatever his self-awareness, was for all humanity. At least, this is likely the interpretation given by much of the Christian tradition.[14] The pre-Shoah Christian theological

---

Studies in the Shoah Series, Zev Garber, ed., volume 5.

[12] cf., Matthew 10:6 and 15:24

[13] Matthew 28:19

[14] cf., Krister Stendahl, "Matthew", *Peake's Commentary on the Bible*

tradition basically ignored the specific role that the Jewishness of Jesus plays in this narrative.

This means that we cannot ignore the Jewishness of Jesus. In fact, we put that factor at center stage as we attempt to understand Jesus' prayer in Gethsemane and Jesus' perspective prior to his trial and death. To say this, however, does not give us a certain clue about Jesus' self-understanding since the meaning of what was Jewish in the first century c.e. was also ambiguous. Thus, I have consistently argued that the issue of Jesus' identity must be taken as a part of the larger discussion in first century Judaism concerning the true meaning of Judaism.[15] As such, Jesus' struggle becomes a contribution to that ongoing discussion in contemporary Judaism. Perhaps our dialogue (for this is an invitation to dialogue) can reveal in what ways this narrative about Jesus, the Jew, does contribute to this conversation about Jewish identity.

Still, this recognition of Jesus' Jewishness, as important as the dialogue on that matter is, remains outside of the issue of how Jesus fits into a post-Shoah Christian theology. The awareness of the Jewishness of Jesus within such a post-Shoah Christian theology becomes an heuristic tool rather than a specific focus for thinking. Lest we be arrogant about Christian theologies of Judaism, that should continue to be the case. Instead, I am suggesting that Jesus' Jewishness be a central criteria for any reading of Christian texts, especially the passion narrative. No reading of these texts can possibly be authentic that serves to deny or circumvent Jesus' Jewishness. Thus, we immediately become dubious about many pre-Shoah readings of Christian scripture including this narrative section about Jesus in the garden.

(London: Thomas Nelson and Sons, 1962), p. 795.
[15] Surely John Pawlikowski as much as anyone has tried to follow this line of thinking, cf.:
John Pawlikowski, *Christ in the Light of the Christian-Jewish Dialogue* (New York: Paulist Press, 1982). and
John Pawlikowski, *Jesus and the Theology of Israel* (Wilmington, DE: Michael Glazier, 1989).

Clearly, Jesus functions, in Christian theology, as the central defining source for what it means to be a Christian. Jesus as a person in history functions to provide a model of what it means to fully follow God's commands. In Luther's terms, Jesus is "true humanity."[16] Thus, Christians can define their self-understanding as fundamentally a discipleship of Christ (or an imitation of Christ). This text from Matthew is often used as an example of what following Jesus means in that Jesus shows in this narrative the courage to risk his own life for the sake of God's will. The Christian life can be pictured as this sort of self-denial for the sake of the will of God.

On the other hand, Jesus is seen as the Christ doing what no other human could do. Thus, Jesus' acts define Christianity not so much by modelling the Christian life but by what they produce for humanity. By denying himself for the sake of God's will, Jesus is said to reverse the pattern of the first Adam (the language of the apostle Paul) and become obedient even unto death.[17] This act, as noble as any similar act might be, has traditionally been seen as unique, as a special part of God's intent for the world.

Both of these ways of reading Jesus' role in Christian theology are background for our reading of this text as a Christian text. These two traditional readings of the passion narrative are also troubling for exactly the same reasons that we were troubled by certain Christian readings of the Jacob narrative. First, they are hidden Christian agenda that work to impose meaning on any given text rather than to allow the text, itself, to give rise to meaning. They are, beside that, quite exclusive criteria, not open to a dialogue between Jews and Christians. If we were to adjust even our hidden criteria to make our theologies dialogical (which is the challenge of a post-Shoah theology), then we would need to re-think these two approaches to the figure Jesus. All our theologies must be re-considered in the light of the Shoah.

Above all, these two agendas do serve to deny the Jewishness of Jesus by ignoring how that Jewishness, that particularity, plays a basic role in Jesus' self-identity. If Jesus models a particularly noteworthy behavior by denying himself for the sake of God's will, that denial of self is surely set into the context of a particular history. Thus, the point may

---

[16] Theodore Tappert, ed. *The Book of Concord* (Philadelphia: Fortress Press, 1959), pp. 413ff.
[17] cf., Romans 5:12ff.

not be primarily an appeal for an imitation of Jesus but rather a call back to faithfulness to the covenant tradition out of which Jesus and his disciples could understand their actions. The implicit appeal to texts such as Psalm 42:6 in the Matthean narrative might help us to see this broader background for understanding Jesus.

We also can say that the uniqueness of Jesus' actions needs to be re-thought as well. The model so often followed that we can see in Pauline theology may not be the meaning of the narrative we are considering. The cup that Jesus speaks of may not be so directly connected to the larger picture of the story of Adam, but rather we may see a connection with the prophetic tradition that turns our attention in quite a different direction. The text also includes an implicit connection with Ezekiel 23:31-34. The connection is more than merely a fascinating new opportunity for reading this part of Jesus' story but makes a specific reference to the Shoah, the destruction of Samaria by the Assyrians. That there is this connection may prove to give us a new reading of this Matthean text.

But finally, if there is a connection to the Shoah of ancient times, we are compelled to ask of this text exactly what we asked of the Genesis text. Is it possible to make such links given the experiences of the Shoah of our century. Indeed, we are led to the threshold of the appropriateness of using the word "Shoah" for both experiences. It is certainly the connection with Ezekiel that allows us to see that as powerful as this text could be for helping Christians to see a post-Shoah reading of the story of Jesus in the garden, this story is also quite different from the Shoah of our time. Jesus is not in the same or even similar position as the Jewish people, his people, were in Nazi Germany.

The Broader Background

Our aim here is to seek for a wider perspective that allows for alternative readings of this text from Matthew. We can gain that wider perspective by following the lead of implicit connections between our text and passages from the Psalms and Ezekiel as I have noted. These alternative perspectives cannot intrinsically hold priority for us except in the way that we find in the text, itself, interpretations that are more adequate for a post-Shoah Christian theology. We gain that possibility by turning to passages from the *Tanach* although again we exercise care to follow the basic criteria for treatment of texts from Hebrew scriptures.

The two texts provide a fascinating contrast of views regarding the Sinai experience for Israel. It is clear from the scant references in rabbinic literature to these two passages that they are both reflections on

Israel's role before God that comes from the covenant promises of Sinai.[18] These are two sides of a coin and both are needed to protect from false readings of Israel's role. It is not surprising then that we see in the Matthean text of Jesus in the garden both of these texts implicitly present. We suspect that the whole scene of Jesus' prayer has to do with more than just Jesus' identity and role but rather with the wider role of all Israel. A closer look at each of these texts can help us sketch this wider background.

The reference to Psalm 42:6 sets Jesus' own sense of the moment into the context of Israel's cry in exile for the glory of God that was placed upon Israel at Sinai. The soul of Israel is deeply troubled because the vision of Sinai has grown weak. Even so, this Psalm draws up this image of God's glory as a means for facing the dread of the moment of exile. The Rabbis argue that this text points to the god-like character of Israel, in the moment of Sinai. Israel is, then, more than human in the larger plan of God. It is this consistent wider perspective that enables Israel to combat the depression of their suffering. The one side of Israel's view of suffering, that this is only a small moment in a larger plan for Israel, is drawn into the Matthean text by this implicit reference to Psalm 42.

The Ezekiel text shows the other side of this theology of suffering. There is very little reference to Ezekiel 23:31ff. in the Midrash, and one can understand why. Ezekiel accuses Israel of abandoning God by whoring after false gods. The imagery of sexual unfaithfulness is a consistent prophetic picture. The notion that Israel will be stripped naked because of their infidelity to the covenant at Sinai is the other side of Israel's theology of suffering. The Ezekiel text defends God's faithfulness by loading the guilt onto Israel. This reading of Israel's theology can lead directly to a typical Christian understanding of the moment of Jesus in the garden. Jesus takes on the cup of affliction instead of those who otherwise deserve it. This has traditionally been a Christian reading of the struggle in Gethsemane. We can see the point, but it works only if Jesus'

---

[18] cf., C.G. Montefiore and H. Loewe, *A Rabbinic Anthology* (New York: Schocken Books, 1974), pp. 132, 435-437, 587.

role is viewed as distinct from that of Israel as a whole. We need a broader look at Ezekiel 23.

The point of Ezekiel is not the substitutionary theology of Christianity, of Christian readings of Isaiah. Ezekiel's words reflect a side of the Sinai picture in which the people of Israel did indeed drink a cup of affliction, but with the result of bringing the people back to repentance. The image of Ezekiel does not lose the other half of Israel's theology, that is, that Israel has been given the glory of God, the image of Psalm 42. Without both halves of this theology we distort the picture always. If we have only Psalm 42, we see Israel always as more than human, as the innocent victims of affliction. If we have only Ezekiel 23, we have Israel as the rejected and condemned sinner. The wedding of the two texts safeguards us from swinging to either extreme at the exclusion of the other. The broader background of the Matthean text is Israel's whole theology of suffering which ultimately finds its meaning in the full and continuing validity of the Sinai covenant.

That Jesus would seek to find his role in light of the images of Sinai is hardly surprising. That his impending suffering would be interpreted by using the dialectical theology of Israel as portrayed in the two texts, Psalm 42 and Ezekiel 23, is also not surprising but enlightening. Jesus understood his potential death as part of the larger picture of Israel's role as defined by Sinai. If we miss this basic fact, we run the risk of missing a vital aspect of the implicit meaning of this important narrative of Jesus in the garden. Even more, the text seems to hold this potential for any Christian theology that would make our understanding of Jesus fit with a philo-semitism, a teaching of respect for Israel.

The Two sides of this Theology Re-thought

We cannot ignore the Christian theological perspective that reads this text in light of the resurrection, nor should we. It is appropriate for Christians to see Jesus in this light as the resurrection is an essential part of Christian confession, indeed, in our understanding of a theology of suffering. It is also likely that the setting of this dual theology I have posed above into the confession of the resurrection is one of the factors that gave rise to the Chalcedonian dogma of the two natures of Christ (divine and human). With all the other factors involved (not the least of which was the hellenistic thinking that forced the categories of Chalcedon), we still can see that our brief journey through the broader background of the Matthean text gives us much more than an alternative reading of the garden scene. We have the potential to re-think our christology, the Chalcedonian formula.

It is possible that the notion of two natures does not arise purely out of the necessity of confronting Hellenistic mystery religions. Perhaps the two natures of Christ holds an affinity to the older tradition that Israel also bore two natures, that essential theology of suffering. Israel was given the glory of God at Sinai. This glory meant that Israel could never be completely destroyed since to do so would be for God to undo God's own plan. We don't have a picture of the pre-existent Christ here (not in Matthew nor in the theology of Israel), but there is already the effort to trace this giving of the glory to Israel back to the Patriarchs. Indeed, one such story can be found in Genesis 32, the story of Jacob at the Jabbok. Matthew, whoever the author was, surely does the same with Jesus by tracing Jesus' lineage back to the Patriarchs (notice Matthew's desire only to do this and not to take the Lucan route back to Adam and thus to God. Matthew only needs to link Jesus with the tradition of Sinai, and thus to Abraham.)

To speak of Jesus' divine nature in this broader context is to *link Jesus with Israel, in a way somewhat mysterious to us, and not to make of Jesus a uniquely independent divine figure*. If we think of Chalcedon in light of Matthew and the dialectic of Psalm 42 and Ezekiel 23, we have a radically different way of doing christology. This, of course, is a Christian concern, but it links with a potential way for Jews to think about Christian texts. Surely this narrative we now consider from Matthew is essentially a Jewish narrative. If taken out of the traditional Christian reading of the text, the narrative is a midrash on Exodus through the use of Psalm 42 and Ezekiel 23. It is not only appropriate for Jews to think about the figure Jesus as a Jew, but it is likely that that perspective is essential for appropriately reading this text, even for Christians. Thus, our dialogue becomes a significant factor in Christian attempts to do post-Shoah christologies.

Having given a route to re-think the shape of christology, and with that the framework of this text for Christian theology, we can move ahead to re-think the content of this narrative, that is, what does this specific narrative mean for us? If Jesus' identity is now to be linked with the larger role of Israel (in Fackenheim's terms *tikkun*), then this narrative has a meaning only in connection with that larger mission of Israel. To work out this theology completely would require looking at the passion narratives as a whole, something I have done in my book. Even so, we can now move to offer a location for the garden narrative in a post-Shoah Christian theology.

It is clear that Jesus and the gospel writers saw this moment in Jesus' life as a critical moment in the history of *tikkun*. Why would that be so? We can understand that only by seeing the historical situation for Israel. Israel was at a moment of crisis in its own land. They were captive, under the thumb of Rome. In that context, the theology of Israel was undergoing open debate between widely divergent positions. Jesus' teaching clearly places him into that controversy. Israel was shaping what its identity would be for generations to come. How that would take shape was critical for the future of Israel. Before *tikkun olam* could take place a healing within Israel was needed. Jesus' teaching and life were thrust into the middle of that struggle.

We can see in Jesus' teaching that he fundamentally aligns himself with one of the strands of Jewish teaching of the time. His words are almost completely reproduced in various places in Rabbinic literature. Jesus was essentially aligned with the pharisees, that group that would later dominate Judaism. Much of this complex picture surely is part of what eventually leads Jesus to Jerusalem and into the confrontation with the priestly group. Many others have more adequately portrayed this whole narrative picture and we need not reproduce that thinking here.[19] The undercurrent of this passion narrative was essentially confrontation on what was to be the true identity of Israel. It is thus, not surprising that the gospel places Jesus into the tradition of Sinai, a true representative of the divine-human encounter that took place at Sinai.

But we must ask why this confrontation? That makes sense only if we see that Jesus saw the alliance between the priests in Jerusalem and the Roman authorities as an unholy alliance (akin to the prophetic plea of Ezekiel). The cup that Jesus envisions is the cup of resistance to this alliance. Could he have known that a confrontation would lead to his execution? Perhaps he knew this and knew that the basic trust that God would not allow God's plan to be destroyed in apostasy was central to his plea in the garden. We cannot assume exactly what Jesus thought God's reaction would be. We cannot assume that he thought God would intervene and save him from death (as with the crucifixion scene and the appeal from the crowd that he save himself). Instead, we have the second image taken from Psalm 42. "My soul thirsts for God, for the living God." Jesus accepts the will of God not in resignation and not in the belief that his lot was unique, but in the full knowledge that Israel had done this before. Israel had drunk the cup of affliction and their trust in God's promises had been rewarded. Jesus' trust is in his belief that his act of

---

[19] cf., Ellis Rivkin, *A Hidden Revolution* (Nashville: Abingdon Press, 1978), pp. 76ff.

resistance was simply right and that God would be a God who rescues Israel.

God Who Rescues Israel

As with the text in Genesis that shifts our view from Jacob to the divine wrestler, the garden scene shifts our view to the divine rescuer with the phrase "not my will but thine be done." And both Jesus and Jacob struggle through the night. Jacob receives a blessing that he has striven with God and with humanity. Jacob's unique experience is the heritage captured in the name "Israel." Jesus receives no blessing except according to the narrative, at the cross. In Matthew, that picture is again possible to see only through an extended application of Psalm 22. While Jacob, the child of a survivor wrestles with God to resist the divine manipulation of Jacob's life, of the life of Israel, Jesus wrestles with God to resist the human manipulation of divine will. We see two halves of Israel's identity by wedding these two texts. Because Israel dares to challenge God because Israel bears God's glory, God blesses Israel. Because Israel (Jesus) dares to challenge human authority because Israel bears the responsibility of God's glory, God rescues Israel.

This reading of the two texts is, however, too simplistic to work as a post-Shoah Christian theology if left with merely these two narrative strands. The theology of suffering that is the broader background of the Matthean text of Jesus in the garden is inadequate for a response to the Shoah. The theology is still true but the picture does not respond to a humanity that has become radically evil nor does it respond to a God who instead of wrestling with Israel through the night is apparently absent, with no blessing even as day breaks. The theology that has served both Judaism and Christianity crumbles in the darkness of Auschwitz. If only there were a divine stranger struggling with Israel through the night. If only there were a rescue that came in the midst of the evil. But the narrative of the kingdom of the night does not produce such potential for meaning.

For Christians the result is at least as traumatic theologically. The challenge is to the central confession of Christianity, to its christology. Without the God who rescues, Jesus is little more than a tragic figure, misled at the point of crisis. And if there is a God who rescues Jesus, who is linked with Israel, then there surely must be a God who rescues Israel in its time of great despair. This is the dilemma of post-Shoah Christian theology, and any genuine post-Shoah reflection on this text of Jesus in the garden cannot circumvent this dilemma. We have potentially lost our assurance of the God who rescues.

Locating the Jesus' narrative

What this means is that Roy Eckardt is correct. We cannot impose a finished redemption on the Jesus narrative.[20] We must return into history with Fackenheim and recognize that any post-Shoah christology must be proleptic,[21] that is we must see that Jesus is a "first fruits" for Christians who have been blessed with the glory of God not because we stand with Jacob at Sinai but because we seek to be disciples of Jesus. Jesus' act to submit to the will of the Father is a messianic deed that begins a process for us of ushering in the kingdom of God. It is the bridge for Christians into joining Jews in the mission of *tikkun olam*. Redemption is complete only when that full healing has taken place. This, of course, is not an explanation of the Shoah for that event remains unexplainable for us. We cannot know why God seemed so absent from Jacob's struggle at Auschwitz and we cannot know why God did not rescue even in the actions of so many Christians who chose to be indifferent. But we can know that especially after Auschwitz no Christian theology of redemption can claim that salvation has been finished in Jesus the Christ. Thus, we must reject theologies that read the garden narrative in this way.

Thus, Jesus becomes a model of resistance for us. This point is also obvious from the rest of the passion narrative, a fact that I have developed through a post-Shoah approach to those narrative strands.[22] That is, Jesus is an appeal to those who would be disciples to resist the forces who would work against God's plan for *tikkun*, especially forces that would deny the message of Psalm 42, that Israel has been given the glory of God, those who would dare to say that Judaism has lost its place in God's plan. Our mission becomes Jesus' mission, to safeguard Israel in all that we do so that we can join with Israel in its mission to the world.

---

[20] A. Roy Eckardt with Alice Eckardt, *Long Night's Journey into Day* (Detroit: Wayne State University Press, 1982), p. 150.

[21] Of course, I mix messages here. Fackenheim extends the call to *tikkun* but it is Rosemary Ruether who has called for a proleptic christology even as she has abandoned that effort to define such a christology. see:

Emil Fackenheim, *To Mend the World* (New York: Schocken Books, 1982). and

Rosemary Radford Ruether, *To Change the World* (New York: Crossroad, 1983), pp. 31ff.

Note that the difference of title for these two books may be more than just coincidence.

[22] cf., again my "Resurrection as Rescue"

CONCLUSION

There is much that is unresolved in this brief re-thinking of Genesis and Matthew, of the narratives of the Jabbok and of Gethsemane, including many of the possibilities for linking our new reading of the two texts. We have worked only to open the door to new interpretations. In so doing we create both essential criteria for any reading of both texts from Hebrew scripture and from Christian scripture for the sake of shaping post-Shoah Christian theologies. At least some of those criteria are clear in what we have said, even as they await even more development. But this open-endeness is exactly the shape of our midrashic approach that can only continue to take form as we engage in dialogue. Still, the extraordinary narratives concerning Jacob wrestling through the night and Jesus struggling with his identity in the garden are equally fruitful for new possibilities in their own right. Thus, I await with eagerness the conversation that we will have concerning these texts.

Chapter 3: Night Encounters: Theologizing Dialogue
Zev Garber

This essay presents a Jewish reading of Jacob at Jabbok (Gen 32: 22-32) and Jesus at Gethsemane (Matt 26: 36-46). The views presented here reflect familiar texts rethought in light of the Shoah. Our inquiry into the two texts will apply the methodology of the Old Rabbis as it was practiced during and shortly after the formative period of rabbinic Judaism. With humility bordering on *chutzpah*, we venture in to the *PaRDeS* (paradise): *Peshat*, meaning of text as received; *Remez*, scriptural understanding bordering on the allegorical and philosophical; *Derash*, homiletic approach characterized by reading into the text; and *Sod*, esoteric inner and mystical meaning, existentially understood and applied, the four approaches to text common to Rabbinic interpretation.

GENESIS 32: 22-32
I. By Way of Introduction

More than the obedient Abraham and the frail Isaac, the figure of Jacob dominates Jewish ancestral traditions throughout the ages. History and fancy blend together in projecting Jacob as the patriarchal body and soul of the Jewish people, in whose personality and image the failures and successes, the dreams and reality, the curses and blessings of a parochial culture are portrayed in microcosm. To understand the Jewish people at any given juncture is to demythologize Jacob in accordance with the historical process and *Zeitgeist* of a given age and place. However, the timelessness of Jacob is anchored to personalities and events --- sibling rivalry, flight, dream, theophanies, reconciliation, Laban, Esau, etc., are all part and parcel of imagining the historical Jacob and living his promise.

Among the events in Jacob's life that tradition assigns an influential role is the patriarch's wrestle with the "angel" at Peniel. The composite picture of Godwrestle at the ford of Jabbok suggested in Torah and *aggadah* involves little historical objectivity and much subjectivity. Overwhelmingly, the wrestle is portrayed in mythical categories, the role of which is to allow one to think constructively and imaginatively about what is not spelled out in history. Of course, the mythicization of history is found in all cultures and traditions. The American cowboy is a contemporary case in point. [1] By demythologizing the divine-human combat, one catches a glimpse of the biblical-rabbinical view of the Jew as victim-fighter-survivor. The historical imagination couched for the most part in symbolic allegory and metaphor can benefit contemporary discussion on the faults and merits of Christian-Jewish memory and responsibility after the Shoah. For it assumes an approach to group and individual feelings suggested in paradigms where the subjective spirit of the interpreter-transmitter is basic to the questions asked and the answers given by historians, theologians, and philosophers.

Aggadic sources embellish the theme of Jacob's encounter with man and Other presented in Genesis 32, 33. The Sages reflect their contemporary history and feelings into the figures of Jacob, Esau, and the unnamed combatant, and draw analogies between the biblical texts and current events, which set forth the agenda for Jewish survival after catastrophe.

Responding to the destruction of Jerusalem and the dispersion of the Jewish people during the Roman occupancy of Eretz Israel, the Rabbis salvaged Judaism by placing it beyond time and history. They elevated Jewish values, practices and thought beyond the daily course of events --- determined by Gentiles --- to a timeless plane. After 70 C.E., in the rabbinic mind, Jews lived between the glories of the past and the messianic restoration to come --the future *Pardes*/Paradise, if you will. Contemporary events were noteworthy only insofar as they were foretold by past generations and/or gave clues about the coming redemption.

More specifically, the midrashic eisegesis on the Jabbok incident brings forth a rabbinic worldview of the non-Jewish world in successive

---

[1] These words are being written as the 65th annual Academy Awards has voted an American western as the best film of 1992. In the literate, tasteful production of "Unforgiven," the myth of the American cowboy has passed from being lionized, to being derided to being revered.

periods: Rome's dominant presence in Eretz Israel followed by the Church's determined and dominant role in the Jewish Diaspora. The ahistorical response of the Sages: Survival with dignity now, survival with dignity then, with little change from the rabbinic epoch to the biblical period, and we may add, likewise to the post-Shoah age.

II. Biblical Exegesis and Rabbinical Eisegesis

Gen 32:25. "And Jacob was left alone (*levado*) ... until the breaking of the day." This is seen in conjunction with "There is none like God, O Jeshurun" (Deut 33:26). Read, "There is none like God *but* Jeshurun," which stands for the patriarch Jacob and his descendants. In history, Israel dwells apart (*levadad*), not reckoned among the nations (Num 23:9), and God alone (*badad*) did guide him (Deut 33:12). And none but the Lord (*levado*) shall be exalted (Isa 2:11) in that "break of dawn" when Israel's subjugation to the Nations of the World will end.

Gen 32:26. "And when he saw that he prevailed not against him, he touched the hollow of his thigh; and the hollow of Jacob's thigh (*yerek*) was stained as he wrestled with him." Jacob is defeated at his thigh, the word can also mean "loins" (see Exod 1:15), the root of his enmity with his brother (Gen 25:26) and sisters-wives (Lev 18:18).

In rabbinic context, these sentiments are interpreted as the angel of Esau/Edom [2] (Peniel, the place of the wrestle --- "for I have seen God face to face" [Gen 32:31] --- is connected to Jacob being favorably received by his brother as "One (who) sees the face of God" [Gen 33:10]), that is to say, Esau/Edom which is Rome was unable to slay Jacob totally but managed "to touch" the righteous men, women, and children during the insurrection of the first and second centuries, and particularly, the Hadrianic persecution, 135-138, which followed the ill-fated Bar-Kochba rebellion, 133-135. In the fire of the Shoah, the "strained thigh" represents the murdered Six Million and their unborn generations and thousands of survivors who betray their ancestral faith and/or chose not the procreate future children of the covenant (*yerek*, a phallic symbol, is the site of the *Brit Milah*, Covenant of the

---

[2] Esau is identified as Edom in Gen 36:1.

Circumcision) due to the holocaustal experience. On the other hand, those who survived this great *Kiddush ha-Shem* and chose to live openly as Jews merit the reward of the lamed Jacob.

Gen 32:27. "And he said, 'let me go, for dawn is breaking.' But he answered, 'I will not let you go, unless you bless me.'" Since Jacob is asked to release his celestial opponent, it follows that the righteous are greater than angels. But Jacob demands a blessing as the price of release. Yet what blessing can Jacob demand from Esau/Edom, who in the rabbinic mind is a synonym for treachery, violence, oppression, and injustice? The blessing, therefore, is a reconsideration of a past malediction: "(Esau) said, 'was he, then, named Jacob that he might supplant me (*'aqav*) these two times? First he took away my birthright and now he has taken away my blessing!'" (Gen 27:36). In light of history and the Shoah, when one-third of the Jewish people were murdered in the *Endlösung* by the children of Edom, Jacob's Children have every reason to fear Esau, but they must also learn the *raison d'etre* of being Israel, to hope eternally and not to fear.

Gen 32:29. "And he said: 'Your name shall be called no more Jacob, but Israel; for you have striven with God and with men, and have prevailed.'"

No longer will Jacob attain the blessing by "supplanting" but as "fighter (*sarita*, connected with the first part of Israel) - with-God (*Elokim*, connected with second part of Israel)," who has earned the divine recognition to become the third patriarch of a people destined to fight "the battles of the Lord" (Num 21:14). In biblical idiom, *shem*/"name" means essence, and the new name removes the stain (curse) of Gen 27:36 (see above). This is a prologue to the incident as Beth-El, where God appeared to Jacob and blessed him and said: "'You whose name is Jacob, you shall be called Jacob no more, but Israel shall be your name.' Thus He named him Israel ... 'A nation, yea an assembly of nations, shall descend form you. Kings shall issue from your loins'" (Gen 35: 10-11). Tradition understand this to be the kings of Judah and Israel, exilarchs in Babylonia, patriarchs in the Land of Israel, and the King Messiah.

Gen 32:30. "Jacob asked, 'Pray tell me your name.' But he said, 'You must not ask my name!' And he took leave of him there." [3] Angels have no set names; names change with the missions entrusted upon them (Rashi).

---

[3] Hebrew, "And he blessed him there." Midrash (Lekah Tob) understands the blessing to be longevity (Job 5:25), priestly (Num 6: 24-26), progeny (Esek 20:40), and messianic (Ps 132:17).

Similarly, forces of destruction and antisemitism are everywhere and anywhere, and they are named only in the eye of the storm. Besides, the death of Jews in Nazi Europe are beyond human terminology and the power to recover from out of the whirlwind (Job 38:1, 40:6) resides in man and God and not in angels.

Gen 32:32. "And the sun rose upon him." In the rabbinic mind, this is seen as an omen for the Children of Israel. Just as the sun has healed Jacob and burned Esau and his chiefs, [4] so will the sun heal the descendants of Jacob and scorch the Nations of the World. It will heal Israel in accordance with the verse, "unto you that bear My Name shall the sun of righteousness arise with healing in its wings" (Mal 3:20), but it will ignite the nations, as the verse states, "The day is at hand, it burns as a furnace. All the arrogant and all the doers of evil shall be straw, and the day that is coming -- said the Lord of Hosts --- shall burn them to ashes and leave them neither root nor branch" (Mal 3:19). Also, in Obadiah, we read, "And the house of Jacob a flame, and the house of Esau for stubble, and they shall kindle them, and devour them; And there shall not be any remaining of the house of Esau; for the Lord has spoken" (Obad v. 18).

By associating Edom with the teachings of *contra-Judaeos* found in Christendom, and evident in the *Voelkische Kulturreligion,* both Protestant and Roman Catholic of Nazi Europe, a post-Shoah theology is born that is intended to ease the Jewish holocaustal pain by suggesting that a day of vengeance exposing the sources of Nazi antisemitism and the Final Solution is at hand. And Christians and Jews in reconciliatory dialogue can ensure that victory is inevitable.

III. Angelophany: Three Faces
Michael

A number of midrashim [5] identify the combatant who injured Jacob as Michael, chief heavenly priest; he did the act voluntarily for the glory of God. The Lord reproached Michael for inflicting harm on "My first born son" (see Exod 4:22, "Israel is My son, my first born") by appointing him as the eternal guardian angel of Jacob and his seed unto the end of history. [6] On the other hand, Michael entreated with Jacob to let him go (Gen 32:27) since he

---

[4] Gen 36 (all) and especially vs. 31-43. "These are the kings who reigned in the Land of Edom before any king reigned over the Israelites" (v 31) is inspirational, i.e., when wickedness falls, triumphant good prevails.

[5] Tanhuma Yelemmedenu Vayishlah 7, Midrash Avkir in Yalkut I, 132.

[6] A biblical example of eternal vigil is provided to a non-betrothed virgin who is taken by force. See Deut 22:28-29.

feared the angels of 'Arabot; they would consume him with fire if he did not start heavenly songs of praise at the proper time -- day break. Jacob replied that Michael who blessed his father and grandfather should bless him too was met with a curt rejection: the servant, who was *not* sent by God, is subservient to the son. Under pressure, however, Michael conceded and took comfort in the thought if God yields to the wishes of Jacob's heirs, how then can he leave Jacob's wish unfulfilled. And he blessed him by saying, may the entire house of Israel be as pious as you are and may their contributions and choicest offerings of sacred things be accepted by the Lord God (see Ezek 20:40).

Jesus

What Jewish tradition ascribes to Michael is often transferred in the writings of the early Church Fathers to Jesus. It follows then that the struggle between the messenger and Jacob at Jabbok makes no sense unless it is seen as the struggle between Christ and the Jews, which is said to reach its classic typology in the gospels. The fight at the river is seen as the contest in which the non-baptized Jews are forever lost in the ignorance of the night. The angel lost the wrestling bout voluntarily to signify the passion of Christ wherein the Jews overpowered him. Likewise, the nameless angel (Gen 32:30) --- the name is not revealed since Jesus was not yet born in the flesh --- gave a blessing, so also Jesus prayed for his executioners. Also, Jacob limped, and the Children of Israel do not cut sinew of the thigh vein (Gen 32:33). This ritualistic act, which in the Jewish tradition is seen as a constant reminder of a people's providential origins, symbolizes in the Christian tradition eternal providential rejection. Another interpretation of Jacob's limping is that his two legs represent Jews and Christians, and the former will have a numbness concerning the grace of salvation. Finally, for others, the lamed Jacob represents the unbelieving Jews and the Jacob who sees "God face to face" (Gen 32:31) represents the true believers, Jews and Christians alike.

Combining the antiquity of Christian and Jewish views that the *'ish* who wrestled Jacob is Michael-Jesus, we are presented with several reinterpretations. First, Michael set out to destroy Jacob but in the end, he harmed and wounded him. Similarly, the Church, the Body of Christ, set out to tarnish the body of Jacob, which in the long nocturnal process has rendered immeasurably to the pain of the Jews as it lessened the value of Judaism in the theology of grace. Yet Michael was *not* charged by God to impair Jacob, and correspondingly, the Church's negative theologizing hermeneutic against the Jews is without a firm divine mandate. Second,

Michael is viewed as the celestial choir master who cannot do his appointed task unless Jacob releases him and this is conditioned by the blessing offered. In like manner, can the Church continue in good conscience liturgy-as-usual without coming face-to-face with its participatory role (mainly as victimizer) in the genocidal night? The blessing requested is two-fold (in the spirit of Gen 32: 27,30): recognition and affirmation that the Chosen People has not been supplanted by the Chosen Church and knowledge that God's truth can never be tied to an eschatology of exclusive salvation. Renouncing supersessionism and antisemitism alike, and critically supporting Jewish survival, this sends forth a powerful stimulus for bringing on the Kingdom of Dawn.

In a post-Shoah age, the exigency of an injured Jacob to survive physically is an alliance with a supportive and protective Christianity; and the need of the Church to rectify morally bankrupt "truth-claims" is to connect Christocentrism with the historical development of Judaism, then and now.

Israel

The mystics of the geonic period speak of a *hayyah* (heavenly being) whose name is "Israel." This *hayyah's* function is to call the hosts of heaven to praise God's Name. He chants: "Blessed You the Lord who is to be blessed," and they reply, "Blessed is the Lord who is to be blessed for ever and ever." [7] In midrashic etymology, the name *Yisrael* in the text of Gen 32 poses four possibilities. The first affirms *'ish ra'ah El*/"one who sees God." The second states *yashir El*/"singing like angels." The third declares *shear El*/"the remnant of God," and the fourth proclaims *yashar El*/"he who walks straight with God." In calling the patriarch "Israel," may this not reflect the identity (*shem*) of the *'ish* (*Yisrael* = "warrior at the bequest of God") transferred now to Jacob? So interpreted, then Jacob's Godwrestling is in reality, self-wrestling.

In assessing the guilt of the Nazis, and the role of the Church and

---

[7] See Hekalot 4, 29; Zohar II, 4b. The *Borechu* is the ancient invocation to public prayer for the *Shema*, and the blessings before and after, in the morning and evening services.

the nations in the most horrific crime directed against the Jewish people in history, the Jew must ask what role --- or lack of role --- did he play in the atrocities. What sin done, what punishment overturned, what signals ignored, what obligations unfulfilled?

In confronting the fire and sacrifice, one senses two faces of the victim of the Night struggle: *Yeshurun*, who walks straight, and *Ya'akov*, who walks crookedly . But the one named *Yeshurun* is "fat and gross and coarse --- he forsook the God who made him and spurned the Rock of his support" (Deut 32:15). Ingratitude to the Source of life and not caring or learning the lessons of annihilation will contribute to ongoing acts of perfidy. However, the one born *Ya'akov* earned the title "Israel" and his limp implies not lacking firmness or strength but represents that Jew who has confronted the holocaustal evil decrees of God and man and has prevailed (Gen 32:29). He is the true surviving remnant who knows that the Teaching given at Sinai, as "the heritage of the congregation of Jacob," [8] to "choose life," [9] is the antidote to the fumes of cyanide. This is the Jacob who can sing, "There is none like God, O Jeshurun, riding through the heavens to protect you, though the skies in His majesty" (Deut 33:26).

Jacob, weakened and yet made stronger in the crucible of the Shoah, is psychologically prepared to meet at the River the other streams of the Abrahamic faith in mutual dialogue and respect. Only the Jacob who can wrestle unabashedly with the curse of the Shoah can hope to emerge with the blessing of *Shalem* (Gen 33:7), totally whole and at peace with the struggle. He has seen the dark face of God and yet he walks upright, refusing to be downtrodden. He is the moral linchpin of Israel's great messianic hope --- the dawning of God's kingdom over *Yeshurun*: "Then He became King in Jeshurun, when the heads of the people assembled, the tribes of Israel together" (Deut 33:5).

MATTHEW 26: 36-46
IV. Unending Seder

The encounter of the Patriarch Jacob and the *'ish* at the ford of the Jabbok is often compared to the account about Jesus in Gethsemane (Matt 26: 36-46; and parallels in Mark 14: 32-42 and Luke 22: 40-46). The Night words in both accounts are riddled with mystery, anxiety, and ambiguity.

---

[8] Deut 33:4.
[9] Deut 30:19.

Jesus, like Jacob, struggles on the eve of a dreadful crisis in solitude and pensive fear; and he is unsure what the dawn would bring. This uncertainty provides fertile ground for scriptural retrospection. How to respond to the indeterminate anguish of Jesus on the night that he was betrayed within a framework of Christian-Jewish dialogue after the Shoah is the intent of this section. What follows is a partisan view of Jesus in the garden read as part of the passion narrative according to the school of Matthew and qualified by the four cubits of the Halachah (Ber. 8a) --- so justified since Matthew, unlike the other Synoptic Gospels, is recognized as a thoroughly Jewish account.

In context, the agony of Jesus is an extension of the narrative of the Last Supper, a Passover Seder meal, involving Jesus and his disciples (Matt 26: 26-29). Though there are halachic disparities with the Matthean Seder (e.g., Jesus blessing first the bread and then wine; at a festive meal, such as Passover, the rabbinic order is *Kiddush* [wine] and *Motzi* [bread]), especially, the Christological insertion, it is, however, traditionally informed with questions, interpretations, and a concluding hymn. It is not clear from the text whether the hymn is one, several, or all of Psalms 113-118 ("The Hallel [Praise] of Egypt"), which the Levites chanted during the offering of the paschal lamb (m. Pesah. V. 7) or Psalm 136 ("The Great Hallel"; Ber. 4b, Pesah. 118a, m. Ta'an. III. 9) is meant.

The formal Seder is extended to the Mount of Olives. "Then Jesus said to them, 'You will all fall away because of me this night; for it is written, 'I will strike the shepherd, and the sheep of the flock will be scattered'" (Zech 13:7).

Like the double-visaged god Janus, a Christological reading of Zech 13: 7, 8 is not only concerned with the realized eschatology expressed at the ceremonial meal (Matt 26:29) and the agony of Jesus at Gethsemane (Matt 26: 36-46) but looks as well to the Shoah. Meaning, the shepherd, for Matthew, is Jesus, and the people who had rejected him will be scattered and will suffer the consequences. [10] And what may they be:

I will turn My hand upon the little ones

---

[10] Compare "the sheep of the flock will be scattered" (Zech 13:7b) and Jesus' charge in sending out of the twelve, "Go to the lost sheep of Israel" (Matt 10:6).

Throughout the land --- declares the Lord ---
Two thirds therein shall perish, shall die,
And one third of it shall survive.
That third I will put into fire ...

(Zech 13: 7b, 8, 9a)

Jewish commentators, however, view the shepherd as the perennial tyrannical antisemite, who will be punished for his opposition of Israel by the dispersion of his people. And the Jewish survivalist views the Shoah simile in terms of a purified surviving remnant:

I will bring the third part through the fire,
And will refine them as silver is refined,
And will try them as gold is tried;
They shall call on My Name,
And I will answer them;
I will say: 'It is My people,'
And they shall say: 'The Lord is my God.'

(Zech 13:9)

The anguish of spirit in the Gethsemane narrative implies images from the Hebrew Bible. The cup of suffering, for example, in Matt. 26:30 recalls a charge to Jerusalem to awaken from the stupor of her cup of affliction and degradation (Isa 51:17, 22); suggests that God doles out fire, brimstone, and burning wind as the portion of the evil-doer's cup, i.e., they are instruments to demolish evil (Ps 11:6); and invokes God's cup of vengeance on Edom, who sided with Babylonia when Judah was conquered in 586 B.C.E. (Lam 4:21).

However, it is Jesus yearning for communion with God (Matt 26:39, 42, 44) that is most inspired by a biblical prototype: the lament by one who is excluded from the Temple in Jerusalem. In Psalm 42, we read:

My soul cries for You, O God (v. 2b)
My soul thirsts for God, the living God;
O when will I come to appear before God! (v. 3)
My tears have been my food day and night;
I am even taunted with, "Where is your God?" (v. 4)
When I think of this, I pour out my soul (v. a)
Why so downcast, my soul,
Why disquieted within me (v. 6a)
O my God, my soul is downcast (v. 7a)
I say to God, my rock,
"Why have you forgotten me,
Why must I walk in gloom,

Oppressed by my enemy?" (v. 10)
Crushing my bones
My foes revile me
Taunting me always with, "Where is your God?" (v. 11)
Why so downcast, my soul,
Why disquieted within me? (v. 12a)

This is not merely a lament of levitical choristers cut off from divine service, [11] but a profound and striking image to Shoah theodicy: the predicament of the anathematized victim who feels further distressed when there is perceived divine silence to the enemy's taunt, "Where is thy God?"

If God is not limited in either power or benevolence, then why? Why the seeming apathy on the part of God, which gives succor to the destroyer. The meditative plaint of the Psalmist is the shattered faith of the survivor; "the unbearable reality that haunts sleep and destroys wakefulness." [12]

Yet festival sleep and not dreadful wakefulness overcame the disciples. On this "Night of Watching" (*Leyl Shemurin*), [13] Jesus' question to Peter, "Could you not watch with me one hour?" (Matt 26:40), a poignant concern which is also suggested in verses 43 and 45, graphically describe his state of abandonment. However, it is the seemingly silence of God (Matt 26:39, 42, 44) that affects Jesus so deeply that he feels emotional pain: "And being in agony, he prayed more earnestly; and his sweat became like great drops of blood falling down upon on the ground" (Luke 22:44). [14] The strong language of sorrow is explained in Christian tradition as the recognition that physical death awaited Jesus and his bearing of human sins as well. Substitute the "Six Million" for "Jesus" and you have a core Christian and Jewish apology for the Shoah: "theology of suffering" on the one hand and "birth pains of the Messiah" on the other explain why the crucifixion of the Jews [15] for the saving of humanity.

---

[11] The heading of Ps 42 is "For the leader, a *maskil* of the Korahites." Korah was the leader who perished in the abortive revolt against Moses (Num 16), but the sons of Korah did not (Num 26:11) and they were part of the Levites who "extol the Lord God of Israel at the top of their voices" (2 Chr 20:19).

[12] Robert McAfee Brown, *Elie Weisel, Messenger to All Humanity*, (Notre Dame, Indiana: University of Notre Dame Press, 1989), p. 54.

[13] Cf. Exod 12:42.

[14] This sentence is wanting in Matthew.

[15] This phrase was first used by Abba Hillel Silver (1893-1963) in addresses before the National Conference on Palestine (May 2, 1943) and the American Jewish Conference, NYC (August 29 - September 5, 1943). But there is little

If the *Sitz-im-Leben* of the abandonment of Jesus is an extended
Seder meal, as we argued, then the above apologia would not do. The proper
parallel to his suffering and forsakeness is the hopeful refrain recited by Jews
after the meal in expectation of deliverance. A closer look at the retelling of
Passover in rabbinic tradition may explain why. In the biblical institution of
the Passover, we read:

> It was for the Lord a Night of Watching
> to bring them (Israelites) out of the
> Land of Egypt; this same night is a
> Night of Watching unto the Lord for
> all the Children of Israel throughout
> their generations.

(Exod 12:42)

The Rabbis interpreted this text and "It came to pass at midnight"
(Exod 12:29) historiosophically, as was their custom. "Throughout their
generations" marked the deliverance of their ancestors from the dangers that
besieged them. By microsophical examination of the biblical text, they found
midrashic authority for suggesting that the whole succession of miraculous
deliverances mentioned in the Bible, from the time of Laban to that of
Sennacherib occurred on Passover night (Num. Rab. XX.12). [16] Similarly,
the final deliverance of all generations, is to take place on Passover eve,
which is a true *Leyl Shemurin* unto the Lord for all generations. Thus, the
great tribulation of Jesus on that night of Passover vigil when abandoned by
his disciples, he experienced Godforsakeness, [17] and this is echoed in the
words at the cross: "*Eli, Eli lamah sabachtani*," meaning, "My God, my
God, why has Thou forsaken me?" (Matt 27:46).

---

doubt that the one man who has done most to establish "The Crucifixion of the
Jews" in the modern Christian consciousness is Franklin H. Littell. Cf. The
Crucifixion of the Jews by Franklin H. Littell (New York: Harper and Row, 1975;
reprinted by Mercer University Press, 1986) for his impacting view on Christianity
and the Shoah.

[16] A supplementary hymn in the Ashkenazi ritual on the first night of Passover,
"And so it came to pass in the middle of the night," is influenced by this midrash.
It is said to be composed by Yannai, one of the principal liturgists of the old
Palestinian *piyyut*.

[17] In Hebrew, *Hester Panin* ("The Hidden Face of God"). See my comments on
"Deconstructing Theodicy and Amalekut, A Personal Apologia," in G. Jan Colijin
and Marcia S. Littell, eds., The Netherlands and Nazi Genocide: Papers of the 21st
Annual Scholars' Conference, (Lewiston, NY: The Edward Mellen Press, 1992),
pp. 407-428.

Yet one is saved from despair by placing invisible trust in the Watchman of the Night. Consider the suffering Psalmist who rebukes his moribund soul with the charge to trust the Lord:

Why so downcast, my soul,
Why disquieted within me?
Have hope in God;
I will yet praise Him
for His saving presence
(Ps 42:6; repeated with slight alteration in v. 12)

In like manner, Psalm 115, recited immediately after the Grace and part of the "Hallel of Egypt" (Pss 113-118 which mirror future deliverance), is a call for national trust in God against the heathen who did not believe in the wonders which God performed in Egypt and at Sinai. The medieval counterpart to the heathen who knew not God and destroyed His Temple are the civilization who believe in Creation, and in the Exodus, and in the moral teaching of Sinai, and still "devour Jacob and lay waste his habitation." Under the stress of persecution by Christians and Moslems during the period of the Crusades, the powerless, wandering Jew denied the rival monotheistic claims that he is cursed by God and man, and invoked the Deliverer to:

Pour out Thy wrath upon the nations
(Christianity, Islam) that know Thee not
And upon the kingdoms that call not upon Thy Name
For they have devoured Jacob (people), And
Laid waste his habitation (Jerusalem).
(Ps. 79: 6,7)

Pour out Thine indignation upon them
And let the fierceness of Thine anger
Overtake them.
(Ps 69:25)

Thou will pursue them on anger and
Destroy them
From Under the Heavens of the Lord. [18]

---

[18] See Zev Garber, "Interpretation and the Passover Haggadah: An Invitation to Post-Biblical Historiosophy," *BHHE*, vol. 2.2 (Spring 1984), p. 27. The paper is reprinted in Duane C. Christensen, ed., *Experiencing the Exodus from Egypt*, (Oakland: Bibal Press, 1988), pp. 51-60. Connecting the "Pour out Thy wrath" paragraph with the Shoah is developed in my "Images of the Shoah in the

(Lam 3:66)

The above reading should not be understood as an expression of vindictiveness toward the non-Jew --- the Halachah instructs the Jew to pray continually for the welfare and success of kingdoms and ministers, and for all states and places in which he resides [19] --- but should rather be interpreted as invoking the Judge-of-all-the-Earth to deal justly with the Nations of the World as He continuously does with Israel (classical Jewish apologia for why Jewish suffering), so that the complete messianic fulfillment of the future, a universal siblinghood inspired by the Torah way, can be realized swiftly in our day. This is not poor theology, as some have argued, but an authentic Jewish understanding of *Heilsgeschichte*, as seen, for example, in Gen 17, Deut 32, Isa 2 and Micah 4.

The significance of the Seder message, retributive not vindictive justice ushers in the Great Redemption, should not be misconstrued by the post-Shoah Christian. It is a necessary wake-up call to the slumbering Christian to rediscover the Jewish roots of his/her faith, which are deep and far reaching, and to live with the *imitatio Christi* without antisemitism. It is an invitation to Christian preaching and catechism to understand Jewish belief and practice without polemics, politics and paternalism. It is a calling to see the Jew not as fossil or ashes but as God's first love in His salvific plan ("As far as election is concerned, they (Jews) are loved on account of the patriarchs. For God's gift and His call are irreversible." [20]). And by encouraging lessons learned from Darkness to Rebirth, Shoah and the State of Israel, it is hoped that the Church can correct an ambivalent triumphalist teaching about the Jews:

Passover Haggadah," a paper presented at the 23rd Annual Scholars' Conference on the Holocaust and the German Church Struggle. See, Zev Garber, *Shoah: The Pragmatic Genocide* (Lanham/New York/London: University Press of America, 1994), pp. 137-154.

[19] Jewish loyalty to ruler and country has its roots in Jeremiah's letter to the exiles: "Seek the welfare of the city to which I have exiled you and pray to the Lord in its behalf; for in its prosperity you shall prosper" (Jer 29:7). Fear of Lord and king is expressed in Prov 24:21 and Ezra 6:10. Mishna Abot 3.2 reports in the name of R. Hanina, the Vice-High Priest, "Pray for the peace of the ruling power (Rome), since but for fear of it men would have swallowed up each other alive." The fourth century amora, Mar Samuel of Nehardea, laid down the biding principle, *Dina deMalkuta Dina*; in civil matters, the law of the land is as binding on Jews as the commandments of the Torah. "Prayers for the Government" are featured in the *Musaf* ("additional") liturgy for Sabbath and festivals by all Jews today.

[20] Rom 11:28b, 29.

> For he (Christ) himself is our peace, who has
> made the two (Jew and Gentile) one and has
> destroyed the barrier, the dividing wall of
> hostility, by *abolishing in his flesh the*
> *law with its commandments and regulations*
> (italics added). His purpose was to create
> in himself one new man out of the two, thus
> making peace, and in this one body to reconcile
> both of them to God through the cross, by
> which he put to death their hostility. [21]

(Eph 2: 14-16)

Then, and only then, can the Church ascend Jesus' conditional query (add, about the state of Christian belief) and proclaim: "My Father, it is possible that the cup passeth, as I will and as You will." [22] This is Christian redemption after the Shoah, any alternative is Christian suicide.

V. Conclusion: The Snake in the Pardes

The Shoah has destroyed Christian and Jewish innocence in reading scriptures. Whether or not there is a direct link between two thousand years of Christian supersessionism teaching and the Shoah, the murder of millions of Jews in the heart of Christendom cannot be denied. The culpability of Christian teaching in fostering cultural and religious antisemitism in doctrine and dogma must be eliminated. To love the Lord Jesus Christ and to walk in his footsteps cannot be out of step to the Jewish, Christian and non-Christian victims of the Austrian Catholic, Adolf Hitler, and his co-religionist (Catholic and Protestant) murderers.

To say that not all Jews of Europe were murdered and that there is life affirmation among the *She'erith ha-Pleita* (saved remnant of Israel), and

---

[21] Other noteworthy examples of supersessionist eschatology are John 4: 21-26 and Gal 3:26-29.

[22] A post-Shoah re-reading of Matt 26:42b.

then invoke Torah as the panacea is naive and misleading. Torah is what it is and not what we make it out to be.

Torah is not the all perfect absolute of the true believers, nor does it provide an instant blueprint to rescue upon distress or demand. In God's creation, there is *tohu vavohu* ("unformed and void"), [23] so that man can redeem an imperfect world. God purposefully hides His face so that man can be free and choose the right ethical action.

God did His job and gave Torah at Sinai so that the Jew and mankind can learn and do. But can the Jew today read the Torah intact? Is he able, does he care? Pogroms, expulsions, crematoria have blackened and scourged its words. Memory of its content is filled with corpses and broken promises. To seek the seer and scribe is to find ashes, shoes and mattresses of hair.

But the Voice of Torah stubbornly refuses to be silent and its deafening words demand a hearing: God and Shoah. Do we read and evil demiurge capable of willing a universe in which Auschwitz can fit or do we say, the horrific Event is less severe by the presence of the Creator? In re-reading the Holy Scriptures after Shoah, do we encounter God and not Auschwitz, Auschwitz and not God, neither God nor Auschwitz, or God and Auschwitz?

In reading Jacob at Jabbok and Jesus at Gethsemane, the fourth option, for me, seems the most probable starting point for post-Shoah ecumenical dialogue. To wrestle with the Night Words of Jacob and Jesus is to confront the snake in the *Pardes*: a continuous *Din Torah* (disputation based on Torah-judgement) with God, self and other, which instead of diminishing the paradox makes the problem more significant and more troubling and thus, more full of hope. It presents a challenge to Christians and Jews towards a true reconciliation accountable to scriptures and responsible to a post-Shoah world. Let the re-thinking on self and reciprocal discovery begin!

---

[23] Gen 1:2a.

Chapter 4: WRESTLING WITH TWO TEXTS: A POST-SHOAH ENCOUNTER
Henry F. Knight

MEETING JACOB AT THE JABBOK[1]

Introduction

What might Jews and Christians discover if they met over a shared biblical text in an honest and forthright attempt to interpret a text each honored as the Word of God? What might they discover if they moved to more problematic ground, namely, a text which for one was sacred and paradigmatic and for the other historically and existentially problematic. The following essay examines these interrelated questions by focusing on two key biblical texts. In the first case (Gen. 32: 22-33), Abraham's grandchildren, Jacob and Esau, are preparing to meet in the context of a twenty year estrangement. Jacob has displaced his older, twin sibling, taking his birthright and blessing. The night before their historic encounter, Jacob wrestles with a mysterious, unnamed figure.[2] Reflecting on this text, the Jabbok story is re-entered and the dynamics which Jacob faced are explored. In the second case, the story of Gethsemene (Matt. 26: 36-46) is explored, focusing on Jesus' night of wrestling and its meaning for contemporary Christians and Jews as they ask how this central story for Christians has been affected by what happened in yet

---

[1] An earlier version of the first part of this essay has been published as "Meeting Jacob at the Jabbok: Wrestling With A Text," *Journal of Ecumenical Studies*, vol. 29, No. 3 & 4, Summer-Fall, 1992, pp. 451-460. It is used here with permission.

[2] Alan Segal, in his historical study of the birth of Judaism and Christianity, has developed a more direct metaphorical identification of Judaism and Christianity with Esau and Jacob. Citing Genesis 25: 23-24, he contends that rabbinic Judaism and Christianity both grew out of the faith world of Israel's Second Commonwealth as critical transformations of Hebraic life and culture. Consequently, he argues, it is appropriate to equate Judaism and Christianity as "twin religions." See *REBECCA'S CHILDREN: JUDAISM AND CHRISTIANITY IN THE ROMAN WORLD* (Cambridge, Mass.: Harvard University Press) 1986. pp. 1-3, 142-181.

another night, the long night of destruction called the **Shoah.**   What
follows is written in a single voice in this encounter -- a Christian one --
and is offered, where it begins, at the threshold of the Jabbok, self-
consciously on the post-**Shoah** side of the history of Jewish-Christian
relations.

Facing the Text
Who was the *ish*, the one with whom Jacob wrestled during the
night at the Jabbok? With whom (or what) did Jacob wrestle on the
banks of the Jabbok? Was it the guardian angel of Esau, as the sage, R.
Hama b. R. Hanina, has suggested?[3] Was it Esau, the estranged brother,
sneaking into the camp under the cover of darkness?   Was it fear
personified? Was it guilt? Was the stranger the haunting and stalking
shadow of Jacob's father, Isaac? Was the stranger God?   Was the *ish*
Jacob himself, that is, the other side or sides of Jacob?[4]   Who was
encountered that night? What was encountered that night?
At the Jabbok, Jacob prepared for meeting his estranged brother
on the following day. He sent his family across the river, out of harm's
way, and prepared to wait and rest. But nightfall brought no rest. Instead
it brought struggle. An unnamed stranger, an *ish,* (literally, a man) came
and wrestled with Jacob through the night, putting his hip out of joint in
the struggle. When dawn approached, the assailant asked Jacob to let go.
Jacob resisted, demanding to be blessed in return. So the figure asked for
Jacob's name, which Jacob offered freely. At that point Jacob received
a new name, Israel, meaning, according to the text, that Jacob had striven
with God and with human beings and had prevailed. Jacob, now Israel,
held his grip long enough to ask for the name of the one with whom he
struggled. But Jacob received no name, only a question, asking Jacob

---

[3] See H. Freedman, trans., *MIDRASH RABBAH: GENESIS*, vol. II, LXXVII:
III, (London: The Soncino Press) 1939, p. 711.
[4] Elie Wiesel, *MESSENGERS OF GOD* (New York: Random House) 1976, p.
123f.

why he wanted to know. Jacob's question was met by another question which forced Jacob to search more deeply within himself asking: Why did he want or need to know?   Once more, Jacob had to face himself, even as he faced the *ish*, in that returning question. There the encounter ended and the stranger blessed Jacob.

Whatever else happened that night, Jacob struggled with his own identity and legacy. Wiesel in his commentary on the story contends that Jacob wrestled with himself, the other Jacob, hidden from view: weak, vulnerable, and dependent on his mother, Rebecca.   According to Wiesel, this Jacob fearfully anticipated the morning encounter with Esau. Surely then, whatever else Jacob wrestled with that night, it included, even if it was not limited to, the legacy and identity he brought to that river bank. Jacob wrestled with *a lifetime in one night.*

The Unnamed Other

Jacob asked for the intruder's name. Instead he received a question: "Why do you want to know?" Jacob's request was returned to him and then he received a blessing. What happened in between? Did the returned question become the occasion for further wrestling? Perhaps Jacob, then, inquired more deeply about his own motives in the encounter: Why did he want to know the intruder's name? Did he want to control the *ish,* which he would be able to do if he learned the name? Did he want to master the encounter and the one whom he encountered? Was he playing a power game of mastery and deceit even in the wrestling? Did Jacob care about the stranger's reality or simply his own welfare? Perhaps all these options fit. Or perhaps, the question was ironic, in effect, asking Jacob, "Do you really need to ask? Certainly, you know whom you have encountered!" The reader can only wonder. Nothing more was said between them, at least nothing recorded in the text. The story reports only that afterward Jacob named the place **Penuel/Peniel,** the face of God.

Why name this place the face of God? The story says because in that place Jacob met God face to face and lived. Does that not imply that God was the assailant? The word used for the assailant was **ish**, man, and is not a name used for God. Neither was the word **malach**, meaning angel, used, although that word is used in other texts which interpret or refer to this one (e.g., Hosea 12: 5), lending increased ambiguity to the encounter and its interpretation. Given what the text reports, then, why name the place **Peniel/Penuel** (face of God)?

First, the story describes a change. The old Jacob, the one who was the trickster, the deceiver, the supplanter -- that one might have stolen the chance to name the other, just like he once usurped his brother's birthright. Up to this point in the story, the text even relates that Jacob had come hoping to placate his brother and redirect Esau's anger -- especially after years of fearing reprisal, even death (Gen. 32: 20). In this episode, however, Jacob respected the limit. Jacob was satisfied not having the name of the other, and yet, somehow knowing in the encounter that he had been wrestling with God as well as with his past, his trickery, his pain, his deception, his shame. So he named the place, the encounter, not the one encountered. He left what or whom he encountered open and rich: never just God, or just the past or just fear or just shame. And yet, never without any of them.

Jacob had encountered, among other things, a legacy of shame and fear, and *in all that* he encountered God as well. They went together, inseparably. The struggle with everything he encountered brought change and a new name, a new identity -- though not without cost. Whatever else Jacob encountered that night, it included the history he brought to the river bank and the consequences of facing that history. So Jacob named the place, that is, the encounter, not the one encountered.

The Limp

The story says that Jacob's thigh was put out of joint. The wound was physical and permanent. Thereafter, he would walk with a limp. For a tradition which speaks of the way of right living as *halakah*, to be permanently hindered in one's walking could never mean just a simple physical wounding. The linguistic echoes penetrate far deeper. Right living, *halakah*, is literally derived from the verb to walk. The lingering limp of Jacob could not have been just in his legs. It would have reached to every fiber of his identity as he stood before God, now as the "Godwrestler."[5] Jacob was marked by the wrestling and by what he had encountered in the struggle -- the shame and fear, as well as by everything else he confronted that night. The limp was and remained psychic and spiritual, as well as physical. His "walk" thereafter would reflect his struggle.

As Jacob left the banks of the Jabbok to face his brother, he brought with him his shame, his fear, his remorse, *and* his strength -- all in a new name and in a new configuration. His encounter with Esau would not be without shame. Neither would it be without everything else.

---

[5] Arthur Waskow, *GODWRESTLING* (New York: Schocken Books) 1978, pp. 1-12.

That night, that place in his life, he named **Penuel/Peniel** -- because there, in that place, Jacob had met God, face to face, as he faced himself, and faced up to his fears, as well as his shame: the lifetime he brought to that river bank. Whatever else Jacob wrestled with that night it included his own legacy of shame. Similarly, the wound he bore thereafter, his limp, was bound to what he faced that night. Jacob would wrestle with that legacy, along with everything else, the rest of his life. That night he learned he could, and that doing so was how he must live thereafter.

A Tragic and Shameful Parody

The legacy of displacement and shame borne by Jacob vis-à-vis his brother, Esau, is not unlike that borne by sensitive Christians setting out to meet their Jewish siblings in the late twentieth century. Yet the journey to this modern Jabbok is a fearful and ironic twist to Jacob's story -- indeed, it is a tragic parody. This encounter takes place on the other side of another night, not unlike Jacob's first night of wrestling. This time, however, the displacement is borne by those who have tried to usurp the place of Jacob in history, stealing birthright and name, as well as blaming the victim for the loss of sacred identity. After Auschwitz, any meeting between Christians and Jews over the biblical story of Jacob at the Jabbok calls forth an awareness of this other historical text and invites further wrestling with the issue of shame and the lifetimes brought to such an encounter.

The dynamics of displacement reach deep into the historic identity of Christianity and penetrate the story Christians tell in describing their place in history as God's people. Paul van Buren has put the issue concisely: "in the Church's story the Jewish people was displaced by the Church as the sole legitimate representative -- and successor -- of Israel."[6] Other theologians, like Rosemary Radford Reuther and Gregory Baum from the Roman Catholic side and Clark Williamson , a Protestant representative following in the spirit of James Parkes, contend that the adversarial treatment of Israel is rooted in the sacred story of scripture, itself, not just in the story of the Church. Reuther identifies this legacy as the "left hand of Christology,"[7] while Williamson characterizes the

---

[6] Paul van Buren, *THE WESTMINSTER TANNER-MCMURRIN LECTURES ON THE HISTORY AND PHILOSOPHY OF RELIGION:* "The Change in the Church's Understanding of the Jewish People" (Salt Lake City: Westminster College of Salt Lake City) 1990, p. 14.
[7] Rosemary Radford Reuther, *FAITH AND FRATRICIDE: THE THEOLOGICAL ROOTS OF ANTI-SEMITISM* with an introduction by Gregory Baum (New York: The Seabury Press) 1974.

canonical image of Jewish life as a caricature rooted in the early conflict between Church and Synagogue and in need of "ideological critique."[8] Van Buren clarifies what is at stake: "If the ... story did not lead directly to the **Shoah,** it surely provided a suitable climate for the development of modern antisemitism; and when the **Shoah** did come, the traditional way of telling the story offered little resistance to it."[9]   He adds, "what is at stake is nothing less than the Christian story."[10]   The point: Christians with no direct linkage to what happened in Nazi Germany, even those born after the **Shoah**, share responsibility for *how* they claim their identity even if they have no direct responsibility for the displacement or theft of identity the story they tell conveys. The issue is bound to identity and not simply to behavior (though for some it may include behavior). Consequently, what must be faced is shame as distinguished from guilt.

Shame is not the same phenomenon as guilt. Guilt has to do with behavior. Guilt is rooted in something someone does to another that violates the covenantal fabric of their shared life. Shame, on the other hand, is rooted in being, in who people are, not what people do. Shame is an expression of identity, not behavior. To be sure, shame and guilt are often related, and one can give expression to the other, but the distinction is essential.[11] For example, even if someone has not committed an act which violates the covenantal bonds shared with another, he or she can participate in an identity that denies another's full participation in community or even provides a foundation for the act of violation itself. The displacement theology on which Christians have been nurtured for centuries is just that sort of identity-related phenomenon.   The displacement is not a behavior consciously engaged in by Christians vis-à-vis Jews; it is *in* and passed on *by* the Story that tells Christians who they are. Unless this identity bearing narrative is transformed, the violence it breeds will remain in-utero, ready to be reborn in another generation. And without shame, it can go unchecked.

In this way, shame, is deeper than betrayal, at least the way

---

[8] Clark M. Willaimson and Ronald J. Allen, *INTERPRETING DIFFICULT TEXTS: ANTI-JUDAISM AND CHRISTIAN PREACHING* (Philadelphia: Trinity Press) 1989, pp. 28-31, 70-72.
[9] van Buren, p. 15
[10] Ibid, p.16.
[11] See Helen Merrell Lynd,   *ON SHAME AND THE SEARCH FOR IDENTITY* (New York: Harcourt, Brace & World, Inc.) 1958, pp. 13-71 for a classic discussion of this distinction. See Robert Karen, "Shame" in *THE ATLANTIC*, Volume 269, No. 2, February 1992, pp. 40 - 70 for a helpful summary of the current literature on shame.

many people think of betrayal. For much of what has happened in the shameful history of the Church's relationship to the Synagogue grew out of fidelity to a triumphalistic mission that sought to convert and finally to eliminate the disconfirming[12] identity of Jewish siblings. Yet in a more critical way, this too is betrayal -- betrayal of the covenantal intention of creation which Christian   traditions tragically distorted in the very expression of that intention.

Facing Shame Without Being Ashamed

When fully faced and forthrightly acknowledged, shame can lead to the kind of wrestling described in this Genesis text. It can wound as well as transform. It can be a deep, identity-penetrating struggle which brings an entire lifetime into the conflict. Such struggle should not be avoided. A lengthy and convoluted history must be faced, rethought, and even transformed. In the case of the **Shoah,** Christians must face not simply what was done during 1933-45, they must also confront a long history of contempt that led to the twelve years of terror dictated by Hitler. Christians must grapple with how they name themselves and their world, asking, what is it about how Christians inhabit the world that can lead to such hatred and contempt? How has the Christian identity, in the way it has traditionally embodied its confessional claims about being God's people, led to the betrayal of its covenantal partnership with the Jewish people and with God? In the shadows of Auschwitz, Christians must

---

[12] See Richard L. Rubenstein and John K. Roth, *APPROACHES TO AUSCHWITZ: THE HOLOCAUST AND ITS LEGACY* (Atlanta: Hohn Knox Press) 1987, pp. 59 ff., for a helpful discussion of the "problem of the disconfirming other" and its embodiment, "exclusivistic intolerance," as a concommitant dimension of the truth claims of Christianity, as well as those of its Abrahamic siblings.

confront the legacy that fed the fires of the **Shoah**, a legacy of supplanting, of claiming a blessing that rightfully belonged to an older sibling. It is one thing to be included in another's blessing, as Paul, for example, sought to extend God's covenantal embrace of life to Gentiles through Jesus.[13] It is quite another matter to usurp that blessing as one's own, forgetting or ignoring the original inclusion on which any claim to the blessing can be based.

How, then, might Jews and Christians engage each other as they meet at the Jabbok a generation after the **Shoah**? Clearly, shame will be a component of their conversation. But dialogue, if it is built only on shame, is built on an inadequate foundation. To be sure, shame is a necessary aspect of such a meeting. However, if only the shame is faced, particularly by Christians, their displacing identity claims remain in place. Christians have learned to identify themselves *over against* Jews in ways which feed antisemitism and contempt and which after doing their violence, then lead to shame. Shame, of course, can lead to repentence. Such has been the prophetic call of responsible Christians wrestling with these matters. But what is meant or addressed by such a call for repentence? If repentence leads only to a shame-based quality in Jewish-Christian interaction, then Jewish partners in such activity will surely be uncomfortable, if not suspicious. The foundation for engagement, then, would be negative and unequal, even paternalistic. What must happen is for the shame to be confronted, as shame, with its identity-bound source likewise confronted and transformed, in repentance.

Repentance is not just an inward attitude of regret, brought on by guilt or shame or both. Neither is it simply an act of soul-searching contrition. Repentance is a turning from sin, a re-orientation of a person's identity, even a community's identity, from sin to life -- more specifically,

---

[13] See Paul van Buren, Otfried Hofius, J. Christian Beker, et al. in *THE PRINCETON SEMINARY BULLETIN*, Supplementary Issue, No. 1, 1990, "The Church and Israel: Romans 9-11" for an instructive look at Paul's treatment of this issue.

the covenantal fabric of life to which Jews and Christians are committed as the divine intention of creation. There is, of course, an inward moment of recognition and acknowledgement, which is essential to the act of repentance. For Jacob, it involved facing his identity as the supplanter, the heel-sneak (**Yaakov**) when he wrestled with the **ish.** For Christians, facing their shame involves naming the source of their shame as forthrightly as they can and acknowledging what has been problematic in their own identity before God and their Jewish siblings. This acknowledgment, however, is only the first moment in a bold, yet vulnerable confession. The second moment involves reframing the way Christians express their relationship with God to include God's continuing relationship with Jews, thereby showing a new face to an estranged sibling. In addition, this confessional task must address what it means for each community to be included in the covenant purposes embraced by God. Christians, together with Jews, must contend not only with shame but also with how to articulate some form of common ground for including one another and their claims as people of God.

How Christians engage Jews and confront their tangled history has implications beyond their own interfaith encounter despite the particularity of the issues they face. Western Christians do not carry a legacy of shame and mixed blessings with regard to Jews only. For example: white, middle class, American males carry a similar legacy in their relationships with women, African Americans, and Native Americans. Those relationships include dimensions of shame that they dare not avoid. Consequently, as white, male, Euro-American Christians learn to face the shame in their faith identities with regard to Jews, they will be called to continue wrestling with shame in other aspects of who they are. Wrestling with their own personal and cultural texts will take them to the Jabbok again and again as they meet African American, Native American brothers and sisters; and, as they meet their own Euro-American sisters as well. Over and over, they will discover they know more than they wish about mixed blessings. And as children of Abraham, Jacob's story will continue to hold them accountable.

Any call to repentance which faces such legacies must confront shame as well as guilt and sometimes shame even when no guilt is experienced. Never again can responsible people of faith accept, for themselves, an unchecked naivete as an acceptable quality for their lives.

By facing the shame and wrestling with the identity issues generating it, responsible persons of faith can learn to face their shame without remaining ashamed. They can break the cycle of shame and transform its source as they discover, perhaps more often than they wish, new ways of naming their relationship with God and their siblings. In the end, this is the hope of sharing such a journey to the Jabbok.

An Unfinished Encounter

In the end, this encounter with Jacob, just as Jacob's encounter with his sibling, remains unfinished. The tale unfolds in the biblical text with Jacob (still identified as Jacob and not yet as Israel) confronting Esau the next morning. Eventually, they embrace, weeping (Gen. 33:4). Some would thereby conclude the two were reconciled. Yet, as the tale continues, a painful distance remains between the two siblings. They do not unite in a shared journey even though Esau invites his brother to accompany him to Seir. For whatever reason, Jacob does not accept his brother's invitation to go with him to Seir. Instead, Jacob promises to come later -- a promise he never keeps. Why? What still separates Jacob and Esau? However much Jacob has faced himself and his past (including his relationship with his brother, father, mother, and God), he has more to face with Esau. After their tearful embrace, Jacob and Esau remain significantly other. Their journeys lead in different directions: Jacob eventually to Bethel; Esau to Seir. And yet, their otherness, because it is familial, remains covenantal. Nonetheless, the biblical tradition leaves the subsequent relationship between Jacob and Esau unspecified and therefore open to interpretation, except to identify Esau with Edom and, thereby, with a long tale of enmity and violence. Later commentaries fill in the open places by identifying Rome with Esau/Edom. The point: though perhaps reconciled in one sense, the distance and conflict between these two siblings remains; their story is, indeed, unfinished.

Any contemporary encounter with Jacob and his story remains similarly incomplete. Jews and Christians, however much they may meet and embrace, even while weeping, still find themselves confronting the distance between them and the tangled history that describes how that history has come to be. At the core of Jacob's wrestling was a mixed legacy which included the burden of shame. To be sure, there was guilt, too, for all he did. Yet deeper still, was the reality (along with his awareness of it) that he was weak, indecisive, and capable of deceiving those he loved. The shame fed the guilt and the fear while the fear and the guilt fed the shame. Likewise, Christians wrestling with who they are in the shadows cast by their legacy of displacement also encounter shame. The task before them, as it was before Jacob, is to confront the shame, wrestle with it, even demand from the wrestling (if not the shame itself) a blessing and a transformed identity.

Still, the wrestling does not end. Further struggle follows, particularly if Christians and Jews choose to face each other over confessional ground they do not share. The next section moves to another night time encounter which for Christians is paradigmatic. Like the episode at the Jabbok, this story focuses on a deep existential struggle, filled with questions of fidelity and vocation. Like the Jabbok, Gethsemene is approached with fear and trembling -- though for very different reasons for Jews than for Christians.

MEETING (JESUS) IN THE GARDEN: GETHSEMENE REVISITED
The Path to Gethsemene
After meeting at the Jabbok, Jews and Christians find a different set of issues when they approach the confessional ground of Christians. This is especially clear in approaching such a place as Gethsemene since it brings into focus the centrality of the passion of Jesus in the context of another night of testing and trial. Moreover, it brings into focus, for Jews, the risk and fear involved in trusting their Christian siblings to embrace their Christian identity without at the same time denying Jews theirs in the process -- the very issues faced in the post-**Shoah** encounter at the Jabbok.

After the **Shoah**, the path from the Jabbok to Gethsemene winds through a problematic as well as life giving, confessional history. On the one hand, the path leads to the heart of Christian confession, the passion story. In and through it, Christians know themselves to be included in God's loving and forgiving embrace of creation. Yet, in and through this same story, Jews know themselves to be recipients of Christianity's accusation of being a displaced and reprobate people.[14] Moreover, Jews have known in practical terms that during Holy Week, when the passion story is dramatically rehearsed by Christians, it is wisest for them to step out of the way of Christian hate and antisemitism. Elie Wiesel's comments illuminate what has been experienced by too many Jews throughout history.

As a child, I wouldn't even come close to the church. I changed sidewalks. It wasn't because of me: it was because of them. Because twice a year they would beat me up.[15] Some of that legacy -- its supersessionist beginnings especially -- was encountered in the post-**Shoah** wrestling at the Jabbok. However, supersessionism has not been

---

[14] See chapter three of Rosemary Reuther's *FAITH AND FRATRICIDE: The Theological Roots of Anti-Semitism* (Minneapolis: The Seabury Press) 1974, pp. 117-182, for a discussion of the patristic roots of Christian antisemitism.
[15] Elie Wiesel, *AGAINST SILENCE: The Voice and Vision of Elie Wiesel*, Irving Abrahamson, ed. (New York: Holocaust Library) 1985, vol 3, p. 110.

the lone problem. The teaching of contempt and "the myth of deicide" also underlie the long history of hate and antisemitism.[16] Again, because the issues are identity-laden and not simply, and sometimes not at all, behavioral, Christians must face themselves and their shame in a critically integrated adjustment of their narrative identity.   This task is nowhere more clearly seen than when Christians who follow such a path make their way to the passion of Jesus. Hence, the next leg of this post-**Shoah,** confessional journey moves toward the Mount of Olives to an olive grove called Gethsemene.   The setting: another night with echoes of yet another.

The Story

At first glance, the story Christians face in Gethsemene appears straight forward. It begins earlier, in an upper room, in the evening setting of the seder. The story of deliverance and its celebration in a ritual meal has led to Jesus dismissing his disciples and moving with them to the Mount of Olives.   There, after asking all but three of his disciples to wait for him, Jesus withdraws with Peter, James and John to pray. He briefly tells them that he is troubled and asks them to remain where they are and "watch" with him while he withdraws further to pray. After a time, Jesus returns to the three disciples who were to be watching with him and finds them sleeping. The story continues with Jesus saying, "so you could not watch with me one hour? [Then] watch and pray that you may not enter into temptation..." (Matthew 26: 40f.) The scene repeats itself three times, with Jesus' prayer requesting that the cup pass him by while at the same time he prays for strength to accept and drink from the cup if it is what God wills. The third time he asks them, "Are you still sleeping and taking your rest? Behold the hour is at hand, and the son of man is betrayed into the hands of sinners. Rise, let us be going; see, my betrayer is at hand." (Matt. 26: 45f.)

---

[16] See William Nicholls, *CHRISTIAN ANTISEMITISM: A History of Hate* (Northvale, N.J.: Jason Aronson Inc.) 1993, for a comprehensive review of this history.

While the action may be straight forward, the story is far from simple. For Jesus, of course, the story is one of anguish and integration. Like Jacob at the Jabbok, Jesus brings his lifetime to the garden as he struggles with the consequences of his work and message. Somehow, he knows it is not going to turn out well for him. The story itself refers to his sense of what lies ahead, utilizing the ritual symbol of a cup and extending the symbolism of the seder, which has preceded his going to Gethsemene. Most typically, the cup has been interpreted to refer to Jesus' impending crucifixion and death, drawing particularly from Jesus' own similar identification with his cup and death in the seder. Gethsemene quite literally overlooks Jerusalem. From there, Jesus ponders the consequences of his life and work as he looks out over the occupied city. He is on a collision course with Roman authorities and he has frightened Temple leaders who rely on the status quo. In the garden, Jesus dramatically faces the probable outcome of his ministry: rejection and death. He prays that this not be the outcome, yet always in the context of giving himself to the divine will which the text implies may require Jesus' death.

What happened in the garden is also the disciples' story: The disciples are asked to go *with* Jesus to his place of prayer and struggle. There, three (Peter, James and John) are singled out to go farther and to *watch with him* as Jesus goes still farther into the garden to pray and wrestle with his destiny. The disciples respond by falling asleep, failing Jesus. they are unable to be *with* him, much less *watch with* him.[17] Their struggle is the struggle to be faithful to their companion in his present need. Jesus has asked only that they stay *with* him or *watch with* him. He asks them to do no more. They fail, falling away as Jesus, as the story remembers it, expected.[18]

Interestingly enough, the stories of the disciples, Jesus, and the overarching passion narrative come together as Jesus confronts his sleeping disciples the third time. Jesus has prayed that the cup pass him by, always with the caveat that God's will be done. After each prayer he

---

[17] Daniel Patte, *THE GOSPEL ACCORDING TO MATTHEW: A Structural Commentary on Matthew's Faith* (Philadelphia: Fortress Press) 1987, pp. 367-369. See also, Donald Senior, *THE PASSION OF JESUS IN THE GOSPEL OF MATTHEW* (Wilmington, Delaware: Michael Glazier) 1985, p. 78.

[18] It is interesting to note that in this episode the characters are all male. Later, as the crucifixion draws nearer, the women of Jesus' circle will emerge from the background of the narrative as those few, in contrast to this scene, who did not fall away or fail to watch with their leader and friend.

discovers his disciples unable to endure the night and its anguish with him. Then the third time he emerges with a sense of understanding not present earlier. "Arise my betrayer is at hand." (Matt. 26: 45) Jesus knows and he is accepting. But what is it that he knows; what is it that he is accepting?

The episode at Gethsemene is surely a boundary story for Jesus, Peter, Judas, and any who would follow this one named Jesus. For Jesus, the boundary is often associated with the physical and spiritual sufferings that lie ahead in the trial, rejection, abandonment, and eventual crucifixion awaiting him. However, in this episode, the moment of crisis is tied specifically to the relationships Jesus has with his disciples. What is the limit of the covenantal existence he has offered his followers? Will their inability to stay awake and watch, their inability to share his anguish, their inability to face what he will face break what they share with him and what he has given them? Will Peter's denial break the bond that ties them together? Jesus has said it would not earlier. Is that not the choice immediately facing Jesus in this episode? How fully will Jesus drink from the cup of covenant life? In a sense, Jesus has promised and advocated a covenantal relationship, a marriage, so to speak, that cannot be sundered by the imperfections of those who accept it. In Gethsemene, that promise is tested with sleep, denial, and even betrayal. Will Jesus choose covenant life in these circumstances, with these people? If so, it will cost his life. And in the larger circle of Jesus' covenantal obligations the issue remains the same. Jesus has chosen covenant life with all of Israel, and he has chosen to focus his embrace with those usually cut off or living at the margins of covenant community. How deeply will he drink from this cup?

The Cup

The central question addressed in the Jabbok story was who or what was the *ish*? In Gethsemene, the parallel question is what was and is the cup which Jesus anticipated with anguish and prayed might pass him by? But, after the **Shoah**, one cannot simply ask what does the cup which Jesus faced signify? One must also, and perhaps first, ask what can it *not* -- or *no longer* -- signify? Clearly, in the ugly light cast by the **Shoah**, the cup cannot signify a divine expectation that Jesus must suffer and die to restore creation. No longer can any human being be used as an instrumental step in some larger scheme of things, even if that grand design is called divine. Nor can suffering, itself, bear the intrinsic meaning it has carried for Christian belief. Just as surely, the cup cannot be filled with supersessionist interpretations of God's covenantal embrace of creation or Israel.

What, then, is the cup which Jesus faced in Gethsemene? After a post-**Shoah** journey to the Jabbok, how can and should the cup which Jesus confronted that night in the garden be identified? With whom and what did Jesus wrestle in the night shadows of that place? And how does this vantage point in the late twentieth century affect the way that cup is named? To be sure the biblical text proclaims that, whatever it was, the cup was a source of anguish. Jesus could feel its presence. In effect, he knew it was coming, but not that it was inevitable, otherwise he would not have prayed as he did. Somehow, somewhere, it involved a choice: his...God's...perhaps his disciples'....perhaps the local authorities, Jewish and Roman, perhaps all of them.

Also, the Matthean text introduces the symbolism of the cup earlier, at the seder where Jesus takes one of the cups of blessing (presumably the last one at the close of the meal) and personally identifies with it. The story associates that identification more specifically with his blood and its being poured out for many for the sake of his covenant with them ("Then he took a cup, and after giving thanks gave it to them, saying, 'Drink from this all of you: for this is my blood of the covenant, which is poured out for many for the forgiveness of sins." Matt. 26: 28.) Traditionally the church has identified the cup in Gethsemene as an extension of this moment, representing Jesus' suffering and crucifixion as a sacrificial death for others. But what of Jesus' own identification?

Jesus does not introduce, *de novo*, the imagery of a cup to his disciples, nor does Matthew do so to his readers. Rather, Jesus takes the cup in the ritual context of the seder wherein the cup is richly bound up with the story and images of Israel, -- more specifically, Israel's deliverance and identity as a covenant people. The cup is a symbol of thanksgiving and recollection of a relationship bestowed and yet still promised. It recalls the Passover gift of freedom and its corresponding relationship of responsible witness. Its meanings are cumulative. Every Passover ritual and experience of this wonderful relationship is poured into this cup. Moreover, every Sabbath meal includes a thanksgiving blessing which is recited with the taking and sharing of a cup of wine. The point: Israel's entire covenantal legacy is bound up, in thanksgiving, with this ritual act. The cup bears multiple meanings, all of which provide gustatory linkage with the covenantal story of Israel. It is this cup with which Jesus identifies his life and passion.

Just as the cup in the seder signified divine deliverance and God's gracious choice to be in covenant relationship with the people Israel, so the cup for Jesus would be identified with his appropriation of that covenantal legacy as well as its and his unyielding commitment to liberation and life. Moreover, Jesus' identification with that cause was an identification that was so complete that he identified his entire life with it. His cause was God's cause and God's cause was Israel and the covenant life that she represented for the world. After Auschwitz, Christians must see this cup in all its fullness, not simply as it has been reduced by selective liturgical memory.

With this more inclusive and self-critical context in mind, how does one answer the question, what was the cup Jesus faced in the garden? While it might include the suffering he was anticipating and the cost of his life, those components would surely be derivative, no matter how important they were. The cup represented the gift and calling of covenant life, embodied in his own life and that of his people. The question confronting Jesus then would be, shall Jesus drink from the cup of covenant life so completely that it would bind him irrevocably to those who follow him as well as to those he sought to reach with his message? Like Jacob, Jesus faced a lifetime in one night, symbolized in the cup. What would it mean for Jesus to drink deeply from this overflowing symbol of his life and everything to which he was committed?

If God intends life, God would not intend that which diminishes it. If the cup was given by God, and that is surely the implication of this imagery, the cup does not represent crucifixion, but all that Jesus chose and embraced in his life and, derivatively, the consequences of those choices -- choices which may very well signify and include crucifixion as well as the quality of life he honored in the choosing. The point: the signification of crucifixion is not primary but secondary.

Another Night

As our encounter with Jacob at the Jabbok made clear, another more recent historical night casts its shadows on our interaction and interpretation of the texts of faith, no less this one. Realizing the power of Elie Wiesel's well known point, "not all victims were Jews, but all Jews were victims," Jesus' followers must face the unsettling recognition that to follow Jesus after the **Shoah** is to follow Jesus into the camps and its kingdom of night. With this in mind, the story takes on a frightening dimension. If the night and its garden now include the world of the whirlwind (or its reverse, the whirlwind now includes this story), then each stage along the path is a stage in the immersion of this world. To be asked to enter the night in Gethsemene with Jesus is frightening enough. To be asked to stay awake and watch, more so. To be asked to go a little farther, and then to watch and pray, increases the challenge even more.

But to draw those two nights together and ponder their relationship is something else altogether. After Auschwitz, following Jesus means following Jesus into a Gethsemene renamed Majdanek or Sobibor or ...some other frightening appellation.

Historically, we know that only a few Christians followed Jesus into the night of the **Shoah** and most of them did so problematically. The Confessing Church, for example, followed Jesus there, but without recognizing the pervasive poison of antisemitism in their land and culture. The issue for them was idolatry and Church autonomy.[19] They, like Peter, denied Jesus -- that is, the *Jew* from Nazareth, whom they called Christ. Most in that time and place who professed to follow, however, simply fell asleep, unable to stay awake even for the briefest time.

And even now more than a full generation later, there is a challenge involved in entering Gethsemene knowing that its night includes this other night of horror. Are those who follow Jesus after the **Shoah** prepared to step into the night of Gethsemene knowing what it now includes for them? Moreover, are they prepared to hear Gethsemene's story ask them to stay awake, perhaps even to go a little farther and follow their leader even deeper into this little understood olive grove that marks the threshold of Jesus' passion?

Elie Wiesel, in telling his story in *NIGHT*, probes the historic question of his faith: "Why is this night different than any other night?" with intensely compounded irony, giving the central liturgical question of his people an unexpected twist.[20] The children of the **Shoah** know another night that mocks the night of deliverance and thanksgiving. In his telling of this story, the character of each challenges the overarching meanings of the other.

In the shadows of the **Shoah**, the double edge of the seder's question can be directed to the account of Jesus' long night of anguish and faithfulness, asking: How is that night different for Christians, especially in the ironic light of the night of the **Shoah**? Typically, Christians have seen the night at Gethsemene as an intensely focused expression of Jesus' passion. Jesus' decisions, actions, anguish and fidelity are all present. In

---

[19] See Franklin Littell, *THE CRUCIFIXION OF THE JEWS: The Failure of Christians to Understand the Jewish Experience* (New York: Harper & Row) 1975, pp. 44-60 for a classic analysis of this chapter in the history of the Christian Church.

[20] See Lawrence S. Cunningham, "Elie Wiesel's Anti-Exodus," *AMERICA*, April 27, 1975, pp. 325-327, for an interesting analysis of the paradigmatic structural qualities of *NIGHT*.

that night, Jesus faced all that he is and has been, all that he is called to be, in the light of what lay ahead for him. Now, after another night, which renders all previous nights fundamentally different, how is the night of Jesus' wrestling different once again?

Clearly, then, what lies ahead is yet another night of wrestling. For Jacob the issues were ones which had accumulated over a lifetime, indeed, they were his lifetime. They included fear, shame, love, hope, healing... For Jesus, the issues were also cumulative. He too faced a lifetime in one night. His issues included his vocation, perhaps his self understanding about any messianic role he might fulfill. Certainly they also included his love and disappointment with regard to the holy city of Jerusalem and its people. As well, they included his relationship with disciples who could not watch with him when he needed them, who even ran away and denied him in his distress.

Now, given their post-**Shoah** vantage point, modern day Christians are faced with the awareness that had this story unfolded in the present century another tragic tale would be laid over this one. Jesus would have been once more asking those who followed him to stay awake and watch with him through the night, this time a twelve year long night. Jesus, a Jew, would have been selected, perhaps turned over by those who knew him. His followers and companions who were Jewish would have been taken with him. But the majority of his followers, now Gentiles, would have been spared. Would they have chosen to go with him into this night? If so, would they have managed to avoid falling asleep during that time. Jesus first asked his disciples "to sit here while I go yonder and pray (Matt. 26: 36)." From a post-**Shoah** vantage point, where is "here" and where is "yonder" whence Jesus goes? And why does Jesus next take Peter, James, and John, his closest companions, a little farther along, asking them to "watch" with him while he goes yet a little farther? Does he take them now -- invite them -- farther into his anguish? And what is it that fills his soul with sorrow and anguish? Then? Now? These are certainly questions that will give critically reflective Christians in this century pause as they ask them self-consciously in the lingering shadows of the **Shoah**.

Crises in the Garden

In Gethsemene, Jesus faced two major crises: one covenantal the other political. At the closest, most intimate level, Jesus had asked Peter, James, and John (his closest companions) to go a step further into the night and to watch and pray with him To be sure, what he faced, he faced alone--as the story relates. Nonetheless, he asked his three intimate

friends to go the extra distance and to stay awake and watch with him --
nothing more. They were not asked to change things, or to do anything
-- simply to be present, awake and to watch. Yet they slept. And the
others, whom he asked to go only a part of the way into his night of
anguish, they too fell asleep, failing to give even a more limited presence.
    In contrast, Jesus was fully present -- to himself, to his cause, to God and
to his sleeping companions.
        The covenantal crisis extended to the people, and the city which
Gethsemene quite literally overlooked. What was Jesus' commitment to
that place and to those people? Would it be as complete and unreserved
as with his disciples? The answer was yes. There was no turning back on
his commitment. There was no holding back on embracing covenant life
as fully and intensely as he had chosen. He had filled the cup full, to
overflowing and he would drink it. The other crisis, distinct from the
covenantal one, was political. Jerusalem was not simply occupied; it was
also not infrequently compromised. At the same time, it remained holy
and the center of his people's life. It was this crisis that swallowed up the
others and then receded in the background in the later stories of Jewish
complicity and responsibility for Jesus' death -- responsibility that most
recent scholarship points out is misapplied to the Jews because of an
operative myth of deicide.[21]
        In other words, Jesus faced a multifaceted crisis. On the one
hand, the crisis was covenantal. It involved those people to whom he was
covenantally bound -- from the most intimate members of his disciples to
the most marginal members of Israel's second commonwealth. On the
other hand, his crisis was political. His beloved city and land were
occupied by Rome. The leadership of the Temple collaborated with

---

[21] William Nicholls, *CHRISTIAN ANTISEMITISM: A History of Hate*
(Northvale, N.J.: Jason Aronson Inc.) 1993, p. xix.

Roman authorities to stay in power and to secure what they thought was needed for their people. Collaboration and oppression were palpable. How committed was he to the message of God's inbreaking reign and to those to whom he was covenantally committed, especially those in Jerusalem, the heart of his world? Absolutely so...even if it cost his life!

Yet the story of crisis has been distorted, confusing some subtle and yet important distinctions. The covenantal crisis which Jesus resolves in favor of those who fall away, deny, reject, and who even abandon him is confused with the political one, especially as it is focused in the breach between Jesus and Judas. The blame for Jesus' death is shifted from the executioners, i.e., the Romans, to an intimate collaborator whose caricature eventually arises to symbolize the central Jewish action in the story -- a fact even the stylized account in Matthew does not support. The political crisis with Rome is all but removed from the story, certainly placed in the background, while parts of the covenantal crisis are brought to the fore.

Given what can be critically discerned about Jesus' situation then, as well as what must be faced about the distortion and hatred carried by Christianity's legacy of anti-Judaism and its myth of deicide, how should the crisis and its conflict now be understood? To be sure, the issue is covenantal, but on a much larger scale. Now it includes not simply individuals and/or parts of the covenantal story of Christianity, but it extends to include the overarching covenantal framework of life to which the Christian story bears witness. The covenantal crisis that confronts critical and thoughtful believers -- Jews as well as Christians -- is whether or not the world can be embraced covenantally at all. Indeed, this is the heart of Irving Greenberg's point that the **Shoah** is a reorienting event moving Israel [and Christianity] into an age of voluntary covenant.[22] According to Greenberg, covenant life must hereafter be voluntary, embracing fully that in "covenant life" God has completely embraced human agency. Divine partnership and presence are to be found in the covenantal experience and process but no longer can the divine partner be expected to act except through the called human response[23] of faithful

---

[22] See Irving Greenberg, "Religious Values After the Holocaust: A Jewish View" in *JEWS AND CHRISTIANS AFTER THE HOLOCAUST*, ed. by Abraham J. Peck (Philadelphia: Fortress Press) 1982, pp. 63-86, esp. pp. 82ff. and "History, Holocaust, and Covenant" in *REMEMBERING FOR THE FUTURE: The Impact of the Holocaust and Genocide on Jews and Christians*, Proceedings of an International Conference, Oxford and London, 10-17 July 1988, Pergamon Press, Oxford (1989) pp. 2920-2926.
[23] Greenberg, "Religious Values After the Holocaust," p. 83.

people.

Choices in the Garden

The hermeneutical issue facing the post-**Shoah** Church is how to read such central and important passages in the canon as this one without participating in those traditions which have passed on and contributed to the teaching of contempt. Only then can it begin to ask, "What rendering of the Gethsemene story emerges post-**Shoah**? How is Matthew's story modified, affected by what happened in the **Shoah**?" Critical faith calls for a hermeneutical self-consciousness that can situate its interpretive dynamics faithfully within the tradition at the same time it is able to avoid making the mistakes of the past, even if such mistakes were once faithfully motivated. What is required is a double-edged hermeneutic, with distinct but related moments of critique and correction. Clearly that is the critical spirit of this midrash and its companion interpretations.

Often hope lies in the text itself, once freed from ideologically straitjacketed readings of it. In this case, two crises, one covenantal and the other political, have been confused in the telling, with the political crisis with Rome driven to the background of the story. Moreover, throughout history, the figure of Judas has emerged as the image in which these collapsed crises have merged. Judas is clearly here a collaborator, who makes a political deal in betraying his friend. Instead of excising the role of Judas from the story one can recover it more fully as that of a collaborator in whom two crises are focused and dangerously confused. The task, hereafter, will be to restore, albeit critically, the fuller political reality that is left in the background -- except for its eventual resolution in crucifixion -- which, unambiguously was a Roman act. Toward this end, the text and its story have been critically reopened.

According to James F. Moore , the twin hermeneutical tasks of a post-**Shoah**, midrashic reading of scripture are
1. To undo the theology of contempt;

2. To provide foundation for the teaching of respect, not by imposing new
meaning on traditional texts but by returning to the text and its narrative
with an increased receptivity to its own ambiguity and plurality. [24]

Utilizing such a midrashic process, one thereby uncovers a narrative
capacity for diverse readings of the story, recognizing that the scriptural
text of Matthew is itself midrash[25] showing how Jesus has embodied and
extended Torah. Moreover, as this essay reflects, the context for such
midrash is dialogical, assuming either the literal or figurative presence of
the Jewish reader/interpreter -- an assumption which Matthew made as
well, albeit in argumentative fashion.

The hermeneutics of midrash are significant. They are at once
confessionally critical and critically confessional. They reflect a lively
interaction between the received tradition, in this case a text, and how that
tradition is experienced, with text and experience each challenging the
other to move toward greater authenticity -- like wrestling with the text of
Jacob at the Jabbok. In essence, midrash is testimony that the story passed
on by the text lives in the interaction of the text with an other's significant
experience of it. Consequently, there is a deep acknowledgment of the
significance of the text on the part of the one engaged with it which
simultaneously addresses the critical impact on each with the other. As
well, there is a presumption of a critical *relationship* with the text (as well
as its interpretive traditions) based on a dynamic and interactive
indwelling of the larger story.

Clearly the double hermeneutic at work here and throughout these
remarks is not unlike that of Paul Tillich's method of correlation.
However, in the age of the *Tremendum*, Tillich's Protestant Principle is
replaced by something at once more intense and critical -- the **Shoah**,
itself.[26] No longer is it enough for the cross to function as prophetic
critique. The failure of the Church and its story during the Third Reich
requires a stronger and more self-critical principle. The second moment
of the dialectic builds on the guidance of covenant life as the divine
intention for creation. 'Covenant life' avoids the dangers of
supersessionism by being more inclusive than Tillich's category of

---

[24] James F. Moore, *CHRISTIAN THEOLOGY AFTER THE SHOAH: A Re-
Interpretation* of the Passion Narratives (Lanham, Maryland: University Press of
America) 1993), p. 29.
[25] Ibid.
[26] Ibid, p. 139.

Catholic Substance while retaining its substantive particularity. Moreover, while positive as well as restorative, covenant life is not without its own critical dimension, a quality one might call its covenantal critique.

A Covenantal Orientation

The covenantal orientation guiding this midrash is dialectically critical and, itself, rooted in a dynamic, interactive epistemology. At its heart, is an understanding that the fundamental intention for creation, which Jesus sought to serve and which Matthew understood Jesus to have fully embodied, was a reality that can be helpfully focused with the phrase *covenant life*. Instead of seeing Jesus in anguish over whether or not God wished him to give his life as a sacrificial offering for others, a covenantal reading, like this one, sees the crisis confronting Jesus to be one of risking probable and imminent death as a consequence of fidelity to a covenantal relationship with God, Jesus' own followers, the people Israel, and even those most marginal in Israel's covenantal community. In Gethsemene, Jesus was, thus, facing the incredible cost of grounding his own life in a radical and inclusive commitment to covenant life at the point of extreme crisis. That crisis included impending death. As well, and perhaps more importantly to this reading, that crisis included the betrayal of one, denial and falling away of the eleven other intimate companions, and rejection by the larger numbers of people whom Jesus sought to embrace. And as the crucifixion scene eventually portrays, the crisis included even the feeling of absolute abandonment in the end. Moreover, a covenantal reading of this story distinguishes this aspect of the crisis from the political crisis, the more direct reason for Jesus' crucifixion. Jesus faced the choice of affirming his covenantal commitments at their point of violation and in the face of a distinct, even if related political cost. His passion was a radical and intense commitment to covenant life. Consequently, this interpretation turns away from seeing Jesus' prayers in Gethsemene as moments of resignation and submission to God's will and sees them instead as moments of wrestling with the implications of embracing covenant life so fully that he embraced even the very violations of it (denial, betrayal, abandonment). Essentially then, this reading sees the underlying question confronting Jesus in Gethsemene as how committed was he to this inclusive and unyielding way of embodying his father's will? The answer, the story reports, is "completely so."

How does such a picture fit with Matthew's overall portrait of Jesus? In a gospel that emphasizes with stylistic consistency that Jesus is the one who has fulfilled the scriptures and is the one hoped for by Israel, the messiah, continuity is maintained by affirming that Matthew's portrait is one of a Jesus that Matthew sees as fulfilling God's covenantal intentions for creation, which are articulated prophetically in scripture. Yet the promise-fulfillment motif is directed toward the covenantal intention that lies behind and in front of[27] the prophetic utterances which Matthew cites. The covenantal intention, while singularly God's originating and continuing purpose for life, is not exhausted by claiming that Jesus fully and completely embodied it in an inclusive and radical fashion. Such a claim does not require asking whose covenant, Israel's or the Church's, is truly the covenant intended by God. Rather, God's covenantal intention, singular and uncompromising, lies behind and ahead of each attempt to embrace, serve, and embody it, no matter how successful the attempt. Consequently, supersessionism can be avoided at the same time one can also avoid any divine requirement of propitiation. Likewise, the divine embrace of suffering as intrinsically meaningful becomes fundamentally unnecessary. Yet the underlying theme of Matthew's portrait, that Jesus is the life that Scripture anticipated and bears witness to, can still be affirmed -- however, not in the mutually excluding categories that have hitherto been employed in interpreting Matthew -- categories with very specific roots in the conflict between two competing claims for the identity of Israel after the catastrophe of the fall of Jerusalem and the destruction of the second temple.

The Cup after the Shoah -- One More Look

After the **Shoah**, the cup with which Jesus' followers have to contend overflows with increased anguish. After the **Shoah**, Gethsemene's locations shift to places with names like Majdanek, Belzec, Sobibor, Ravensbrück, and questions of *staying awake* and *staying with* Jesus during the night take on new, unsettling meaning. The notion that suffering might contain inherent meaning requires refocusing on Jesus' choices and concerns in Gethsemene in a more self-consciously Jewish framework -- one even more Jewish than that of Matthew. The point: It is essential to clarify that Jesus' choices and anguish are life directed, both individually and on behalf of his people, even if they were made in the

---

[27] The same covenantal intention also grounds a critical *relationship* to the text and the larger canon. Scripture itself can and has grounded antisemitic attitudes. Consequently a critical relationship as well as a critical reading of the scriptural witness is required.

face of death. That is, they were not acts of resignation and giving up, but moments of resistance to death and its power as it was experienced in denial, rejection, abandonment, and betrayal. Jesus was choosing life, covenant-oriented life, even if the consequence of his fidelity to covenantal existence risked probable death.

The issues of transcendence and power are another matter no less important to the issues raised by the **Shoah** but not treated here. Nonetheless, they spill out from the cup facing Jesus' followers. The options facing Jesus all emphasize that the covenantal framework of his life was now completely in his hands. Divine intervention did not come from some place else, heaven or otherwise, to confirm or deliver Jesus from his night of anguish. The cup from which he chose to drink did not contain a magical potion capable of removing Jesus from his circumstances. Instead, what lay within his power was whether or not he would choose the covenantal quality of life that characterized life with God and neighbor in an ecology of faith, even if it was confirmed by no one else. In a sense, this is Irving Greenberg's point, confirmed in Jesus' choices in Gethsemane. Intervention does not come; nonetheless, covenant life is confirmed and extended at its point of crisis. In other words, the transcendence experienced in the garden is one of meaning. A power from outside does not intrude or intervene in the situation. Rather, the power of covenant life is disclosed in Jesus' choice for covenant life in the very moment it is unconfirmed by any significant other, divine or human. At the same time, Jesus is not delivered from the situation by virtue of his action, in contrast to Esther's historic action which did bring her people liberation and serves as Greenberg's example of a noninterventionist paradigm for voluntary covenantal existence. There remains a real distinction between an authentic Jewish expectation of the Messiah and the Christian assertion that something happened as a consequence of Jesus' actions as he approached and endured the cross. Nevertheless, such a reading, by virtue of its non-interventionist, covenantal perspective [28] does not require a supersessionist nor contemptuous reading of Jewish action then or now.

---

[28] See my essay "Choosing Life Between the Fires: Toward an Intentionalist Voice of Faith" in *REMEMBERING FOR THE FUTURE: The Impact of the Holocaust and Genocide on Jews and Christians* -- Proceedings of an International Conference, Oxford and London, 10-17 July 1988, Pergamon Press, Oxford (1989) pp. 641f. where I develop a critique of the interventionist perspective and analyze how post-**Shoah** theology can move beyond simple interventionist and intentional options to a more self-critically dialectical one I identify with the term intentionalist.

Summary

    When Jews and Christians meet in Gethsemene after the **Shoah**, the issues increase. Each brings a difficult history to this confessional garden, compounded by the historic night of the **Shoah**. Gethsemene, of course, is an essential step in their walk of life, for Gethsemene guards the threshold of the passion of Jesus, the very heart of their story.   For Christians, the post-**Shoah** journey to the Jabbok is a choice they must make to face themselves in a new and unsettling way.   After the **Shoah**, Christians who undertake their journey to Gethsemene by way of the Jabbok walk with a limp born of spiritual humility.   Moreover, they approach Gethsemene with a responsibility to avoid any victimizing readings of what happened there and after.   For Jews, the path to Gethsemene represents a significant and vulnerable choice to accompany their Christian siblings into new and unnerving territory.   For them, Gethsemene can be a place that symbolizes fear, as historic memories of persecution are recalled.

    To choose to meet there by means of a post-**Shoah** midrash requires a critical re-interpretation that is able to challenge and correct past antisemitic readings at the same time it is able to establish a legitimate ground in the biblical story of Gethsemene itself.   Any post-**Shoah** midrash, if the encounter at the Jabbok has any lasting merit, will re-enter the story itself, not simply the text, to extend Gethsemene's reality into ours and ours into it.   Such a meeting will recognize that this story, like Jacob's, is not neatly bound and contained by the specific biblical text.   Neither is it solely contained within the larger, scriptural canon, for it is clearly the Church's liturgical story as well.   It is a living, breathing, and life changing narrative, which like the story in the seder that it originally extended, is annually rehearsed in liturgical fashion such that it continues to fund the understanding and piety of those whose lives are grounded in the passion of Jesus.   Finally, such a meeting will contend with the ongoing wrestling that the **Shoah** has provoked for people of critically reflective faith.   In the end, approaching Gethsemene by way of the Jabbok may not be sound geographical wisdom, however, it is good critical advice.   Critical faith, especially in the age after the **Shoah**, has no less a mandate than this.

Chapter 5: WRESTLING WITH BIBLICAL TEXTS AFTER THE *SHOAH*
Steven L. Jacobs

I. WRESTLING WITH *BERESHIT*/GENESIS 32:22-33
A. First Thoughts

The "textual essence" of the religious struggle after the *Shoah* is attempting to reconcile the "oughts" of theology and religious faith with the <u>realities</u> of experiential history. Both the sacred texts of both Judaism [Torah equalling *Bereshit*/Genesis through *Divre Hayamim Bet*/II Chronicles] and Christianity [Bible equalling Torah + New Testament] attempt to present a cogent *weltanschauung*/worldview consistent with what we may term the "historically-traditional" understanding of both faith communities--i.e. a loving, caring, protective, interactive God who [1] exists in a covenantal/familial relationship with Jews and/or [2] familial relationship with Christians through the unique experience of the person of Jesus the Christ. Both faith communities have, throughout their histories, affirmed and re-affirmed the centrality of these messages of this "God-who-acts-in-history"--despite, at times, overwhelming evidence to the contrary--while, at other times, denying the validity of the other.

The nightmarish horror--and worse--of the events of 1933-1945, specifically 1939-1945, has called into question this historically-traditional understanding of God, God's relationship with both Jews and Christians, and the "oughts" of these two faiths. The "uniqueness issue" of the *Shoah* simply refuses to go away.[1] By

---

[1] See, for example, Alan Rosenberg, "Was the Holocaust Unique" A Peculiar Question" in Isidor Walliman and Michael N. Dobkowski, Editors, <u>Genocide and the Modern Age: Etiology and Case Studies of Mass Death</u> [New York, Greenwood Press, 1987], pages 145-161, wherein he writes of the "four kinds of evidence" in stressing the uniqueness of the <u>Shoah</u>:....the simple fact of the size and scope of the destruction....the means employed in the Holocaust....-the varied physical and psychological qualities used to reduce intended victims to their barest physical qualities as "objects"....the vast and determined attempt by

extension, these events have raised anew the problematic of the reinterpretation of the sacred texts in lights of these new experiences. For better than two thousand years, Jews have chosen to interpret Torah in light of their historically-traditional understanding of God as the Author/Inspirer of the text; for slightly less than two thousand years Christians have interpreted both Torah and New Testament in light of their historically-traditional understanding of God and Jesus. A post-*Shoah* interpretation of both Jewish and Christian Scriptures requires, therefore, at first blush, a "re-thinking" of the whole notion of God in relation to sacred text, the specific implications of such re-thinking, and the meaning of specific texts themselves--the focus of this and other papers.[2]

B. Wrestling with *Bereshit*/Genesis 32:22-33

I would begin by noting, at the outset, that I am not one who could be characterized as a "scriptural literalist," that is, one for whom the Torahitic text is God-authored and dictated, Moses-written, and error-free, and thus evidence of Divine revelation at Mount Sinai to the collective community of Israel both willingly and unwillingly present at that moment. Rather, I understand these texts which comprise Torah to be an evolving, ongoing struggle of authors and editors, religionists all, at times human to a fault, to their changing perceptions of the Divine

---

the Nazis to transform the victims into the image that the Nazis had of them. [page 156]

[2] For a Jewish re-thinking of the categories of faith--specifically those or God, Covenant, Prayer, Law and Commandments, Life-Cycle, Festival Cycle, and Israel and Zionism, see my [forthcoming] book Rethinking Jewish Faith: The Child of a Survivor Responds [New York, SUNY Press, 1994]. For a Jewish reflection on Christian rethinking, see, especially, Chapter Eight: "Rethinking Christianity: An Outsider's Perspective."

Additionally, I find myself in complete agreement with Emil L. Fackenheim, who, in the "Forward" to The Jewish Bible After the Holocaust: A Re-Reading [Bloomington, Indiana University Press, 1990] writes:

A re-reading: after the Holocaust, Jews cannot read, as once they did, of a God who sleeps not and slumbers not; and after the resurrection of a Jewish state that includes Jerusalem, they cannot pray for the city as though, if not there, they could not get there by an easy El Al flight. So enormous are the events of recent Jewish history--this is the central conviction informing this book's hermeneutic--that the Jewish Bible must be read by Jews today--read, listened to, struggled with, if necessary fought against--as though they had never read it before. [pages vii-viii]

over the course of centuries, written down after oral transmission, and inspired by those changing perceptions of a reality greater than their own. Additionally, textual errors, transmission and other, humanly-crafted, do not diminish either the sacred nature of the Torah text or the profound and time-honored insights contained therein.[3]

Having said this, I would focus on the text in question--*Bereshit*/Genesis 32:22-33--along the following five avenues: [1] the time the "wrestling match" between *Ya'akov*/Jacob and the *ish* takes place; [2] the question of the identity of the *ish*, as well as that of *Ya'akov*/Jacob himself; 3] the nature of the *bracha*/blessing offered by the *ish*; 4] the proper understanding of the Hebrew verb *vatuchal* in verse 29; and, lastly, [5] the nature of the conflict/contest itself.

[1] Dark Time

Rabbi Sampson Raphael Hirsch [1808-1888], German Orthodox Jewish leader and a prime proponent of a kind of Western neo-Orthodoxy which attempted to merge European culture with strict Jewish observance, made much of the time the conflict/contest took place in his Torah commentary *T'rumath Tzvi*:Jacob's experience that night was the answer to his cry of distress: as long as night prevails on earth, as long as man's consciousness is clouded, and as long as things are intermingled beyond recognition so that they cannot be understood for what they really are, Jacob will have to expect struggles and conflicts.[4]

Dead one year before the birth of Adolf Hitler, Hirsch lived long enough in Germany to see the rise of the Pan-Germanist movement in Austria which called for union with Germany and the preservation of the "German character" of all "German territory," as well as the anti-Semitic German political parties begin to make political headway.[5]

---

[3] If anything, the sacred nature of the Torah is enhanced and elevated by the commitment of the Jewish People during the course of centuries to translate its truths into everyday realities, to live by its insights, and to die to preserve its contents both physically and spiritually.

[4] Trumath Tzvi: The Pentateuch with a Translation by Sampson Raphael Hirsch and Excerpts from the Hirsch Commentary, Edited by Ephraim Oratz; English Translation from the Original German by Gertrude Hirschler [New York, The Judaica Press, 1986], page 150.

[5]For example, Adolph Stoecker [1835-1909] founded the notoriously anti-Semitic Christian Social Workers Party in 1878 and himself served in the

How prophetic, then, how appropriate, then, his comments to the *Shoah*! *Ya'akov*/Jacob wrestles at <u>night</u> with his *ish* because the world itself is still experiencing night: cold, foreboding, alone, impending doom. And the darkest of nights for Israel the people occur during the *Shoah* when the non-German world huddles together, as it were, refusing, in the main, to venture out into the night and do battle until it is almost too late.

Were this not enough, night itself affords those who commit their heinous crimes, now so well known, the privilege of literally hiding behind them, of placing them under the covers of darkness whereby secrecy is maintained and those who would oppose them stand in ignorance. Night, too, affords the victimizers the singularly unique ability to perform those crimes against their victims without having to look directly at their victims and see the results of their handiwork.

Lastly, night affords both the victimizers and the bystanders--and, sadly, to a lesser degree, the victims themselves--the mask of not having to look directly at each other or themselves. Victimizers do not have to look directly at victims--Nazis do not have to look directly at Jews. So-called "good" Germans and/or "good" Christians do not have to address their inactivity under the cover of night's darkness. Thirdly, the Jews themselves, finding relief and respite as well as momentary safety In the dark of night, do not have to look with clarity at a world of which they are now its premier *korbanot*/scapegoats.

Contemporarily, what do we now say? What implications do we now draw? Firstly, the world remains embattled between the forces of darkness and the forces of light; the most troublesome locations In our world--Bosnia-Herzegovina, Somalia, Iraq, etc.--relish the dark as the place wherein they can ply their genocidally-destructive acts. Bringing to light evidence of their continuing crimes is all-too-often <u>after</u> the facts of death, rape, murder, starvation, torture, etc. Secondly, therefore, bringing to light now require the development of the kinds of "genocidal early warning systems," of which Leo Kuper and Israel Charny, among others, have extensively written.[6]

Reichstag from 1881-1908. Also, in 1887, Otto Boeckel's openly-espoused anti-Semitic views served to get him elected to the Reichstag.

[6] See, for example, Leo Kuper, <u>Genocide: Its Political Uses in the Twentieth Century</u> [New Have: Yale University Press, 1981]; Leo Kuper, <u>The Prevention of Genocide</u> [New Haven: Yale University Press, 1985]; Frank Chalk and Kurt Jonasson, <u>The History and Sociology of Genocide: Analyses and Case Studies</u> [New Haven: Yale University Press, 1990]; Isidor Wallimann and Michael N.

[2] The *Ish* and *Ya'akov*/Jacob

The late Chief Rabbi of the British Empire, Joseph H. Hertz, in his own Torah commentary, is of the opinion that the *ish* is "a Heavenly Being" or "God's Messenger," and adds:

> Maimonides is of opinion that the whole incident was a 'prophetic vision;' and other commentators likewise have in all ages regarded the contest as symbolic, the outward manifestation of the struggle within the Patriarch, as in every mortal, between his baser passions and his nobler ideals.[7]

Hirsch leaves the matter unresolved by referring in his translation to the *ish* as "someone."[8] Both The Oxford Annotated Bible and Plaut's The Torah: A Modern Commentary translate *ish* literally as a "man."[9]

If, indeed, the *ish* is "only" a "symbolic man," then the *ish* is, indeed, *Ya'akov*/Jacob/*Yisrael*/Israel who now struggles/wrestles to "make sense" of the world post-*Shoah*. And we return to our original opening premise: that of the struggle between the "oughts" of faith and the realities of history. Because *Yisrael*/Israel wants to continue to

---

Dobkowski, Editors, Genocide and the Modern Age: Etiology and Case Studies of Mass Death [New York: Greenwood Press, 1987]; Erwin Staub, The Roots of Evil: The Origins of Genocide and Other Group Violence [New York, Cambridge University Press, 1989]; Jack Nusan Porter, Editor Genocide and Human Rights: A Global Anthology [Washington, DC: University Press of America, 1982]; Israel W. Charny, How Can We Commit the Unthinkable: Genocide: The Human Cancer [Boulder: Westview Press, 1982]; Israel W. Charny, Editor, Toward the Understanding and Prevention of Genocide: Proceedings of the International Conference on the Holocaust and Genocide [Boulder, Westview Press, 1984]; Israel W. Charny, Editor, Genocide: A Critical Bibliographic Review [New York, Facts on File]: Volume I [1988] and Volume II [1991]; and, most recently, Helen Fein, Editor, Genocide Watch [New Haven, Yale University Press, 1992].
[7] Joseph H. Hertz, Editor, The Soncino Edition of the Pentateuch and Haftorahs With Hebrew Text, English Translation, and Commentary [London: Soncino Press, 1966, Second Edition], pages 123-124.
[8] Sampson Raphael Hirsch, T'rumath Tzvi, page 150.
[9] Herbert G. May and Bruce M. Metzger, Editors, The Oxford Annotated Bible [New York, Oxford University Press, 1962], page 41; W. Gunther Plaut, The Torah: A Modern Commentary [New York, Union of American Hebrew Congregations, 1981], page 217, though on page 216, Plaut does refer to the ish as a "man."

affirm both its faith and its God--as well as itself--It continues to try and make sense of the world post-*Shoah*, fearing, perhaps, to admit that, just maybe, the world no longer makes any sense whatsoever, and that, indeed, is the ultimate <u>meaning</u> of the *Shoah*. Christians, too, thus wrestle and struggle with the meaning of the world post-*Shoah*, realizing only too well that the *Shoah* denies the very presentation of faith that is Christianity: the death of Jesus the Christ, a gift given in love by both Father and Son, His subsequent resurrection and the <u>redemption</u> of faltering and pitiable humanity.

If, however, the *ish* is not symbolic man, not *Ya'akov*/Jacob himself, but a representative of the Divine Presence, we now admit of two possibilities, all the more so since *Ya'akov*/Jacob is himself "wounded" in the process and by the experience: Either this Divinely-appointed messenger represents the forces of "good" with which *Ya'akov*/Jacob must struggle/wrestle-- or, Heaven forfend, he represents the forces of "evil" with which *Ya'akov*/Jacob must contend, and which, perhaps, also, are narrowly defeated.

To regard the *ish* as representative of good is to ally him with *Ya'akov*/Jacob himself and his life's journey, wrestling/struggling in Hertz's words between the "base" and the "noble." It thus becomes, too, the Divine Presence entering indirectly into the fray, realizing that humanity In general and *Ya'akov*/Jacob in particular will not grow humanly or humanely without such contest. [The exact physical appearance of this external *ish*--his form, size, skin and hair coloration, appearance, etc.--become irrelevant in this process.]

If, on the other hand, the *ish* is representative of the evil which exists in our world and with which both humanity and *Ya'akov*/Jacob must wrestle/struggle, then the"historically-traditional" Jewish and Christian theology of the "God-who-acts-in-history" is at risk: For can such an evil messenger be Divinely-appointed? If so, then do not the Nazis themselves and their leader Adolf Hitler--and all previous and subsequent enemies of the Jewish People--becomes "agents of God," doing their work in response to a Divine purpose of which we are still unaware? Jews and Christians want very much to deny such a prospect, yet the affirmation of such an interactive God using such evil agency remains a profoundly disturbing possibility.

And what of *Ya'akov*/Jacob himself? The operative sentence is, of course, verse 29: "*Vayomer: Lo Ya'akov ye'amair od sh'mecha; ki im Yisrael, ki sarita im elohim [Elohim?] v'im anashim vatuchal.*/And he said: No longer will your name be called Jacob; but rather Israel, for you have wrestled/struggled with divine beings [God?] and human beings and have prevailed." [More on this last verb *vatuchal* below.]

Ya'akov/Jacob is changed, profoundly changed, by this encounter/experience, as has been the Jewish People by the *Shoah*. He is not who he was prior to the contest; he has been wounded severely, and will ultimately die carrying his wound with him. He has emerged victorious from his conflict, and both Biblical and Rabbinic traditions regard him the better for it. Indeed, his very name change from Ya'akov/Jacob [i.e. Heel-Grabber] to Yisrael/Israel [i.e. Overcomer-of-beings] is indicative of this victory and the very appellation by which Jews are known today.

Israel, too, the Jewish People, is not who it was prior to the *Shoah*. All manners of Jewish expression and Jewish life have been significantly affected by the *Shoah*. No one--Jew or Christian--would be so bold to say that Israel has emerged <u>victoriously</u> from the *Shoah*; the wounds are still far too fresh, the pain still too intense, the losses still too great. Generations of Jews will continue to limp to their graves carrying with them the scars of the *Shoah*.[10]

Finally, we note, that, in limping away after the contest, there is no indication that the struggle now concluded will end such a tortuous journey. Indeed, following the patriarch himself, Israel the people continues to struggle with the post-*Shoah* realities of both faith and history. Ya'akov/Jacob is now more fully Yisrael/Israel, yet Ya'akov/Jacob is not totally absent from that reality. The Jewish people post-*Shoah* carries with it what it was prior to the *Shoah*, dreaming of what it was and could have been, realizing only too well what it will never be.[Parenthetically, the Christian, child too of Ya'akov/Jacob now Yisrael/Israel, limps away from the encounter and into this post-*Shoah* world, burdened by both guilt and shame for active involvement, for silent acquiescence, for bystanding, wanting to stand again in God's

---

[10] My own personal position is that the <u>Shoah</u> is a wound form which the Jewish People will <u>never</u> recover. For example, if demographers are correct that the loss of approximately six million Jews--one and one-half million below the age of eighteen--represents in terms of present and future Jewish births a figure two and one-half times that number--and we are today between fourteen and sixteen millions persons world-wide--then the <u>real loss</u> represented by the <u>Shoah</u> is approximately <u>fifty percent</u> of our people. Given all the pressures to which Jews are subjected at the close of this Twentieth Century, we will never be numerically what we could have been. And such figures do not even begin to address the unrealized dreams of those murdered or never born.

presence, however re-defined, knowing that where once he/she stood, he/she can do so no longer.][11]

[3] What *Bracha*/Blessing?

Of the four commentaries cited, only Hertz addresses the actuality of the *bracha*/blessing itself, referencing it alluded to in the *Haftarah*/Additional Scripture read in the synagogue on the Sabbath where it is found, ,the text itself strangely silent as to its actual content:

> In the words of the Prophet chosen as the Haftorah for this Sedrah, 'He [Jacob] strove with an angel, and prevailed: he [Jacob] wept, and made supplication unto him.' That supplication for mercy, forgiveness and Divine protection is heard. Jacob, the Supplanter, becomes Israel, Prince of God.[12]

Following upon verse 27, the indication is that the change-of-name is the blessing. Why, then, the need for the author/editor to have the wrestler bless *Ya'akov*/Jacob now *Yisrael*/Israel in verse 30? Could it be that the change-of-name is not the *bracha*/blessing, but only opens the door to the blessing? Could It be that, having come through this wrestling match successfully, the doorway to *bracha*/blessing is now opened--whatever it will be? And the absence of its actual words is the text's dramatic emphasis that each generation will have to determine for itself what its *bracha*/blessing will be--but only after it has engaged in the wrestling, only after it has been wounded in the fray, only after it limps away now more fully prepared to meet the challenges of the new day?

That is the predicament of post-*Shoah* Jewry: We have come through the years 1933/39-1945--not "successfully"--and have earned the *bracha*/blessing for which we seek, not yet truly knowing what It is, still nursing our wounds and exploring our possibilities, still attempting to "make sense" of what has transpired. It may very well be too early--fifty years hence--to state with absolute certainty what our *bracha*/blessing is. Our world has been irrevocably torn asunder and we are still attempting to put the jagged pieces back together In some semblance of normalcy. Only now--half a century forward--have we begun to ask the questions [theological, religious, historical,

---

[11] I am indebted to Dr. Henry F. Knight, Associate Professor of Religion at the University of Tulsa for this insight.

[12] Joseph H. Hertz, Op. cit., page 124.

philosophical, ethical, political, etc. which may very well result in our *bracha*/blessing.[13]

Both the textual encounter and the "*Shoah* encounter" are extra-ordinary in *Ya'akov*/Jacob's life and in the life of the Jewish People. *Ya'akov*/Jacob becomes *Yisrael*/Israel and the Jewish People begins its collective journey forward. This same Jewish People experiences the *Shoah* and the journey almost comes to its end. Once again, *Yisrael*/Israel limps forward, uncertain of where it is going as at the first, knowing far less what the future holds in store. But it goes forward.

[4] *Vatuchal*: Mistranslation and Misunderstanding?

Verse 29 ends with this verb. Hertz's translation, paralleling King Jamesian English, reads "....and hast prevailed."[14] Hirsch's more poetic German, rendered into English, reads "....since you have prevailed."[15] Both the Oxford Annotated Bible[16] and Plaut's The Torah: A Modern Commentary[17] read "....and have prevailed."

Yet, understanding the root of this verb to be the Hebrew *yachol*/"to be able," do not these translations reflect rather the biases of the authors/editors/translators? Is not a more accurate and logical translation/rendering of this verb, past tense, "and you have been enabled?" Is this not more consistent with the reality of what has transpired between *Ya'akov*/Jacob now *Yisreal*/Israel and the *ish*? Is this not what, in truth, has happened to the Jewish People since the *Shoah*: Both have been enabled subsequent to the wrestling match to go forward, both changed and wounded, in quest of the blessing, whatever it is, to continue the journey wherever it will lead. To be "enabled" is not to "prevail;" it is, rather, to recognized who one is, what one is, upon what resources one can draw, and go even at risk. To refuse to go forward after the encounter is to become impotent, and, ultimately, to die. Neither *Yisrael*/Israel or the Jewish People have chosen to do either.

---

[13] It would be far too simplistic and theologically and religiously offensive to speculate upon the re-creation of the State of Israel as the bracha/blessing to come out of the Shoah. Other possibilities--such as a revitalized Jewish life, both in this country and abroad--remain equally problematic.

[14] Joseph H. Hertz, Op. cit., page 124.

[15] Sampson Raphael Hirsch, Op. cit., page 151.

[16] Herbert G. May and Bruce M. Metzger, Editors, The Oxford Annotated Bible, page 41.

[17] W. Gunther Plaut, The Torah: A Modern Commentary, page 218.

[5] Why the Need to Wrestle?

The last point I would raise with regard to this *Bereshit*/Genesis passage is one to which I have alluded earlier [page 9]: Namely, that it is significantly important that the confrontation be in the nature of a <u>wrestling match</u>, without which the event itself looses much of its power, appeal, and meaning.

Kohelet/The Preacher writes *Ayn kol hadash tachat hashamesh*/"There is nothing new under the sun" [1:9],. The author/editor of *Bereshit*/Genesis 32:22-33 fully understands this verse as do we today, post-*Shoah*, both literally and symbolically: Without such wrestling, without such struggling, without such pain, humanity, being whatever it is that we are--the Jewish People no exception--can go forward. It is our fate that the common life's journey we share is not one of total bliss or total pain, but, rather, a mixture of both joy and sorrow. It is our fate that, sadly, only when tested do we rise to the nobility of which we are capable and descend to the depravity of which we all-too-often give evidence. We wrestle only to succeed on occasion, only to fail on others; but we wrestle nonetheless.

The *Shoah* now remains for *Yisreal's*/Israel's descendants, Jews, Christians, Western humanity, its ongoing wrestling match, not yet over; its protagonists and antagonists, however, all-too-well defined. Who will, ultimately, emerge victorious is still as yet un- clear. The nature of the *bracha*/blessing equally unclear; the <u>meaning</u> of the wrestling match also unclear. Light slowly begins to dawn after this darkness--but only in the distance and only barely. *Yisrael*/Israel/The Jewish People has been <u>enabled</u> by this experience to go forward, where as yet unknown, hopefully, with eyes opened; more aware of the fragility of its own and others' existence, more sensitive to the cries of others, more compassionate to their pain, but, perhaps, also, more frightened, more unsure of its own footsteps as it limps into its future, more anxious than before. But there is no turning back, no nostalgic look again at life pre-*Shoah*; there is only life post-*Shoah*, but <u>life</u> nonetheless.

II. "WRESTLING WITH MATTHEW 26:36-46"
A. First Thoughts

Inherently, for a Jew to "wrestle" with this or any New Testament text--religiously and/or theologically--is problematic at the outset: This book which tells the "story" of Christianity in the person of the resurrected Christ is <u>not</u> part of Jewish sacred literature, and, therefore, possesses less sacred meaning and import for Jews than for Christians.[18] A religiously-sensitive Jew, therefore, must approach this task with a certain trepidation, not unwarranted given the previous history of what has been called euphemistically "Jewish-Christian relations."

Then, too, there are "issues of concern" to any Jewish-Christian discussion which, while not directly germane to this paper, need to be enumerated here and explored elsewhere. I would outline them as follows:

[1] Can any dialogue whatsoever between Jews and Christians, between Judaism and Christianity, take place which excludes discussion of the religio-theological import of the *Shoah* as well as the rebirth of the State of Israel in 1948?

[2] Is the New Testament "anti-Semitic?" That is, what role have those passages and/or books which negatively portray the Jewish community of Jesus' day played both in the development of Western anti-Semitism and the *Shoah* itself?

[3] What now do Christians mean when they speak of God the Father, His Son Jesus the Christ, and an unredeemed world which could and did countenance the *Shoah*?[19]

[4] What, then the very "mission" of the Church, specifically towards the Jewish People and generally towards all non-Christian peoples In the aftermath of the *Shoah*, as well as towards each other?

[5] What, then, is to be the proper relationship between the "parent" Judaism and the "child" Christianity, between Jews and Christians, given the long, sad, and tragic history of that relationship, or, rather, non-relationship?

[6] In our post-*Shoah* world, what meaning is to be attached to a serious historical look-see at the birth, growth, and development of Christianity, the person of Paul and others, through the Nazi period, up to and including our own day?

---

[18] Obviously, the reverse is not the case: The Christian Bible is Torah plus New Testament [page 1], and, thus, both "parts" are sacred to the Christian. And, while unequally worthy perhaps, both parts are worthy of serious analysis and reflection.

[19] A related question which strikes at the very heart of the matter is the following: Is Jesus the Christ, the One and Only Begotten Son of God, only for those who accept Him as such? Or, is He the Christ, the Only Begotten Son of God, for all those who do not accept Him as such? And what, then, do you do with those who neither accept Him as such or reject Him outright, or stand in ignorance of Him? What then is the proper Christian response first to the Jews?

B. Wrestling with Matthew 26:36-46
[1] The Heart of the Matter

Jewish *midrashic*/interpretive tradition records that when the Children of Israel went into slavery In Egypt, the Divine Presence was with them in pain and in sorrow, following them; and when they celebrated their liberation and redemption in joy and gladness, that same Divine Presence was with them, leading them. As a Jew, the heart of this passage, it seems to me, is Jesus' thrice-offered prayer to God, repeated twice with minor variation [verses 39 and 42] and alluded to once [verse 44], offered by one who knows his own death is imminent [verse 38 joined with verses 45 and 46]. Acknowledgement of impending death is interwoven with resignation, acceptance, and trust [verse 38].

Is it too much a stretch of the imagination to see this Jesus not as a divine personage, as he is so perceived by the various Christian communities, but as a fellow Jewish traveller, sharing the fate of his own people even in the oppressive Roman period? equally, too much a stretch of the imagination, post-*Shoah*, to see the agonies of this individual Jew as giving voice to the thousands of other Jews [and Christians] in the death camps which punctured the landscape of Poland and elsewhere? Is it too much a stretch of that same imagination to see in Jesus' words the words of those persons of faith who met their own deaths with dignity and courage [Hebrew: *al k'dushat Hashem*/for the sanctification of the Divine Name/Presence], refusing to commit suicide themselves, still believing in that historically-traditional God and His plan and purpose for Jewish humanity?[20]   I think not--regardless of one's own personal theology. Rephrasing verse 39 with this understanding, therefore, yields the following:

> O my Father/God: If it be possible, let this cup [of sorrowful life] pass from me. Nevertheless, not as I will it [i.e. by my own hand], but as You will.[21]

---

[20] What is, perhaps, additionally so difficult to realize is that this martyred "death with dignity" in the face of overwhelming depravity is, quite validly, a form of resistance to both enemy and oppression.

[21] This and the following interpretations/rewritings are based upon my reading of both William Barclay, The Daily Study Bible: The Gospel of Matthew, Volume 2, Revised Edition [Philadelphia: The Westminster Press, 1975] pages 347-350; and The Interpreter's Bible, Volume 7: Matthew-Mark [Nashville: Abingdon Press, 1978] pages 578-581.

Rephrasing, however, verse 42, with the above-noted understanding in mind, yields the following:

> O my Father/God: If this cup [of sorrowful life] may not pass away from me except I drink it [I.e. by my own hand], instead [the disjunctive 'but'] [I reject this course of action] Your will be done.

Verse 41, then, becomes an exclamatory declaration not only to those who were with Jesus at the time, but, also, to those in the death camps, surrounded by the most vile of human actions, not to succumb and be like those who inflict both pain and death, but to remember that humanness itself is a divinely-given gift:

> Watch and pray that you enter not into temptation [to be like those who debase, degrade, and destroy], for though the spirit is indeed willing [you truly do not wish to do so], the flesh is weak [it is an all-too-easy trap into which to fall].

Indeed, there were those who did fall into the trap: Kapos who terrorized their victims more so than the Nazi guards themselves; ghetto police who relished and enjoyed the power they held over their fellow Jews; Jews who exploited others for profit or other self- serving ends; and those who own base vileness enabled them to derive pleasure from the pain and suffering of others--or worse, those who surrendered whatever humanity they possessed in exchange for callous indifference--not as a defense mechanism for personal survival--but because they genuinely could care less about others. That such, however, is not a description of the vast majority who found themselves inside the death camps is a tribute to the nobility and dignity of the human spirit.

[2] *Betrayal*

The significance of the word *betrayal* in verses 45 ["the Son of man is *betrayed* into the hands of the sinners"] and 46 ["my *betrayer* is at hand"] is particularly poignant when, again, Jesus, the Jewish human being, suffering along with his own people, is juxtaposed with the contemporary reality of the *Shoah*. Jewishly understanding "Son of man" [Hebrew *ben adam*?] as the Jewish voice of humanity crying out inside those concentration and death camps, did not those awaiting their own deaths see there the very betrayal of humanity itself? Did they not conclude that the forces of darkness had, indeed, conquered humanity itself? Ironically, the acknowledged purpose of the "system" was to dehumanize the Jews [and others] physically, so that, when put to death, the Nazis were able to rationalize that those exterminated were, in fact, not truly human beings: After all, they did not look nor act like human beings.[22] And yet, perversely, it was the Nazis themselves and their henchmen, in carrying out their deeds, who betrayed the nobler aspects of their humanity and stand condemned eternally because of it.

> Behold, the hour is at hand, and our [Jewish] humanity is betrayed into the hands of the Nazis....my betrayer is at hand.

Then, too, the silence, acquiescence, and/or complicity of those who could have rescued but chose not to do so itself bespeaks a form of betrayal, the end-result of centuries of teaching that the Jew is "other than human." Since the death of the Jew Jesus two thousand years before, the perception of the Jew as "demonological," allied with Satan, century after century, bore tragic fruit in the very unwillingness to aid the Jews under Nazi hegemony even in their moment of greatest need. Is it any wonder, then, that verse 38 of this text can now be read and understood with a different and yet similar poignancy than when it was first uttered:

> My soul is exceedingly sorrowful, even unto death.

In the darkest of nights, robbed of both hope and a future, no one rallying to their defense, feeling cut off, isolated, alone, their own people impotent to act in the face of such overwhelming evil, what continues to inspire is the nobility with which death itself was met, coupled with the determination to survive even this if at all possible--but not at the expense of personal degradation and debasement.

III. CONCLUSION

---

[22] The very term used by the SS to describe their captives prior to death-- 'Musselmanner' ["musclemen"] --is itself the classic statement of perverse irony.

A. Final Thoughts

Questions of so-called "contemporary relevance" aside, wrestling with
the sacred texts of any religious tradition and/or faith community in
light of historical experiences strikes at the very essence of religion:
Whether or not faith itself can be affirmed as it was prior to this new
experience; re-affirmed in light of this new experience, now changed
and/or modified; or abandoned altogether because of this new
experience. The "*Shoah* experience" of 1933-1945 challenges all three;
yet both Jews and Christians continue to be Jews and Christians after
the *Shoah*. For some, their historic faith and understanding of God and
God's relationship to humanity has been little changed by the *Shoah*.
For others, both their faith and their understanding continue to change
because of the *Shoah*, yet nowhere near a final resolution. And for
others, it was and remains the *Shoah* itself in all of its grotesquerie
which has resulted in both loss of faith and loss of faith-community.[23]

"Wrestling with Biblical texts after the *Shoah*" is, in truth,
something of a new beginning for both Jews and Christians. It is a
journey forward through as yet-uncharted territory, bursting upon as
yet-uncharted land. If Emil L. Fackenheim is, indeed, correct, that
"....the Jewish Bible must be read by Jews today--read, listened to,
struggled with, if necessary fought against--as though they had never
read it before," so, too, must the Christian Bible--encompassing that
same Jewish Bible--be equally read, by both Jews and Christians, as
though, together, we have never read it before. In light of the *Shoah*, we
may never have.[24]

---

[23] Interestingly enough, Reeve Robert Brenner's pioneering study of <u>Shoah</u>
survivors themselves now living in Israel reflects this tripartite division. See his
<u>The Faith and Doubt of Holocaust Survivors</u> [New York: Macmillan Publishing
Company, 1980].

[24] See Footnote #1 for the full text. Later on in <u>The Jewish Bible after the
Holocaust: A Re-Reading</u>, Fackenheim relates the following:

'Reformation' turns the mind to the country of the Reformation--and
of the 'Aryan/non-Aryan' abyss. In 1939 I had fled from Germany,
the land of my birth. In 1983 I returned, not for my first but for my
first theological visit. There the Roman Catholic theologian Hanns-
Hermann Henrix affirmed that Christian anti-Judaism will not end
until Christians find a positive relation to Jews, not despite their non-
acceptance of the Christ, but because of it. On his part, Martin Stoehr,
a Protestant, spelled out the following: 'We Christians have lived
along side Jews for nearly two millennia. But we have never listened
to them, and our Christian faith has not helped us in this regard. Then
why do we want to listen to them now? Not because of our Christian

faith, but because six million Jews were murdered. He ended his major address as follows: 'We Christians must begin all over again, with the first two questions of the Bible. "Where are you, Man?" and "Where is your brother?" Events have revolutionized the thinking of these two German theologians, one Roman Catholic, the other Protestant. No longer able to begin with a New Testament superseding the Old, they began once more with the beginning--an 'Old' Testament as old-new for them as the Ta'anach has been for Jews all along. In this, we learn from Eberhard Bethge, they had a precursor in Dietrich Bonhoeffer. [pages 72-73]

Chapter 6 - FACING THE HOLY WHOLE
Henry F. Knight

In the course of too many centuries, people of faith have rendered the holy in ways that deny the claims and confessions of others, justifying in the process their indignation toward and condemnation of unbelievers. The polemic of John 8 punctuates the biblical witness of the fourth Gospel and makes this unavoidably clear, particularly as Jews are portrayed as the very enemy of Christ. To be fair, the Jewish Scriptures are not free from the rhetoric of contempt and the violence of conquest. But Christians would do well not to pursue pointing out the speck in the eyes of their covenantal siblings before undertaking to remove the log from their own. In other work I have drawn on the hermeneutical strategies of midrash as an instrument of critique and retrieval capable of securing an honest and vulnerable integration of this negative strand within the foundational scriptures of Judaism and Christianity. Offering a plural voice to the scriptural witness, midrash recognizes the wide variety of interpretations that may legitimately be carried by biblical testimony. Further still, midrash supplies a biblically rooted way of resisting prior expressions of covenantal fidelity that maintain the very fidelity that is threatened by the rhetoric in which it is framed.

In an earlier reflection on the summons of Moses at the burning bush I ventured into this territory with some fear and trepidation, trying to step carefully on the hallowed ground of sacred origins. I noted in that essay several key features that a post-Shoah return to this foundational story must not overlook-indeed, with which it must contend:

1. Ex. 3: 1-15 is a survivor's/survival story. The figure of a burning bush cannot be anything less than a threatened, living entity engulfed with flame. To say this bush is not consumed can mean either that it has survived after the fire is over or that it is resisting its demise while the fire is still raging.

2. The summons from God occurs in and through the burning bush, not in and through the bush by itself. Moreover, it occurs in and

through it. The burning bush mediates the call of God. It is the means by which the I AM-you are for others is heard.

3. The summons is a dialogically/covenantally constituted (I AM-you are) event. The hineni of its summons is mutually constructed. The I who summons Moses is heard as the I of Moses faces the Thou of the Summoner.

4. The hineni is fulfilled in return for the sake of liberation. Moses recognition of his standing before the Holy One of Israel is not for his sake alone. It is for the sake of his people, for others. He is called not simply into being but into being in relation for the sake of those with whom he lives in relation.

5. Their liberation leads to the land of others, beginning and returning to Sinai in order to be on the way to the land of promise. Beginning, passing through, and returning to the Mountain of God.

In his case, Moses stood before a burning bush and through it he was approached, albeit enigmatically, by the Eternal One of his forebears, the God of Abraham, the God of Isaac, the God of Jacob. Christians approach the holy by way of their burning bush-Jesus of Nazareth. They have learned to do so cautiously, even tentatively, removing their shoes as it were, proceeding with care. In some instances, the approach is too facile and tramples on the mystery of God's presence mediated in and through this figure. At other times, the mystery encountered in and through Jesus is so identified with him that it overwhelms and consumes the historical figure through whom it comes. In classical Christian language, Christian approaches to God in and through Jesus still contend with the vestiges of adoptionism and docetism (particularly, monophysitism).

In the remarks that follow, I intend to read John 8 asking if its anti-Jewish rhetoric is an essential component of its Christian witness. I want to ask if Christians must approach the holy by denying the approach of their quintessential other in the process. After Auschwitz, this issue cannot be avoided. It will undoubtedly involve those who face it with theological issues posed long ago. But the urgency is current and focused nowhere more clearly than in the testimony of John 8.

READING JOHN 8

The eighth chapter of John begins with Jesus in the Temple teaching a group of his followers, and undoubtedly some curious onlookers. A group of religious leaders from the Jerusalem area bring before him a woman caught in the act of adultery and ask Jesus how he would dispose of her case, citing religious law that she should be stoned/killed. The scene, familiar to many, unfolds with Jesus drawing or writing on the ground and saying to the assembly that the one who is without sin may cast the first stone. The group disperses and Jesus turns to the accused, asking her where her accusers have gone. Then he sends her away, admonishing her to "sin no more."

The scene shifts back to Jesus teaching his gathered assembly in the Temple as he tells them "I am the light of the world. Whoever follows me will never walk in darkness but will have the light of life." (John 8:12) Then the Pharisees (who earlier had left Jesus alone with the woman) challenge Jesus' testimony. In the exchange that follows, Jesus declares that he judges no one; however, he hastens to add a word of clarification, stating that if he were to judge, his judgement would be valid, since it is confirmed by his Father in heaven, whom his interlocutors could not know since they did not recognize his authority nor his relationship with his Father.

The exchange concludes with an editorial comment that Jesus was not yet arrested since "his hour had not yet come." (John 8: 20) The narrator then describes Jesus explaining that he will be "going away," but where he is going they, this time identified as "the Jews," cannot come since they are "from below" while he is "from above." He then adds in response to their query regarding his identity, "I have much to say about you and much to condemn." (John 8:26) Another editorial comment follows, explaining that they ("the Jews" this time) did not know Jesus was speaking "about the Father." Then Jesus, in an apparent allusion to the crucifixion to come declares, "When you have lifted up the Son of Man, then you will realize that I am he." As this portion concludes, John points out that as Jesus was saying these things, "many believed in him." (John 8:30)

Next Jesus says to the very same group, "the Jews who had believed in him," (John 8: 31) "If you continue in my word, you are truly my disciples; and you will know the truth, and the truth will make you free." Instead of seeing this as a confirming statement, the very ones "who had believed in him" resist his implication that they are not free. They are, they declare, "descendants of Abraham" and are therefore already free. Jesus clarifies his comments and his understanding of the enslaving character of sin. Then he declares, "I know you are descendents of Abraham; yet you look for an opportunity to kill me, because there is no place for you in my word." (8:37) Then Jesus links his comments to what he has "seen in the Father's presence" grounding his authority in that of "the Father."

The conflict deepens further as the accused answer that "Abraham is [their] father," which Jesus then disputes, saying if they were Abraham's children they would not be doing what they are doing, "trying to kill me." (8: 40) they are, Jesus claims, "indeed doing what [their] father does." (8:41) "You are from your father the devil, and you choose to do your father's desires." (8: 44) "You are not from God." (8: 47).   The conflict intensifies as Jesus' opponents, now clearly identified as "the Jews" accuse Jesus of being "a Samaritan and [having] a demon." (John 8: 48) Jesus defends himself adding that whoever keeps his word "will never taste death." (v. 51) The accusation deepens, with Jesus' accusers asking "Are you greater than our father Abraham, who died?" (v. 53) The exchange intensifies further until Jesus in his expression of relationship with Abraham evokes the question, "Have you seen Abraham?" (v. 57) He responds, "before Abraham was, I am," alluding, as his does, to the divine name. As a result, his accusers pick up stones to throw at him as Jesus hid himself and left the Temple.

CONFRONTING THE POLEMIC
When we look critically at John 8 we notice a progressive identification of the opponents of Jesus, first with "the scribes and the Pharisees" (8:12-13) then with "the Jews" (8:21-22). Whether or not this is a developmental progression or a stylistic one, they are equivalent groups that are being portrayed. George Smiga argues that John actually intends a variety of Jewish leaders and not "the Jews" in general Smiga, 156-57).[1] Nonetheless the damage is done, at both the

[1] George M. Smiga, Pain and Polemic: Anti-Judaism in the Gospels (New York:
Paulist Press, 1992) 156-157.
"An increasingly clearer picture emerges from all these studies grounded in the hypothesis that the Gospel was written in response to the exclusion of the Johannine church from the synagogue and the subsequent dialogue between these two religious parties. The subject of the picture is a defensive and threatened Christian community, attempting to reshape its identity isolated from the synagogue and its Jewish roots." Robert Kysar, "Anti-Semitism and the Gospel of John" in Craig A. Evans & Donald A. Hagner, editors, Anti-Semitism and Early Christianity: Issues of Polemic and Faith (Minneapolis: Fortress Press, 1993) 120. Kysar, citing the seminal work of J. Louis Martyn, explains his thesis that the Gospel of John is "a two-level drama" depicting "two sibling religious communities, each with its own identity issues," (121) portrayed in the gospel narrative as "thinly-disguised opponents of the writer's own contemporary Christian community." (124) John Gager, recognizing the

contextual level of the Gospel's composition (toward the end of the first century CE) and as Jesus is portrayed in his conflict with his own religious leaders in Jerusalem.   Indeed, the identification of Jesus' opponents as "the Jews" (Ioudaios) is an indication of the two levels at which the entire gospel text works.   The contemporaneous conflict between Jesus and his opponents is in large measure grounded in the later conflict between the nascent Christian and rabbinic communities of the narrator's time at the turn of the first century C.E.   With each community's identity at stake, the evangelist told his story of Jesus and his conflict with the Temple as a veiled expression of the conflict between the Johannine Church and the (a?) synagogue of his time. The point: John's polemic is rooted in a struggle for the heart and soul of the descendents of Second Temple Judaism. On one side are the followers of Jesus who see him instituting a new religious identity replacing the covenantal symbols of Temple (which had already been destroyed) and Law, and redefining Torah. On the other side were the descendents of the Pharisees finding in Torah and Law the symbols which would sustain them in the wake of the Temple's destruction. Clark Williamson has put the matter well.[2] The animosity in John 8 is one pole of a two-sided family fight "of the worst kind."[3]

While it is helpful to identify the polemic as rooted primarily in a later conflict between synagogue and church, it does not diminish the violence in the biblical text. The expression "the Jews" has been incorporated as a category and is no longer used to designate a people. The world is divided into those who are for Jesus and those who are Jesus' opponents, with the quintessential opponent bearing the designation "the Jews." They are even deemed, in mythic fashion, to have been opponents of God's way from the very beginning as evidenced by John 8: 44-45.

RESISTING TEMPTATION

---

categorizing dangers of this critical thesis, renders the possibility that the veiled conflict could be specific to a single local synagogue with whom John's community was experiencing mutual conflict. See John G. Gager, The Origins of Anti-Semitism: Attitudes Toward Judaism in Pagan and Christian Antiquity (New York: Oxford University Press, 1983) 152.

[2] Clark M. Williamson, Has God Rejected His People? Anti-Judaism in the Christian Church (Nashville: Abingdon Press, 1982) 84.

[3] Williamson, 82.

More than rhetoric is at stake here. John's polemic expresses a deeper, problem in which the world view of John's Gospel is steeped. There is a dichotomizing, bifurcation of reality into either-or categories of eternal life/the world, followers of Christ/opponents of Christ (with Jews being the quintessential opponent).[4]   The accuser-accused dynamics separate John's world into categories that do not allow its inhabitants to accept the other who chooses not to join them in their way of being faithful. John's world is dualistic, ontologically as well as morally and spiritually. George Smiga has captured these dynamics well: John's exclusive christology obliterates all that does not acquiesce to its demands.[5] Attempts to limit the referent of "the Jews" are overwhelmed by the christological sense which divides all into a dualism apportioning life to those who believe and rejections to those who do not. The either-or dualism of the gospel will allow no other place to stand.[6]

In other words, John 8, with its polemic of abrogation, forces us to recognize that religious exclusivism cultivates a violent attitude toward the other that is a faithful expression of orthodox Christian identity. Rosemary Ruether calls it the "left hand of Christology:"[7]

By mythologizing the theological division between 'man-in-God' and 'man-alienated-from-God' into a division between two postures of faith, John gives the ultimate theological form to the diabolizing of 'the Jews' which is the root of anti-Semitism in the Christian tradition. There is no way to rid Christianity of its anti-

---

[4] Gager, 152.

[5] Smiga, 173.

[6] Smiga, adapting categories he derived from D.R.A. Hare and John Gager, differentiates between three types of anti-Jewish polemic. The first two categories are intra-Jewish: prophetic critique and subordinating intra-Jewish polemic. In neither case are the central symbols and realities of Judaism questioned. Rather, the polemic is based on fidelity to those symbols (prophetic critique) or on which group has most faithfully represented and incorporated those symbols and values into their lives. A third form, abrogating polemic, aims to replace the central symbols and meanings of Judaism with new ones in order to establish a new theological entity/identity. See Smiga, Pain and Polemic, 136.

[7] Rosemary Reuther, Faith and Fatricide: The Theological Roots of Anti-Semitism with and introduction by Gregory Baum (New York: Seabury Press, 1974) 116.

Judaism, which constantly takes social expression in anti-Semitism, without grappling finally with its Christological hermeneutic itself. (Faith and Fatricide,116)

Faced with the embedded violence of John 8, thoughtful post-Shoah Christians stand before a critical summons. Because of its embedded violence, there is a moral imperative to disassociate with the face value/plain meaning of its testimony. At the same time, we are confronted what Levinas calls the "temptation of temptation."[8] In other words, as confessing Christians we are summoned first by the text and its witness. As we answer the summons, we encounter the violence embedded there and we subsequently wrestle with its meaning. If we approach the text already prepared to disassociate ourselves from it, then we approach the text

already admitting that we are not summoned by it, but by something else. That is the "temptation of temptation" as Levinas terms it. Of course, one option is to reject the text out of hand, and many Christians have surely chosen this option, most often by not including it in their canon within the canon. One might also choose to amend, pointing to a variety of translations that demonstrate such a strategy. Again, one must ask if this strategy dodges the matter of violence embedded in the narrative identity given by the biblical text. One could also opt for critical embrace as well, searching for a place to stand within the text that allows, or even invites, resistance to the primary voice of the text. This last option is the way of midrash and the way our panel has dealt with similar matters in our dialogue. The problem now is whether or not there is such a textual place from which to engage the matter in John 8, while at the same time resisting the violence in the text. In other words, we are looking for another voice, intrinsic to the text that can challenge the dichotomizing polemic of its majority witness. An intra-textual move such as this allows for a form of self-criticism that can stand in solidarity with external critique without abandoning the authority of the text in one's confessional life. In that regard, let us turn to the opening scene of John 8.

STANDING ACCUSED

The opening lines of the chapter take us to the Temple where a woman caught in the act of adultery is brought before Jesus. He is

---

[8] Emmanuel Levinas, "The Temptation of Temptation" in Nine Talmudic Readings trans. by Annette Aronowicz (Bloomington: Indiana University Press, 1990) 30-50, esp. 35, 48.

asked how he would handle the situation, more specifically: how
would he read the Law in her regard? His answer: to draw in the sand
and declare, honoring the Law while pushing beyond it: he who is
without sin, cast the first stone.

Most scholars in the critical tradition understand this opening
scene (7:53-8:11) not to be originally from the Johannine corpus. It
does not appear in the earliest manuscripts John 8 and is only located in
this text in later editions of the canonical tradition. Many scholars note
its similarity to Synoptic concerns, pointing out its affinity to Luke,
even suggesting its thematic linkage following Luke 26: 38.   Even so,
Ray Brown cautions against scholarly dismissal of the episode as an
inauthentic expression of the Johannine witness.[9] He calls it an
interpolation that is nonetheless linked theologically by theme to John
8.[10]   Still, its admonition not to judge stands in ironic contrast to the
scenes in John 8 that follow it. Indeed, its anticipatory counterpoint to
the accusational contempt that follows may be, for Christians, like me,
its primary virtue and saving grace.

Because of its imported status these twelve verses are often
placed in an exegetical parenthesis. However, when this is done the
episode is too often read in isolation from the remainder of the chapter
even though most interpreters will retain reading it with John 8's
dichotomizing logic and accusatory mentality.[11]   There is another
option, however, rooted in the recognition that the episode is most
probably imported from outside the Johannine tradition.[12]   The text
may very well be a midrashic wedge, placed there by others who, while
wanting to honor the witness of John, found the polemic to be
problematic for them as well. When read in this fashion, the opening
episode challenges the scenes that follow by referring to a thematically
linked event that while not Johannine is still authentically rooted in the
historical Jesus.

READING MIDRASHICALLY

This strategy is important. Scripture, even with its flawed
rhetoric, claims our allegiance. That is where we begin. But we do not
remain there.   The introductory episode in which people of faith,

---

[9] Raymond E. Brown, The Gospel According to John I-XII (New York: The
Anchor Bible/Doubleday, 1966) 336.
[10]   Ibid.
[11]   Brown, 336.
[12] Kysar 119ff.

leaders even, bring one of their own caught in the act of infidelity before Jesus and each other, provides ironic leverage for responding to the summons to responsibility that the subsequent witness of John seems to disregard. In the several verses of John 8:12 and following fellow travelers of the covenantal way accuse another of covenantal infidelity. In the biblical text she is a Jew caught in adultery and brought before Jesus and other Jews who had sought his counsel. In the subtext that Martyn calls its second level, the followers of Jesus are confronted by the leaders of the synagogue as they join the woman, accused of infidelity. However, in subsequent generations of Christian testimony, as in the verses that follow, the ones brought before Jesus and accused of adulterous infidelity is always "the Jews." Indeed, Christian testimony of 8:12ff accuses "the Jews" (i.e., the covenantal siblings of later generations of Christians) of covenantal infidelity regarding Jesus as the representative one of Israel's God. Indeed, "Jews" are even rendered as joining themselves in a progressively more intimate way with the enemy of all creation. They are caught, as it were, in spiritual adultery from the very beginning. And the Jesus of this later testimony sounds sharply different from the Jesus who earlier challenges any of God's representatives to cast the deadly stones of judgment and death at the one caught in adultery. Instead, they and the woman are sent away and told to put away their infidelities: "sin no more."

We may probe deeper, reading these opening twelve verses not simply as midrash but reading them midrashically as well-midrash on midrash. When Jesus was confronted with the woman before him and her accusers asking Jesus what he would do, he stooped and drew or wrote on the ground. We may wonder what Jesus was drawing/writing in the sand. The text, of course, does not report. Many exegetes have speculated, using the silence of the text in this regard as an occasion to suggest Christologically driven readings of the Hebrew scriptures. Some even go so far as to link Jesus writing with his finger with God's writing of the Ten Commandments in stone with God's finger! We might do better to pay attention to the fact of an absent text and to ask what might be significant about the actual text not being reported. Ray Brown draws the conclusion that it must not have been important or that it was doodling or insignificant. We do know that whatever it was, it was temporary, drawn in the sand. It was not written in stone and meant to be permanent.

From work done in conflict mediation, we might recall that the use of a temporary text can often serve to refocus accusatorial conversation on a common object, a common text as it were, that allows disputants to withdraw accusations, save face, and disengage from unhealthy conflict. The problem is separated from the person and the accusative voice of conflict is freed to become a problematically focused indicative voice. The closing lines of the episode suggest that something like that happened after Jesus made his comments, while drawing, doodling, or writing in the sand. His finger was pointed at whatever he was drawing, not at those who had confronted him. The accuser-accused dynamic that they brought to him was reconfigured. And then the woman was sent away along with the accusers, after which Jesus rather ambiguously commented to the one left before him, go and sin no more. To whom was Jesus speaking? The woman? Surely. The scribes and Pharisees? Most probably, though the text is unclear about their location. The text reports in verse 9 that they had departed; however, as John continues his narration in verse 13, they are still present. Regardless, Jesus was also addressing his followers and anyone else close enough (literally and figuratively) to overhear. And if we read the insertion of this story as a midrashic wedge placed before a number of troubling , though important verses in the Johannine witness, we are invited to hear an unknown midrashic editor addressing the Johannine followers of Jesus regarding the accusations that follow. What else are the accusations of John 8: 19, 23, 37, 44, 48 but a progressive case that "the Jews" who have not chosen to follow Jesus have been caught in adultery and betrayed their Lord? As we read these verses at the cusp of a new millennium, we cannot avoid seeing that they have functioned as verbal stones which have been held and thrown at Jews for centuries. Read as midrash John 7:53-8:11 should lead attentive Christians to recognize themselves hoist on their own petard. It should lead them to put down the stones and to go their way (our way) leaving the polemical way of accusation behind.

FACING THE I AM

When John 8 is read this way, confessing Christians stand once more before their burning bush, Jesus of Nazareth, who, bearing the I AM that constitutes their being, calls them to face up to the violence in their witness and to move beyond it in search of new relationships with the quintessential other in their lives. This is an interesting hermeneutical turn, since John builds his Christology from a similar base, seeing Jesus to be the incarnation of the One who speaks creation into existence.

Even if the I am's of John are not midrash on Exodus 3:14, but verbal hot text,[13] as it were, to a variety of references to the divine name throughout the Hebrew scriptures, the episode at the burning bush lies behind them and informs how they might be read and heard more fully. In that regard, we should remember that I AM is more than reflexive assertion of divine identity. It is a dialectical/dialogical constituted summons to life that is recognized in the dialogical circumlocution I AM-you are.

I AM-you are is a confirmative summons to life, that is more than a constitutive and dialectical summons to being. I AM-you are is a summons to responsibility-first for Moses' own people, then for others. Moses is called to return to the place of his people's oppression and to bring his people forth in freedom, acting in partnership with the One who has called him and who will accompany them along the way.

Furthermore, the summons to responsibility is a call that extends to leading this liberated people in establishing their covenanted life in a land already populated by others. They are summoned to embody covenantal responsibility/right relations with their neighbors-- all their neighbors--in a realm of others.

For this reason, I AM-you are for others is a summons to representative responsibility for others in a land already populated by others, with the understanding that such a place is their land of promise.

In other words, we are called upon by John's testimony to ask, "Who is the I of Jesus' I am if the I AM-you are [for others] of Ex. 3 is the summoning gestalt that lies behind John's hot text. The summons

---

[13] Brown, 334.

By referring to the phrase *ego eimi* (I am) as hot text, I am suggesting that the phrase opens up to an intratextual multiplicity of associations in the biblical text related to occurences of the divine name like hyper text on the Internet. This intratextual association is essential to the way of midrash making every occurrence of the divine name contemporaneous with every other. That is, the phrase *ego eimi* is an intratestual link with every other occurrence of the divine name rendered in Greek. This is a link upon which midrash depends and builds. Exodus 3 and its story of the giving of the divine name lies behind each of these links at the same time it also participates as one of them.

Ray Brown in his examination of the use of *ego eimi* (I am) in John explains that there are four occasions in which the phrase is used in absolute form without any predication, indicating that the divine name would clearly be associated with such usage. Three of those occasions occur in John 8. See *The Gospel According to John I-XII, Appendix VI*, p. 533-538.

of/at the burning bush is an I Am-you are for others. It is holy in and through the constitutive summons to life that calls forth life lived in response to the Other on behalf of others. At Israel's burning bush that summons is mediated through their very particular experience of oppression, indignation, and near annihilation. Moses was summoned to return in solidarity with his people to call them, in turn, to freedom and then to lead them into the land of promise, their promise-"the land of the Canaanites, the Hittites, the Amorites, the Perizzites, the Hivites, and the Jebusites." (Ex. 3: 8, 16) Moses was summoned to return to the land of oppression, Egypt, and to lead the people out, to freedom. And not just freedom, to the gift of covenant partnership and its covenanted responsibilities. That too is holy. Furthermore, that summons calls the people of Israel to live differently than other peoples, yoked in covenant to the Eternal One Who Is and Is Yet To Be, blessed thereby with the responsibilities of that relationship. What does this mean? While there is a significant strand of tradition that leads to a theology of conquest, there is also textual support for a minority voice, claiming that the land of promise is a land in which others dwell and the people of the covenant must come to terms with how to live with their neighbors in such difficult circumstances. Because of their past, they know they can be enslaved and destroyed. They, more than once, have been the object of genocidal violence. Still, they call the others amidst whom they dwell to a different way of living, a way which bears forth the promise of life in barren times and places. What does it mean to hear John identify Jesus with the I AM-you are of creation, the constituting word of life, that punctuates the prologue of John so magnificently and then hear Jesus identify with it in chapter 8? We may ponder two ways of reading this. If Jesus is re-presenting the constitutive word of God, then he is one through whom the I AM-you are is encountered. He is the Christian burning bush who in his passion is not consumed as he bears witness to the One he makes present. One may even oppose Jesus (fall away, deny, even betray) without intending to oppose the one he represents. On the other hand, if Jesus is identical to the constitutive I AM-you are, then when one encounters Jesus, one encounters God, not a burning bush. And those who oppose Jesus, would oppose God. The latter option is the one followed by John in chapter 8. When viewed in the light of the burning bush, however, we see that he his Christology is in danger of overwhelming and even losing the historical figure of Jesus in the process.[14]

---

[14] See my book Confessing Christ in a Post-Holocaust World (Westport, CT: Greenwood Publications, 2000) chapter three, for an examination of this

While John is distinguishing that which is of God from that which is not, he divides the world into opposing camps and forces that reduce people to categories and view those who are other as an enemy to be opposed not a neighbor to be loved. The summons to life lived in full covenant partnership in the presence of and on behalf of others is undermined by the by his dualistic framework. In the process, even Jesus of Nazareth, the Christian burning bush, is consumed by the symbol that stands in his place. In other words, we are faced with the problem of monophysitism, this time framed in the witness of scripture.[15] A representative Christology, had John employed it, would still affirm that Jesus embodies the eternal logos that intends creation. And that when one meets Jesus one encounters the very intention of creation embodied before them. But Jesus of Nazareth would not be consumed in the process, and the full force of the I AM-you are for others would be honored as well. In other words, the integrity of the other is intimately bound to the integrity of a truly incarnational faith. To address those who are other as categories for opposition is to lose as well the very one through whom the Christian summons to covenant life/responsibility is mediated.

READING AND FACING THE HOLY RESPONSIBLY

After the violence of the last century, reading biblical texts responsibly increases in importance. We know the impact of unexamined prejudice being passed on in sacred texts. We know the levels to which religious animosity can rise/sink. We know how critical it remains for human beings to learn how to live with those who are other, culturally and religiously. In the case of John 8, we must read aware of its context, recognizing the two levels of its composition. But that is not enough. Our encounter with John 8 forces us to recognize that religious exclusivism and its violence to the other are faithful expressions of orthodox Christian identity. While unnerving, it is true. We are guilty as charged. But there is another voice, hidden in the text, bearing witness to another way. Too easily we read over or past it. Or instructed by the consensus of others, we recognize it as an imported scene, out of place with the witness that follows, only to place it in an exegetical parenthesis, noting that it should not guide the reader in interpreting the Gospel. But we may

---

option.
[15] Gail O'Day's comments in The New Interpreter's Bible makes precisely this point. See Gail O'Day, the New Interpreter's Bible, vol. IX (Nashville: Abingdon Press, 1995) p. 628.

read otherwise, recognizing that being out of step may be precisely the point-a signal to the reader to proceed carefully, attentive to the irony that follows.

From this particular midrashic vantage-point, we are provided a place to gain critical perspective on the troubling testimony of John 8 yet still granting the witness of John authority in our lives. As well, while standing on John's midrashic ground we are invited to do our own midrashic work, configuring a temporary text in the sand, as it were, and seeking a way to move beyond accusation and contempt by reconsidering the dualistic framework of John's guiding Christology. In turning to the story of the burning bush, the story behind the I am's (ego eimi's) of John, we are able to ground a confessional relationship with Jesus that does not force his followers to view those who see Jesus differently than they do to be seen as enemies. And we can make such a confession drawing on the constitutive I AM-your are that has intended creation as life lived in responsible relationship from the beginning. To be sure there are some very practical implications we should honor. Whenever we read John 8, in whole or in part, we should supply a sense of context-its two levels, especially, its intra-family conflict and an awareness that survival was the issue for both groups in this familial argument. In liturgical settings, when extended explanations of context may not be possible we should consider either not using the reading or using with necessary and interpretive translations (e.g., translate "the Jews" as religious leaders). And importantly, we must remember that the problem involves more than correcting for polemical language. In the end, it is our responsibility to learn to face the holy always remembering that when we do, we deal with real persons, each of whom bears in his or her face a reflection of the Holy One who has given each of us life and breath. Furthermore, we must learn to face the holy in holistic ways, attending to all that is integrated in the oneness of God, not just this or that aspect that we have only partially glimpsed. We must discipline ourselves to be fully attentive to the wholeness of the holy. And throughout, we must face the holy as wholly as we are able, facing ourselves, even those aspects of ourselves that we dislike or find shameful. We must ourselves be whole if and as we approach the holy. To be sure, this task remains unfinished as we learn to face the holy whole.

Chapter 7 - Wrestling with God and the Devil
Steven L. Jacobs

Introduction

Now, more than fifty years after the conclusion of the Second World War, and the horrifying nightmarish events now known as the Holocaust or *Shoah,* with the reality of genocide problematic on the world scene lingering into this new century barely three months old from the "century of genocide" just completed, the full impact of *religion,* both theological and institutional, upon these events remains little explored at best. It is "the story remaining to be told." Despite all the bridge-building and good faith efforts of sincere Jews and Christians willing to meet in dialogue over this most painful of topics, we have only begun to hesitantly scratch at this scabbed-over surface of our wounds, still, perhaps, truly afraid to launch a bold and daring frontal assault on our own flawed religious and theological traditions. Even these post-Holocaust/*Shoah* public readings of selected passages of both the Hebrew Scriptures and the New Testament are fragile beginnings, but beginnings nonetheless, all-too-often drowned out by the pathetic indifference of Jewish and Christian religious communities more attuned to irrelevant issues and passing, faddish concerns than to the central issues of our collective survival. The Holocaust/*Shoah* is, equally, our sure inheritance and legacy as Jews and Christians, just as our evolved and evolving rituals and ceremonies, our changing ethical systems, our unique insights on the Divine-human encounter, and our scriptural texts are welcome parts of that same inheritance and legacy. That the 20th Century began with the genocidal slaughter of the Armenians (despite continuing Turkish denial), proceeded through the genocidal slaughtering of Jews and Roma, and ended with the genocidal slaughtering of Bosnian Serbs, Croats, and Moslems, as well as the Rwandese, remains a stinging indictment of the supposed "power of faith" to move the hearts of humanity in a positive direction.

And yet, as one ordained to the liberal rabbinate of the Jewish Religious Tradition (but whose roots remain strongly intertwined within the German Orthodox Jewish Religious Tradition), whose entire professional career, both scholarly and congregational, has been in dialogue with those both inside and outside the Jewish Community, I *do* continue to affirm both the *potential* "power for good," not only of our own faith traditions to affect both the present and future courses of human events, but of those of us willing to reach out to the "others" among us who are not like us. And I *do* affirm the central insight of Jewish philosopher of dialogue Martin Buber (1878-1965): that where two persons truly meet, there, in that interstitial place, there, the very presence of the Divine may be found. Standing, therefore, on holy ground together with my three beloved colleagues--Zev Garber, Hank Knight, and Jim Moore, let me proceed.

Exodus 3: Wrestling with God
First the verses that occasion this wrestling match:

> "Then the Lord said, "I have observed the misery of My people who are in Egypt; I have heard their cry on account of their taskmasters. Indeed, I know their sufferings, (8)and I have come down to deliver them from the Egyptians, and to bring them up out of the land to a good and broad land, a land flowing with milk and honey....The cry of the Israelites has now come to Me; I have also seen how the Egyptians oppress them....(16) "I have given heed to you and to what has been done to you in Egypt. (17) "I declare I will bring you up out of the misery of Egypt....(2) So I will stretch out My hand and strike Egypt with all My wonders that I will perform in it; after that he will let you go."

The "truth" of these words is affirmed by the Jewish commentators consulted and their commentaries: Abraham Cohen[1], Harvey J. Fields[2], Everett Fox[3], Joseph H. Hertz[4], Samson Raphael

---

[1]   Abraham Cohen (1947). *The Soncino Chumash.* London: The Soncino Press. Cohen, in addition, also raises two substantive issues which necessitate responses: (1) That the Egyptians were, in truth, agents of God in their overly-zealous oppressive work (pg. 330); and (2) That God's physical salvation of Israel was both present *and* future (pg. 332).
[2] Harvey J. Fields (1991). *A Torah Commentary for Our Time.* New York: Union of American Hebrew Congregations Press.

Hirsch[5], Malbim (Meir Leibush ben Yehiel Michel)[6], W. Gunther Plaut[7], Rashi (Solomon ben Isaac)[8], and Nahum M. Sarna[9]. And, of course, many, many others!

However--and that is an exclamatorily large "However!"--in 1994, I wrote in my book *Rethinking Jewish Faith: The Child of A Survivor Responds:*

> If God did, in fact, rescue the Jewish People from the hell of Egyptian slavery, why not rescue us from the hell of Auschwitz or Buchenwald or Maidanek or Mauthausen?[10] If God did, in fact, redeem the Jewish People from our exile in Babylonia, why not redeem us from our exile in Riga or Kovno or Lidice or Lvov? If God saved us after our departure from Spain only 450 years before, why not save us after our departure from the cities, towns, villages, and countries throughout Eastern and Western Europe, where we have lived for over 1,000 years and from where we were taken to ghettos and on to concentration camps and murderous death?[11]

For me, the haunting, troubling, gut-wrenching questions posed by this scriptural text remain as haunting, troubling, gut-

---

[3] Everett Fox (1995). *The Five Books of Moses.* New York: Schocken Books.

[4] Joseph H. Hertz (1961). *The Pentateuch and Haftorahs.* London: Soncino Press.

[5] Samson Raphael Hirsch (1986). *T'rumath Tzvi: The Pentateuch.* New York: The Judaica Press.

[6] Malbim (1984). *Commentary on the Torah.* Israel: M.P. Press/Hillel Press.

[7] W. Gunter Plaut (1981). *The Torah: A Modern Commentary.* New York: Union of American Hebrew Congregations Press.

[8] Rashi (1998). *Complete Tanach with Rashi.* Chicago/New York: Davka/The Judaica Press. (CD-Rom)

[9] Nahum M. Sarna (1991). *The JPS Torah Commentary.* Philadelphia: The Jewish Publication Society.

[10] (Footnote #1) To regard the former as a *singular event* incapable of repetition still remains problematic: Why one and not the other? Did God, somehow, therefore, expend whatever energy committed to human interaction on the *Pesach* (Passover) liberation and have none left during the *Shoah* even though Jews and Christians regard *all* prior rescues as Divine interventions? (pg. 21)

[11] Steven L. Jacobs (1994). *Rethinking Jewish Faith: The Child of A Survivor Responds.* Albany, NY: State University of New York Press, 16-17.

wrenching now in 2000, as they were in 1994, and as they were between the years 1939 and 1945:

Could it be that God did not rescue, redeem, save us during the *Shoah* because God *chose* not to do so for reasons either unfathomable or too monstrous to contemplate?

Could it be that we, somehow, *merited* such punishment as the result of our own errant way or the ways of the rest of humanity, serving, once again, as their *korban,* their sacrificial offering?

What possible sin or sins had we or they committed that necessitated the deaths of so many innocents along with the guilty, especially children, Jews and non-Jews alike,   in   ways   so horrific as to border on the unspeakable and unbelievable?

Or could it be that God did not rescue, redeem, save us during the *Shoah* because God *could not* do so, however much God wanted to do so?[12]

Thus, as a "scriptural non-literalist"--that is, one for whom neither the Hebrew Bible nor the New Testament are literally the words of God, but, rather, the evolving responses of the communities of the faithful, Jews *and* Christians, to their changing perceptions and understandings of the Divine over the course of the centuries, every bit as sacred and holy to me as to the scriptural literalist--my *rejection* of the *truth* of these central core verses of Exodus 3, and the 4,500 Israelite and later Jewish theology implicit in them, has, equally, already been addressed in that same text in 1994:

After the *Shoah,* it is no longer religiously creditable to speak of God's liberation of the Jewish people from Egypt but not from Germany or Poland or Russia or France. It is no longer morally creditable to give thanks for one liberation, that of Egypt, but not for the other, that of Nazi terrorized Europe.[13]

And while there are many issues to be addressed throughout this chapter, I will confine myself, briefly, to two, both raised by Abraham Cohen in his commentary:

Commenting on the latter half of verse 9--"*v'gam Raiti et halachatz asher Mitzraim lochatzim otam*/moreover I have seen the

---

[12] Steven L. Jacobs (1994). *Rethinking Jewish Faith: The Child of A Survivor Responds, 17.*

[13] Steven L. Jacobs (1994). *Rethinking Jewish Faith: The Child of A Survivor Responds, 66.*

oppression wherewith the Egyptians oppress them"--Cohen writes: "*The Egyptians, as the instruments of God*, exceeded the degree of oppression which had been foretold (Gen. Xv. 13); and for doing this they must be punished."[14]

Is it, therefore, bordering on either the heretical or the obscene to equally conclude that the Nazis and their minions under Hitler--*Y'mach sh'mo*/May his name be forever blotted out!--paralleling the Egyptians under Pharaoh, were, equally "instruments of God?" That is to say, that the God of Israel *used* such evildoers to accomplish Divine purposes, i.e. to punish a wayward Israel for its seeming and supposed lapses and failures of covenantal responsibility? To teach an errant Israel, as well as an errant Christianity, Western civilization, that the power of God brooks no immorality?[15] Quite obviously, for me, the answer is a ringing "No!" The God of Israel does *not* use evildoers to accomplish Divine purposes. Evildoers are in their very personhood a rejection of the power of God to influence their own lives; to, therefore, impute their truly filthy work to Divine manipulation is to both raise their standing in the community of humanity and lower that of God.

Secondly, commenting on the answer of God to Moses' plaint in verse 13 for God's true name to share with the children of Israel, to which the Divine Presence enigmatically responds "Ehyeh asher Ehyeh/I Am that I Am," and goes on to insist "Ko tomar livnei Yisrael Ehyeh shlachane aleichem/Thus shall you say to the children of Israel: 'I AM has sent me to you'" Cohen cites a Talmudic tradition, wrongly attributed to Rashi, that

...the repetition of the words I Am signified God's assurance to Moses that not only would He save Israel from their present sufferings, *but also deliver them from any future troubles.*[16]

Again, it is this issue of the all-too-easy acceptance by both Jews and Christians of the historically-traditional understanding of the

---

[14] Abraham Cohen (1947). *The Soncino Chumash*, 330. (Emphasis mine.--SLJ)
[15] This is exactly the issue raised by Richard Rubenstein's profoundly troubling essay "The Dean and the Jewish People" in his 1966 book *After Auschwitz: Radical Theology and Contemporary Judaism* (Indianapolis: Bobbs-Merrill).
[16] Abraham Cohen, *The Soncino Chumash*, 332.

God of Israel who interacted once to save the children of Israel from that hell of Egyptian servitude, but who failed to do so during the six murderous years of 1939 to 1945, that forms the core of this rejectionist protest and warrants a *rethinking* of not only Jewish faith but of Christianity as well, to which we now turn.

John 8: Wrestling with the Devil

There is no way to minimize the venomous rage attributed to Jesus in the following verses:

> (42) "If God were your Father....(44) "You are from your Father the devil, and you choose to do your father's desires. He was a murderer from the beginning and does not stand in the truth, because there is no truth in him. When he lies, he speaks according to his own nature, for he is a liar and the father of lies....(47) "....The reason you do not hear them (the words of God) is that you are not from God....(55) "....you do not know Him (God)."
>
> (43)

Nor can we minimize the historical and contemporary *implications*[17] associated with the commentaries on this overall passage.   To cite but two examples, first *The Jerome Bible Commentary,* and second *The Oxford Annotated Bible.*

> Commenting on verses 43 and 44, St. Jerome writes:
> (43)They do not receive his word because they cannot: *They have closed their ears to the Word of God.* This, in turn, identifies them as the children of a father whom he will now name explicitly for the first time. (44) *the devil is the father you spring from:* This must be, for it is the devil who is the very antithesis of the God to whom they claim to belong.[18]

---

[17]   For example: The *Miami* (FL) *Herald* reported on 31 January 2000, in an article entitled "State investigating Bible history courses in 14 districts," by Robert Sanchez, "A lesson on John 8 used in Levy County asks, "Who, according to Jesus, is the father of the Jews? The devil."

[18]   Raymond E. Brown, Joseph A. Fitzmyer, Roland E. Murphy (Eds.) (1968). *The Jerome Bible Commentary.* Englewood Cliffs, NJ: Prentice-Hall, pg. 442.

And *The Oxford Annotated Bible:*

> *(39-47)*   *Their* (the Jews) *desire to kill Jesus forfeits their claim to be heirs of Abraham's faith and true children of God.* They insist (v. 41) that *God* is their father. Their murderous intention and resistance to the truth belie this and brand them as children of *the devil* (v. 44). *The fault is in them and not in Jesus.*[19]

Before proceeding further, however, it is crucially important to heed as well the words of the late Roman Catholic New Testament and Jesus scholar Raymond E. Brown:

> Perhaps here we should re-emphasize that a chapter like John viii with its harsh statements about "the Jews" must be understood and evaluated against the polemic background of the times when it was written. *To take literally a charge like that of vs. 44 ("You are from your father the devil") and to think that the Gospel imposes on Christians the belief that the Jews are children of the devil is to forget the time-conditioned element in Scripture.*...Lest the picture seems too dark, we must remember that this same Fourth Gospel records the saying of Jesus that salvation comes from the Jews (iv 22).[20]

Accepting Brown's notion of the "time-conditioned element in Scripture," are we, therefore, correct in our understanding that this text from the Gospel of John is *antisemitic?* As I have, also, written in *Rethinking Jewish Faith:*

> "They condemn the New Testament as "antisemitic," it seems to me, is both to misread and misunderstand the text and *tendenz* of the anti-Judaic portrait painted therein. A much more accurate understanding of that negative depiction would be to see the controversy as "in-house, intra-family Jewish debate"....later taken over by non-Jews, gentile successors to Paul, who, in their burgeoning desire both to separate themselves from their Jewish

---

[19]   Herbert G. May and Bruce M. Metzger (Eds.) (1962). *The Oxford Annotated Bible.* New York: Oxford Publishing Company, pp. 1297-1298.
[20]   Raymond E. Brown (1966). *The Anchor Bible: The Gospel According to John.* Garden City, NY: Doubleday and Company, 368. (Emphasis mine.--SLJ)

beginnings and further to create a new and distinct *religious* response to the times, lost sight of the original meaning of those words, with disastrous future results."[21]

No, this text is *not* antisemitic, but it is anti-Judaic--though it has been *read* antisemitically for two thousand years! And it is that *fact of reality* with which we must grapple as Jews and as Christians, as Craig A. Evans of Trinity Western University, Langley, British Columbia, CN, pointedly reminds us:

> "First of all, there appears to be a lack of awareness of the polemic within the Jewish Scriptures themselves. Secondly, many Jews and Christians read the New Testament writings in the context of medieval and/or modern non-Jewish Christianity....New Testament polemic should be viewed as part of the intra-Jewish polemic that took place in the first and early second centuries. *Finally, the New Testament can be read, and, tragically, has been read in an Anti-Semitic manner*....But divorced from their original context, these expressions do readily lend themselves to Anti-Semitic ideas. Yes, the New Testament can be understood as Anti-Semitic if it is taken out of its early Jewish context. But if it is interpreted in context, as it should be, the New Testament is not Anti-Semitic."[22]

The explosive nature of vss. 31-59 and the antisemitic reading of them over the last two centuries, most especially and particularly in light of the *Shoah, regardless of the historical context which gave rise to this passage and/or the accuracy of the reporting of the confrontation between Jesus and his fellow Jews*, strikes at the

---

[21]   Steven L. Jacobs, *Rethinking Jewish Faith: The Child of A Survivor Responds,* 90. I remain indebted to the writings of Professors Ellis Rivkin (Emeritus) and the late Samuel Sandmel, *alav hashalom,* both of the Hebrew Union College-Jewish Institute of Religion, Cincinnati, OH, as well as others, for much of my thinking about the New Testament text and the environment of First Century Judaism which produced it. These ideas, as well as others, are contained in my paper "Rethinking Jewish-Christian Relations Because of the *Shoah"* in Marcia Sachs Littell, Erich Geldbach, Jan G. Colijn (Eds.) (1994). *The Holocaust: Remembering for the Future II.* Stamford, CT: Vista InterMedia Corporation. (CD-Rom)

[22]   Craig A. Evans (1993), "Is the New Testament Anti-Semitic or Anti-Jewish," *Explorations: Rethinking Relationships Among Jews and Christians,* 7 (2): 3.

very heart of the various understandings of Christianity and their relationship to the New Testament text, and forces a confrontational response to a series of painfully difficult questions, (as Exodus 3 forces such an equally difficult and painful confrontation within the Jewish community, one which has yet to take place) to wit:

- What *now* is to be done with this text within the Christian communities of the faithful?
- Does one confine the question of historically-contextual knowledge to the classroom only, be it church or college/university or seminary?
- Does such knowledge *mandate* dramatic and drastic revisions of all biblical curricula in the above settings?
- What does such knowledge say in a post-Holocaust/*Shoah* world about the *sacred nature* of this New Testament text, regardless of whether or not one is a scriptural literalist or non-literalist?[23]
- What about the *liturgical and lectionary responsibilities* of those who are called upon to address this text and others like it directly?
- For example, does one "preach the Word" with a thoroughly revised text reflective of this more accurate historical understanding of the New Testament, and, in doing so, draw the worshipper's attention to such

---

[23] Blu Greenberg offers a somewhat different suggestion:

The conclusion that I draw from the Holocaust and from the four decades following it is that Christianity needs a Talmud and Midrash that deal with the foundation documents of its faith; that Christians of the next two thousand years ought not to be able to read or teach or understand first century Christianity without these hermeneutic texts of quasi-canonical status; that in the year 2500 a Christian child standing at any point along the religious denominational spectrum will not and need not know where Scripture leaves off and quasi-Scripture begins. Why do I use terms such as Talmud and Midrash, so particular to the Jewish tradition? In order to precisely convey the notions of power and sacredness, as Talmud and Midrash have done for Jews for so many centuries until this very day.

Blu Greenberg (1989), "The Holocaust and the Gospel of Truth," *Holocaust and Genocide Studies*, 4 (3): 273-274.

painfully problematic passages such as this one and raise questions and doubts as to their efficacy?

- Does one simply "share Scripture" without commentary, albeit with this revised text?
- Does one *reconstruct* the lectionary of one's own denominational religious tradition to *exclude* those passages which raise these issues, concentrating, instead, on those passages which reflect the highest moral, spiritual and religious values of Christianity?
- Indeed, how *does* one incorporate this understanding liturgically and lectionarily?

Returning to the text itself, Jesus' assault upon the *covenantal integrity* of the children of Abraham (vss. 31 ff), affirmed at Har Sinai/Mount Sinai and continuously celebrated by countless generations of Jews since--*despite* periodic abuse, cannot be Jewishly accepted, and must, therefore, be unconditionally rejected. The questions remain: How will Christians (and Jews) in this post-Holocaust/*Shoah* and genocidally-continuing world deal not only with this text but which others in the New Testament which equally denigrate the parent-faith of Judaism and the people who refuse to surrender it, providing religio-theological foundational support for the worst excesses of Western Civilization? Can there truly be open, honest, respectful, and sincere dialogue on the part of both Christians and Jews *beginning with the sacred literatures of both faith traditions,* despite, or, perhaps, because of, all those passages of text which cause pain--and worse!? The response is "Yes!" and the answer is "Because we must!"

Conclusion: Searching for the B'racha/Blessing

Seven years ago, 1993, at the 23rd Annual Scholars Conference on the Holocaust and the Churches, in a setting similar to this one, in the presence of my beloved colleagues, I re-translated B'raisheeth/Genesis 32:29--the conclusion of *Y'aakov's*/Jacob's, *Yisrael's*/Israel's wrestling match with the *ish*--"No longer shall you be addressed as *Ya'akov* (Heel-grabber), but, rather as *Yisar'el,* (Israel) for you have wrestled with beings both human and divine *and have been enabled.*" As this text informs us, there was, in truth, no victor in the wrestling match; *Ya'akov* was now enabled (empowered) to go forward in search of the blessing, which had thus far eluded him.

So it is with us, Jews and Christians, both children of Ya'akov: Wounded in the frays of the past, all too often responsible for wounding each other, together, we *must* go forward in search of the blessing which has thus far eluded us. As persons individually and collectively committed to the integrity of our own faith traditions, our shared commitment is to seek and find that *b'racha*/blessing which is, most assuredly, "out there." *L'chu l'shalom*/let us go in peace.

Chapter 8 - Torah and Testimony: Making Sense of Disputation in Dialogue
Zev Garber

Dialogue, A Learning Exchange

Dialogue gives insight to the temper of our age and to the temper of our tradition. In the field of scriptural studies, it means to go beyond acquiring bits of information to a critical exchange of ideas and experience. It means to take seriously the four sequential steps of a learning exchange:

Confrontation, where the participant experiences the text superficially; *Analysis*, where the participant seriously probes the text in light of previous knowledge; *Interaction*, where the participant's mutual or reciprocal communication with others helps him/her benefit from their views; and *Internalization*, where by turning the sharing of ideas upon oneself, the participant rethinks the text as it relates to him/her as an individual and as a member of a religious community.

Biblical exegesis clothed in dialogue has all the possibilities and dangers inherent in any real communication. On the one hand, it can extend one's experience at the most profound level of his/her religious sensitivities. On the other hand, it can devaluate one's past attitude and ideas and develop a new orientation of what it means to be scripturally informed. Comparisons are inevitable, and this may lead to a crisis in faith interpretation. That is to say, the old meaning/orientation may have to disintegrate while a new one emerges. Clearly, visions of the other are altered when Christians and Jews read Scriptures in dialogue.

Rabbinic Torah

Various biblical verses point to the Pentateuch as Torah distinct from the rest of the Scriptures. The verse "Moses charged us with the Teaching (Torah) as the heritage of the congregation of Jacob" (Deut 33:4) suggests the inalienable importance of Torah to Israel: it is to be transmitted from age to age, and this transmission has become the major factor for the unity of the Jewish people throughout their wanderings.

The Sages of the Talmud kept the Torah alive and made its message relevant in different regions and times. This has been done by means of the Rabbinic hermeneutic of a Dual Torah that has been read into verses from the book of Exodus. Regarding God's words to Moses on the covenantal relationship between Himself and Israel, it is said in Exodus, "write down (*ktav*) these words, for in accordance (*'al pi;* literally, 'by the mouth') with these words I have made a covenant with you and with Israel" (Exod 34:27), and, "I will give you the stone tablets with the teachings (*torah*) and commandments which I have inscribed (*ktav-ti*) to instruct (by word of mouth) them" (Exod 24:12).The Sages saw the words "write, accordance, instruct" as the warrant for the Written Torah (*Torah Shebiktav*) and the Oral Torah (*Torah Shehb'al Peh*). In their view, the Written Torah of Moses is eternal and the Oral Torah, the application of the Written Torah to forever changing historic situations, continues to uncover new levels of depth and meaning and thus make new facets of Judaism visible and meaningful in each generation. Take the laws of tithing, for example.

Ma'aserot and *Ma'aser Sheni*, the seventh and eighth tractates in the order of *Zera'im* in the Mishnah, Tosefta and Jerusalem Talmud (Babylonian Talmud lacking) contain Rabbinic rules and regulations in performing scriptural demands for agricultural tithing, that is, when and under what conditions payments are due and by whom and to whom and how a common Israelite may proceed to eat from his own crops after payment of agricultural taxes.

Specifically, *Ma'aserot* ("Tithes") deals with the laws concerning which kinds of fruits and plants of the Land of Israel are tithed to benefit the landless Levites (Num. 18:24), who, in turn, provide for the Priests (*terumat ma'aser*) and the regulations protecting produce misappropriation. *Ma'aser Sheni* ("Second Tithes") discusses (1) the tithing of all yearly produce that is set aside for the benefit of the farmer and his household -- after separating the first levy in the yearly produce given to the Priest (*terumat gedolah)* and the levy parsed to the Levite (*ma'aser rishon)* taken to Jerusalem in the first, second, fourth, and fifth year of the *shemitah* (seven-year) cycle and eaten there (Deut. 14:22-26); (2) legislation to redeem monetarily the *ma'aser sheni* by a second party or by the owner himself, who is required to add a 20% surcharge to the crop value (Lev 27:30-31), and in both situations the capital must be spent in the capitol (Jerusalem);

(3) the rules regulating the fourth year harvest of tree or vine fruits sanctified by the Torah (Lev 19:24), whose produce or its redemption money must be used by the farmer and household only in Jerusalem; and (4) the instructions regarding the elimination (*bi'ur*) of the *ma'aserot* (Deut 14:28-29; 26:12-15), whereby at the termination of the third and sixth years of the *shemitah* cycle, the *ma'aser sheni* is devoted entirely to the poor and destitute (*ma'aser 'oni*) are noted and explained.

In reading *Ma'aserot* and *Ma'aser Sheni* in the Jerusalem Talmud (*Yerushalmi*), one sees (1) how Torah-based agricultural laws, written and oral, are understood by the Sages as legalism and teaching; (2) how the *Yerushalmi* editors augment Scripture and this in turn becomes the pattern for the Tradition (e.g., "You shall certainly tithe all the produce of your seed "[Deut 14:22], understood by the Yerushalmi to be whatever is found and is guarded and grows from the soil, which Maimonides interpreted as all human food which is cultivated from the soil – the Torah states only cereal, wine and oil – is liable to *ma'aserot* [*Hil. Ter.*2:1]; and (3) how the talmudic *sugya* (rhetorical unit) is seen as a living interpretation, reflecting changing times and events by adding and subtracting, thus modifying the Torah of Sinai to the *torah* of the Rabbis.

Arguably, the crowning achievement of the Sages was the preservation of Judaism following the destruction of the Second Temple and Jerusalem in 70 C.E. The Jewish War against the Romans ended disastrously; the religious center and national life were in shambles. Nonetheless, the Sages extended the Temple rites into the community and ritualized ordinary acts into sacred activities. Hence, agricultural laws, table fellowship and tithing were seen as supreme religious duties and as a hallmark of the *Weltanschauung* of the Rabbis. Ultimately, the *Tanna'im* of the Mishna and Baraita and the *'Amora'im* of the Gemara salvaged Judaism from the Roman pillage of Eretz Israel by placing it beyond space and time. They moved Jewish values and thought from the catastrophic events of everyday to timeless wisdom – planting a portable homeland for the fertilization of the mind and spirit. This, in a nutshell, is the theology of the Rabbinic mind.

Testimony of Jesus[1]

There is a line of basic continuity between the beliefs and attitudes of Jesus and the Pharisees, between the reasons which led Jesus into conflict with the religious establishment of his day, and those which led his followers into conflict with the Synagogue.

Two of the basic issues were the role of the Torah and the authority of Jesus. Rabbinic Judaism could never accept the Second Testament Christology since the God-man of the "hypostatic union" is foreign to the Torah's teaching on absolute monotheism. As the promised Messiah,[2] Jesus did not meet the conditions which the prophetic-Rabbinic tradition associated with the coming of the Messiah. For example, there was no harmony, freedom, peace and amity in Jerusalem and enmity and struggle abounded elsewhere in the Land. This denies the validity of the Christian claim that Jesus fulfilled the Torah and that in his Second Coming the tranquillity of the Messianic Age will be realized. As Rabbi Jesus, he taught the divine authority of the Torah and the prophets,[3] and respect for its presenters and preservers,[4] but claimed that his authority was equally divine and that it stood above the authority of the Torah. We agree with others who see this testimony as the major point of contention between Jesus and the religious authorities that ultimately led to the severance of the Jesus party from the Synagogue However, we maintain, that the quarrel began in the words of Jesus on the roads to and from the Torah.

For example, the distinction between the positive articulation of the Golden Rule as given by Jesus[5] and its negative form as given by Hillel.[6] Jesus' ethic is seen in Christianity as altruistic and denies the

---

[1] Our view on the historical Jesus is spelled out in Zev Garber, "Know Sodom, Know Shoah," in Z. Garber and R. Libowitz, eds., *Peace, In Deed* (Atlanta, GA: Scholars Press, 1998), pp. 83-98, and especially, pp. 89-93.

[2] Cf., among others, Matt 26:62-64; Mark 14:60-62; Luke 22:60-70.

[3] Cf. Matt 5:17-20.

[4] Matt 23: 1-3a

[5] Cf. Matt 7:12 and Luke 6:31.

[6] The origin of the Golden Rule is Lev 19:18.Evidence of the Golden Rule as an essence of the moral life is found in Jewish tradition long before the period of Hillel and Jesus. E.g., the books of Ben Sira and Tobit (both second century B.C.E.) expound: "Honor thy neighbor as thyself" (Ben Sira) and "What is displeasing to thyself, that do not do unto any other" (Tobit). Similarly,

individual objective moral value and dwarfs the self for the sake of the other. Hillel's moral code as understood within Judaism eliminates the subjective attitude entirely. It is objectively involved with abstract justice, which attaches moral value to the individual as such without prejudice to self or other.

Hillel's argument is that no person has the right to ruin another person's life for the sake of one's own life, and similarly, one has no right to ruin one's own life for the sake of another. Both are human beings and both lives have the same value before the heavenly throne of justice. The Torah teaching, "Love your neighbor as yourself,"[7] means for the Sages just that, neither more nor less; that is, the scales of justice must be in a state of equilibrium with no favorable leaning either toward self or neighbor. Self-love must not be a measuring rod to slant the scale on the side of self-advantage and concern for the other must not tip the scale of justice in his/her behalf.[8]

Hillel's point stands in contrast to the standpoint of Jesus, whom Christians believe is above the authority of the Dual Torah. The disparity of self and other in the ancestral faith of Jesus is abolished in the new faith in Jesus: "There is neither Jew nor Greek, slave nor free, male nor female, for you are all one in Christ Jesus."[9] This may well explain the words of Jesus on retaliation,[10] on love of one's enemies,[11] and on forgiveness at the crucifixion.[12]

The difference between Hillel and Jesus, the Synagogue and the Church, on the purpose of Torah and the person of Jesus, acquired new intensity after the passing of the Jewish Jesus and the success of Pauline Christianity.

'Ani Hu'/ I Am He

Testaments of the Twelve Patriarchs (first century B.C.E.), warns: "A man should not do to his neighbor what a man does not desire for himself."

[7] Lev 19:18

[8] Cf. the Baraitha in *B. Mes.* 62a, which pits the view of the altruistic Ben P'tura against R. Akiba, and *Pesah* 25b where a man asks Raba (280-352) what he should do if an official threatened to kill him unless he would kill another man.

[9] Gal 3:28. Also, 1Cor 12:13; Col 3:11.

[10] Matt 5:38-42; Luke 6:29-30.

[11] Matt 5: 43-48; Luke 6:27-28, 32-36.

[12] Luke 23:34.

No matter how composite is the figure of the historical Jesus and how rudimentary is the concept of the Christ-event in the Second Testament, there can be no doubt that the Jewish and Gentile believers bestowed divine attributes and power upon Jesus and venerated him above all creatures. Such an attitude towards the person of Jesus as God incarnate led to conflict with the Sages, who revered only Torah-from-Heaven. This is illustrated in the exegetical dissimilarity between Church and Synagogue in how one is to submit to God's righteousness. Reading the nature of God's commandment (Deut 30: 11-14), the Apostle Paul comments that Christ is the subject of "Who will ascend into heaven? ... Who will descend into the deep?" and confessing "Jesus is Lord ... in your mouth and in your heart"[13] is the justified salvation for all. For the Sages, however, salvation is in believing and doing the commandments. "Surely, this commandment that I am commanding you today is not too hard for you ... it is not in heaven,"[14] is the raison d'être of Rabbinic Judaism. That is to say, the Torah is not in heaven, it is here and near so that Israel can hear "the blessing and the curse" and do the 613 Commandments[15] in order "to choose life"[16] and live.

As persuasive as such arguments on faith in Christ or observance of the Torah may seem to be disagreements between Jewish Christians in how to reach Gentiles,[17] the fallout is decisive and divisive in the

---

[13] Rom 10:6 commenting on Deut 30:13-14.

[14] Deut 30:11-12a

[15] The Talmud states: "613 Commandments were revealed to Moses at Sinai, 365 being prohibitions equal in number to the solar days, and 248 being mandates corresponding in number to the limbs of the human body" (*Mak.* 23b). Another source sees the 365 prohibitions corresponding to the supposedly 365 veins in the body thereby drawing a connection between the performance of Commandments and the life of a person ("choose life"). The standard classification and enumeration of the *TaRYaG Mitzvot* (613 Commandments) follows the order of Maimonides (1135-1205) in his *Sefer ha-Mitzvot* ("Book of Commandments," originally written in Arabic and translated several times into Hebrew).

[16] Deut 30:19.

[17] Galatians, for example, which I discussed in my paper, "How Believable Is the Allegory of Hagar and Sarah (Gal 4:21-5:1)," given at the annual meeting of the National Association of Professors of Hebrew (NAPH), meeting in conjunction with the annual meeting of AAR-SBL, in Nashville, Tennessee, 18-21 November 2000.

disputations between the Church and Synagogue beginning with nascent Christianity, as John 8 seems to suggest. The destruction of Jerusalem and of the Second Temple was sufficient proof for believers in Christ that God has pronounced dire judgment upon his stiffnecked people and that the God of promises dispensed His countenance to those who accepted Jesus as Messiah. Hence, "Christ is the end of the law,"[18] in "(whose) flesh the law with its commandments and regulations"[19] are abolished. But Torah and its Commandments are the matrix in which Rabbinic Judaism was born and it proved to be the mighty fortress to withstand danger of extinction from without (Rome) and from within (non-Pharasaic philosophies, including Jewish Christianity). Thus, in the Rabbinic way, to despise an individual precept of the Torah is tantamount to rejecting the whole Torah; and this explains the measures taken by the Synagogue, e.g., the second century Birkat ha-Minim (prayer against Jewish sectarians inserted in the Eighteen Benedictions), to preserve its national and religious character in the face of adversity and catastrophe.

The pivotal points of the polemics between Jesus and the Jews in John 8 (indeed, throughout the Fourth Gospel) reflect his and their disparate views on the yoke of the Torah (temporary or eternal) and the separation of a specific Jewish Christian community in the late first century from the Jewish society to which its members had belonged and are now excluded by Synagogue fiat. On the former, consider Jesus' words to the Samaritan woman at the well, "(S)alvation is from the Jews. Yet a time is coming and has now come when the true worshippers will worship the Father in spirit and truth...,"[20] and on the latter, the intensity of conflict between the Jewish Christian community for which John was composed and the reigning religious authority is reflected in the hostile and vindictive language placed on the mouth of Jesus accusing his Jewish detractors of not accepting the truth, plotting to kill him, and being the children of the Devil.[21]

In the long history of Christianity there exists no more tragic development than the treatment accorded the Jewish people by Christian believers based in part on the anti-Judaism in the Gospel of

---

[18] Rom 10:4a.
[19] Eph 2:15.
[20] John 4:22b-23.
[21] John 8:31-59.

John. The cornerstone of supersessionist Christology is the belief that Israel was spurned by divine fiat for first rejecting and then killing Jesus. This permitted the apostolic and patristic writers to damn the Jews in the rhetoric of John 8, and more, to assign the worst dire punishment on judgment day. These are not words, just words, but they are links in an uninterrupted claim of antisemitic diatribes that contributed to the murder of Jews in the heartland of Christendom and still exists in a number of Christian circles today. How to mend the cycle of pain and the legacy of shame? The key is a midrashic interpretation informed by an empathic and emphatic dialogue between siblings, Christian and Jew, individually and together.

Let us explain. It is a fact that Church-Synagogue relations turned for the better when the Second Vatican Council (1963-1965) issued the document *Nostra Aetate* ("In Our Times"), the first ever Roman Catholic document repudiating collective Jewish responsibility for the death of Jesus. In the Roman Catholic world, this inspired many dioceses and archdioceses to implement *Nostra Aetate* and to rid the anti-Jewish bias of Christian teaching. To illustrate, consider the sentiment of the Italian Bishops to the Jewish community of Italy (March 1998): "For its part, the Catholic Church, beginning with Second Vatican Council – and thanks to the meeting of two men of faith, Jules Isaac and John XXIII, whose memory is a blessing – decisively turned in another direction (from teaching divinely sanctioned punishment of the Jews –ZG), removing every pseudotheological justification for he accusation of deicide and perfidy and also the theory of substitution with its consequent 'teaching of contempt,'[22] the foundation for all antisemitism. The Church recognizes with St. Paul that the gifts of God are irrevocable and that even today Israel has a proper mission to fulfill: to witness to the absolute lordship of the Most High, before whom the heart of every person must open."

Few can rival Pope John Paul II's twenty-three papacy (as of this writing) in ridden the Roman Catholic Church of antisemitism. He more than any predecessor has condemned "the hatreds, acts of

---

[22] Term associated with Jules Isaac (1877-1963), French Jewish authority on antisemitism, who in an audience with Pope John XXIII in 1960, persuaded the Holy Father to consider the errors of the Church's teachings on the Jews. Isaac's writings on *l'enseignement du mépris* played a key role in the declaration of *Nostra Aetate*.

persecution, and displays of antisemitism directed against the Jews by Christians at any time and in any place (Yad Va-Shem, March 23, 2000). He has labeled the hatred of Jews as a sin against God, referred to the Jews as Christianity's "elder brother,"[23] with whom God's covenant is irrevocable, and established diplomatic relations with the State of Israel (1994). The Vatican documents *We Remember* (1998) and *Confessions of Sins Against the People of Israel* (St. Peter's Basilica, March 12, 2000) are major milestones in the Roman Catholic Church's efforts to reconcile with the Jewish people. And, we might add, main line Protestant denominations in the World Council of Churches, in different degrees, have done likewise.

We welcome this gesture of professing and confessing spoken in the spirit of *teshuvah* (repentance) from the largest member-church in the "Body of Christ" and it bodes well for Jews to offer *teshuvah* (response) in kind. Jews must be true to their Torah, distinct from other sacred scriptures and religions. At the same time, they must do their homework and cleanse the People Israel of any conceived and/or perceived anti-Christian bias. Jews must see the Roman Catholic Church's altering attitude and action toward them as good omens done in the spirit of humility and contrition. Jews need to be reminded that the Roman Catholic Church views the encounter with Judaism and the Jewish people, in the words of Rabbi Joachim Prinz on Swiss Catholic scholar, Clemens Thoma's ground breaking work, *A Christian Theology of Judaism* (1980), "not merely one of historic importance but an organic part of Christian unity." Christianity is a legitimate dialogue partner in *tikkun 'olam,* endowing the world in peace, understanding and unity.

Admittedly, dialogue at times creates unexpected friction, of a kind found in chronicles and hoary debates, if aggressively done for the purpose of settling a score. Progress not regress in Christian-Jewish dialogue is only possible if old canards are exposed and reciprocal teachings of respect are encouraged. So proper dialogue on John 8 neither overlooks the harsh statements against the Jews and explains them in a setting in life of that time, nor allows misguided judgments of mean-spirited hermeneutics pass by unchallenged, nor allows a conjunctional albeit controversial thought go by untested. The "I am " of John 8:24, is such an example. It reveals an aura of divinity by Jesus because his words, "I am the one I claim to be," can be

---

[23] Phrase introduced by Pope John XXIII.

equated with God's identity to Moses, "I Am that I Am."[24] For the
Christian divine, this can be interpreted as "I Am" (God) is revealed in
"I Am" (Jesus). But the text continues, "He (God) said, 'Thus shall
you say unto the children of Israel: I Am has sent me (Moses) to
you."[25] This can translate that God as God not God as Jesus is the
absolute and sufficient revelation of the divine pathos for the Jewish
people.

The significance attached to the Name of God in the above
midrashic discussion dispels illusion by illustration. The holiness,
sanctity and power of God's call are heard equally and necessarily
differently by Church and Synagogue. One by Christ and the other by
Torah. However, the completeness of God's Name, meaning His
essence and plan, is hidden in this world forever,[26] but in the fullness
of time it will be made known: "Therefore my people shall know my
Name; therefore, on that day, that *'Ani Hu'* (Name of God, the *shem
ha-mmephorash)* is speaking: here am I."[27]

It is incumbent upon Jew and Christian together in dialogue to
bring that day speedily in our lifetime.

---

[24] Exod 3:14.
[25] *ibid.*
[26] In the unvocalized Hebrew of the Torah, "this is my Name *l'lm"* can be
read not as "forever" but "to be hidden." See Exod 3:15b.
[27] Isa 52:6.

Chapter 9 - Confronting Antisemitism: Exodus 3 and John 8
James F. Moore

Violence on Children: a Memory for the Future

A gunman enters a Jewish day school and community center in southern California and randomly opens fire wounding several including five young children. Which of the images is more frightening to us – the children in pain shot for no reason that makes sense to them or the children running for their lives not knowing who will be shot next? And I remember this event clearly since it happened on my birthday in the summer of 1999.[1] But I think about memories and I wonder what of the memories of these children? Just a little more than a month earlier a shooting spree conducted by one man in Illinois and Indiana started with a similar random shooting in a Jewish neighborhood on the north side of Chicago.[2] The story that was told also spoke of children of a black man, a former basketball coach at Northwestern University, who witnessed their father gunned down in the same shooting spree later that same evening. I will remember this because we have a penchant for remembering these events as they are broadcast for days after as we speculate on why this could happen. Yet the memories of those who saw and experienced the fear of random shots in an otherwise peaceful neighborhood is quite another thing. Naturally, there is much talk about hate crimes and we begin to shape stories of the gunmen rather than the victims as we try to understand. We have come to see events as hate crimes. We remember with great clarity the images of the Shoah that remind us that hate exploding in violence is all too real, all too possible. And despite our desire and efforts to prevent such things happening again, the daily news seems to

---

[1] "Shootings in Los Angeles: The Overview," *New York Times*, August 12, 1999.
[2] "Suspect Sought in Attacks Said to Kill Himself," *New York Times*, July 5, 1999.

remind us of the futility of these efforts. In the midst of so much violence and hatred, we see, hate crimes become just another group of acts of violence of men on women, neighbor on neighbor, children on other children and teachers, and one group on another group. The events of the Shoah only serve to help us see these acts of violence all the more clearly.[3]

Even so, if we take a closer look at the events that I described above, there is still a sense of difference, at least for us. The difference is that the two men, who acted in a random way, it seems, really acted in a calculated way. The words of hatred that marked their activity were words that are written and spread by groups, hate groups, whose existence and identity and purpose is hatred of a very specific form. This is the hatred that can isolate targets, particularly Jews, and identify them as the enemy, the scourge of the earth, the devil in disguise. These are the groups that can repeat the refrain of death to all Jews and can see this as the solution to the protection of the "white" race. The strangeness of this line of thinking and acting still boggles our minds a full 50 years after the Shoah. This is not random hate but well organized and clearly aimed hatred.

John 8

These stories are the background that shows the urgency of our efforts to expose the sinister nature of John 8 and its use in the history of a religious tradition that becomes sinister in the forms that are these hate groups but is hidden and yet clearly present in all forms of Christianity.[4] Such a claim that many like Jules Isaac and Rosemary Ruether have long ago substantiated for us and made us see is the most pressing concern for Christians of any stripe or set of beliefs at the end of the twentieth century.[5] It is still our obligation to humanity to strip our thinking, teaching and acting of all hatred toward the "other" especially the Jew, even when that hatred is implicit or seemingly eradicated. That is, it is still our task to overtly, explicitly reshape the religious spirit of Christians and Christianity in all its forms into a teaching of respect for all others.

---

[3] I am referring to our belief that the Shoah makes painfully clear the possible use and abuse of a history of Christian antisemitism. Among many who identify this issue is:
Emil Fackenheim, *God's Presence in History* (New York: Harper and Row, 1970) and Emil Fackenheim, *To Mend the World* (New York: Schocken Books, 1982).
[4] Again among many who assert this approach to post-Shoah theology is:

It is not enough for us to decry the militant hate groups and to shout that they are no authentic Christians when the very words they spout are a replica of the words that the gospel of John puts into the mouth of Jesus. This interchange that we now engage will look deeper into this text and explore how teaching can be altered, but we must not forget that the real goal is not a discussion about what might happen but action to change and to challenge all forms of hatred spread in the name of Christianity. That is a different task than re-thinking the tradition. This is the task of recreating the tradition.

So we must recognize that the gunmen of the above stories are like so many others who act "righteously" because they hear unmistakably the words from John 8 and other such texts:

> "You are from your father the devil, and you choose to do your father's desires. He was a murderer from the beginning and does not stand in the truth, because there is no truth in him. When he lies, he speaks according to his own nature, for he is a liar and the father of lies. But because I tell you the truth, you do not believe me." (John 8:44-45)

Johann Baptist Metz, *The Emerging Church* (New York: Crossroad, 1986), pp. 20ff.
[5] Isaac, Jules. *The Teaching of Contempt: Christian Roots of Anti-Semitism.* New York: Holt, Rinehart and Winston, 1964. & Ruether, Rosemary. *Faith and Fratricide.* New York: Seabury Press, 1974.

Such a text is worth our consideration because it so thoroughly illustrates the tradition of a teaching of contempt and reinforces this with the authority of Jesus and, through him, God. An exploration of this text and its meaning, thus, becomes our focus. Nevertheless here, I follow the pattern of a midrashic reading in several ways.[6] First, I take the text of John 8 as a Midrash on both Exodus 3 and Genesis 12, 15. Thus, I will read the Johanine text as an interpretation of the Torah. Second, I read John 8 as a text that shapes Christian attitudes even still and a text that, in spite of efforts to eliminate the explicit teaching of contempt continues to implicitly reinforce this teaching among Christians. Third, I read this text as a means for re-thinking not by offering a preferred Christian meaning but by throwing the text into the plurality and ambiguity of meaning suggested by both the text itself and the history of interpretation. That is, I aim to challenge any secure use of this text as a means for authorizing action. But fourth, I do aim to initiate a new ethic that moves beyond a Christian ethic toward a human ethic that is authorized not so much by texts but by the dialogue on texts that we exemplify in our discussion. It is this model that will lead us back to explicit responses to the hate that is so obviously shown in the examples I mentioned above.

The Text as Midrash

The interchange from which the text I have isolated comes surely connects Jesus' claims to the Abraham cycle in Genesis 12-22. That connection together with a number of allusions to other texts is the apparent background for the charge that the Pharisees who have come to dialogue with Jesus are children of the devil. Nevertheless, it seems far more likely that the larger context stretching back to John 8:12 gives the real issue to us ("I am the light of the world. Whoever follows me will never walk in darkness but will have the light of life.") This passage represents one of a series of similar claims based on the Greek 'ego emi', I am. It is to this claim that I will turn for a reading of John 8 as Midrash.

---

[6] Among many excellent sources on Midrash are:
Barry Holtz, "Midrash," in *Back to the Sources*, (New York: Simon and Schuster, 1986), pp. 177-211. & Gerald Bruns, "Midrash and Allegory: the Beginnings of Scriptural Interpretation," in Robert Alter and Frank Kermode, ed., *The Literary Guide to the Bible*, (Cambridge: Harvard University Press, 1987), pp. 625-646.

Of course I do not mean that this reading of mine will be Midrash in the strict sense – following the rules of interpretation of the Rabbinic literature.[7] I do claim, though, that the whole of Christian scripture is a commentary on the Torah tradition and will assume that this text is yet another example of this. Indeed, this text is a prime example of this fact if Johannes Schooneveld is correct.[8] He argued at an earlier "Remembering for the Future" in Oxford that the gospel of John is a case based on the belief that Jesus is the oral Torah. That is, the debate throughout the gospel is based on the claim that Jesus' understanding of Torah was the true expression of the oral Torah as opposed to the faulty interpretation offered by the Pharisees.

Now this argument seems to be close to an early form of the teaching of contempt unless we were to grant that the debate in John is an internal Jewish debate. Then, the teaching of Jesus becomes a legitimate alternative to other rabbinic interpretations (pre-Talmudic). This, then, assumes that the argument is truly open and Jesus' words are not an effort to dismiss the Pharisees but to invite, indeed, challenge them to an honest re-thinking of their positions. Nevertheless, the text of John 8 is a harsh accusation, many, in fact built on to each other. Taken out of the context of an inner-Jewish debate, the words become the foundation for real contempt.

Thus, by taking the words to be midrash, I am forcing the conversation back into the Torah tradition and reversing the pattern of Christian interpretation in order to strip Christian theology of its anti-Jewish bias and show real ambiguity in Jesus' understanding of Torah. The shift changes the focus from the words of Jesus to the words of Torah, essentially Exodus 3:14. Jesus' words offer a reading of this text. Above all, John 8 appears to be a quintessential example of the sort of interpretation that Jesus was to offer. At least it is for the gospel of John.

If Exodus 3:14 is the root text, then we need to look for the point of that text in its original setting. Exodus 3 is the narrative of

---

[7] I have developed this approach more fully in:
James Moore, *Christian Theology after the Shoah* (Lanham, MD: University Press of America, 1993). & James Moore, "Introducing the Dialogue," *Shofar*, James Moore, special editor (Volume 15:1, Fall 1996), pp. 3-12.
[8] This very important argument can be found in:
Jacobus Schooneveld, "Torah in the Flesh," in *Remembering for the Future*, Franklin Littell and Yehuda Bauer, ed. (Oxford: Pergamon Press, 1988), vol. I, pp. 867-878.

Moses encounter with the burning bush and the voice of God. This encounter is first of all an intervention by God in order to use Moses as a mediator of God's intent to investigate whether the cries of the people of Israel require action. Indeed, the voice from the bush is a powerful statement about the identity of the God of Abraham, Isaac and Jacob:

> Exodus 3:7, 13-14: The Lord said, 'I have indeed seen the misery of my people in Egypt, I have heard their outcry against their slavemasters. I have taken heed of their sufferings, and have come down to rescue them from the power of Egypt, and to bring them up out of that country...But Moses said to God, "If I am to come to the Israelites and say to them, 'The God of your ancestors has sent me to you,' and they ask me, 'What is his name?' what shall I say to them?" God said to Moses, "I am what I am. [or, I will become what I will become]" (Translation for the most part taken from the NRSV)

The text is clearly aimed at action. The only suggestion about whether the text is about truth is Moses' concern that the people believe what he says. It is to this concern that the voice identifies itself as "I am (or will become)". Otherwise the text is about the liberation of God's people from their misery and sufferings. If the John 8 text is a quintessential interpretation of Exodus 3, then it is aimed at answering the issue of liberation from misery and sufferings. That is the issue and we are left to ask who are the slavemasters in Jesus' rendering. The error of some of Christian reading of this text is to say that the slavemasters are the Pharisees who speak lies and do not liberate while Jesus makes free. This is, most obviously, mistaken if the issue is an internal Jewish debate. We are left to accept that the issue is the new slavery of the people under Roman rule. The issue is again how to liberate the people from their slave masters.

Of course, this puts the rest of the text of John 8 in a new light. In this reading, Jesus places himself into the role of Moses as the one who speaks for God to the people and the issue becomes how does one know that. The appeal is made to the earlier text and to the I am (the ego emi) to show us clearly that Jesus directs the discussion to the revelation of God's identity in the Torah. The point all along is how to interpret such a mystical and elusive text as the I am. Nevertheless, the shift in the Exodus text from a question of Moses' authority to the issue of the identity of God seems to be inverted in the John 8 text and this inversion becomes the crux of the basic problem with this gospel text. If the issue is no longer what is God's identity but becomes more an authorization of Jesus' identity, then there are at least three major issues that arise from the John 8 text concerning identity.

The Issue of the Messianic

Of course the John 8 text is more explicit in its reference to the Abraham cycle and thus to that form of addressing the matter of identity. However, I have argued that the principal basis for the claims in John 8 is found in Exodus and not in Genesis. I can return to the explicit references to Genesis below after confronting what I believe is the crucial matter to be resolved in any reading of the John 8 text. The text in John appears to be a discussion about the identity of Jesus. Indeed, the discussion appears to be a discussion about the authority of Jesus set in such a way so as to pit the authority of Jesus over against that of the Jewish leaders. In that regard, the text's implicit connection with Exodus 3 seems much more central to this argument.

The problematic is that Jesus' claim seems to set the issue of identity outside of the tradition (even before Abraham I am). Thus, the authority of Jesus in this text appears to be rooted in some basis prior to the covenant tradition of Israel. If this is true, and it seems to be true, then the debate seems to be false from the outset. We have a shift from an understanding of God as given to Moses (I will become what I will become) which is an historical claim, a claim based on the notion of the covenant while the claim suggested by this conversation sets Jesus' identity prior to that thus in the past not as in the Exodus text in the future, or at least in the developing future. Thus, this text could not be understood as a claim about the messiahship of Jesus but rather something completely different.

In fact, this seems to be the basic flaw of much of the reading or claiming that Jesus is the messiah since the argument is almost always based on the past, what has been, rather than on the future, what will be becoming. The central flaw in this line of thinking that has so often been the route of Christian argument is that it cannot be a case about the messiah which is always a case for what will be and not about what has been. In fact, this is why the notion that the Jewish leaders have only Abraham as father really remains irrelevant to the issue of the messianic. The relationship to Abraham has to do with the covenant and is born out in the Sinai narrative with the covenant agreement. That is quite another matter and probably the heart of the debate if it is a real historically accurate debate at all.

Thus, the text of John 8 cannot be a text about the identity of Jesus at all whichever way we try to take the meaning of the conversation.

It must be about the identity of God and if so we must ask why such a debate is crucial or could be crucial for the participants. Above all, we must count as a distortion, then, all efforts to make the text a narrative about Jesus' identity except insofar as the text can represent an internal Christian debate about how to understand Jesus. If the original discussion is about the identity of God, then we need to ask what perspective does this conversation provide on the Exodus 3 text.

The debate about the messianic is, however, fascinating in that the distinction between Christianity and Judaism as it has been perceived from the Christian perspective has usually revolved on this point. The claim has been that the messiah has come in Jesus and that Jews have simply missed the prime opportunity for which they had been waiting. I am not going to offer a Jewish perspective on this supposed question letting my colleagues provide necessary insight, but I can point to the complexity of a Christian response. First, I have argued that the debate over the identity of Jesus is a distortion of the texts themselves, thus is a false posing of the issues. Second, I would suggest that the notion that John 8 is a prime example of this debate is simply mistaken. Third, and most importantly it seems to me, the move to make the question of the messiah an ahistorical question is simply insidious. It is insidious first of all because it transforms the notion of the messiah into a vacuous notion that has meaning only in some heavenly realm. Thus, it is protected from any form of challenge by historical developments but in the same fashion cannot be defended by any form of historical argument. In the end, such a view leads to either simply dismissing history altogether as having any ultimate significance or twisting and thus justifying all of history as part of a larger messianic plan. After the Shoah, this sort of view is unthinkable even if it persists, largely because of certain ways of reading texts like John 8.

Once we accept that the messianic must be an historical claim, then we open up the argument to the historical evidence and no such ahistorical defense of the messianic claims of Jesus can be defended. Jesus is not the messiah because the messiah language is tied to the unfolding of covenant history in the fashion that we can see implied in Exodus 3. There cannot be closure to the messianic but only genuine expressions of the covenant. The argument must be about that matter and not about the messianic.

The Apparently False Debate

The second major distortion of readings of John 8 is the assumption that this argument represents an authentic debate between

Jesus and the Jewish leaders. There are surely clues in the line of discussion that falsify such a view of the debate. The Jewish leaders are portrayed in ways that are simply impossible to conceive even though this has been basic to Christian teaching, the teaching of contempt. The most obvious problem is the notion that the Jewish leaders would have begun this debate as they are reported to have done. Surely no Jew of the first century would have said that "we have never been slaves to anyone. This phrase shows how likely it is that the whole discussion is constructed and links with a later period (even then it is a discussion for Christians and not between Jesus and the Jewish leaders or between the church and Jewish leaders).

We are clearly led to see that the meaning of this text is found in its church use and not in its depiction of Jesus' views or of early Jewish views or of some actual Jewish-Christian dialogue. If we would grant the notion of dialogue (an interesting midrashic move), then the text takes on entirely different meaning. If we ask the hard post-Shoah questions, the text becomes an entrée into a discussion of the credibility of the church. If those questions are asked, then the full message of Christianity is brought to ruin. If we sustain this text as a litmus test set in dialogue, history proves the point made by the Jewish leaders -- "you have a demon." It is only clear that the demon emerges in full force in our own time.

Thus, this is a false debate based on claims that have no truth in themselves either as a true depiction of dialogue or a true depiction of Judaism or a true depiction of Jesus. In reality there could have been no such debate and no conflict, especially of this sort between Jesus and other Jewish leaders. All other aspects of the record of Jesus' teaching shows emphatically that there was no essential conflict between Jesus and the Judaism of his time. We are, thus, compelled to see that the conflict is manufactured by the church and it is the teaching of contempt constructed by the church in a rush to respectability in the Roman-Hellenistic world that carries this lie through the centuries only to be resurrected over and over again in incidents like the shooting spree of Benjamin Smith or the similar attack on the Los Angeles Jewish center.

Only a Thoroughgoing Reconstruction Will Do

An entire generation of Christian scholars aiming to build a post-Shoah theology has shown that a retreat to the texts to find meaning is itself a meaningless gesture. We misread the point, the scenario, if we think that such re-reading of texts accomplishes anything. This is why an exegesis alone cannot suffice. An exegesis alone only serves to reset an historical context frozen in time and fails to see both the lie of the text and the construction of false reality by the text in its persistent liturgical and pedagogical use. To set Judaism and Jesus, thus Christianity, overagainst each other has no possible context for re-interpretation. The idea is itself a lie and must be simply rejected and with this rejection the text must also be rejected. An exegesis alone will only lead us to the threshold of this rejection but only a thoroughgoing reconstruction can possibly answer the tremendum of the Shoah for Christian theology.

So what is this re-construction. Let me assure you that this Midrash is ready to deconstruct Christianity as we know it and this is its truth. We cannot reclaim Jesus the Jew as our teacher unless we give up the claim that begins this narrative – "I am the light of this world. Whoever follows me will never walk in darkness but will have the light of life." And with this radical new direction we can reject the other claims that have been so damaging – "You are from your father, the devil..." and "The reason you do not hear them is because you are not from God." Indeed, history shows that it is likely that the opposite is true. Only an inversion of this text can be true to this history, the history of Shoah.

Another Way – The Dialogue Community, Building a New Community

The way to reconstruct is to open the multi-logue that redoes the scene of John 8 in a way that inverts the narrative. This dialogue begins with a recognition that the light that might lead us to truth is found in the soul of all touched by God. We begin our discussion by recognizing that wisdom shared by all who speak the truth will set us free. We continue our conversation by saying that we know you speak the truth because you words are from God. We then conclude by admitting that we hear them, the other, because finally we reject the pride of exclusivism and come to respect all who would speak truth and seek the freedom and wellbeing of humankind. This is dialogue, actually multi-logue since it invites a plurality of voices who can speak. And this can happen simply by entering into two millennia of inverting the dialogue of John 8, creating a dialogue community. This has already begun but it is so early in this new age we seek and the dialogue must be emphatic and we must teach about it from our classrooms and from pulpits and in meetings and live it in standing on the barricades for respect for all others. Is this a dream? Yes, but is there another way?

The Remaining Issue

One more issue remains, the issue we began this paper with. An inversion of this text in dialogue does effectively invert the teaching of contempt in the production of a dialogue community and in the denunciation of the teaching. I have argued that this requires us to see that the center of Christian teaching cannot be a teaching about the identity of Jesus, certainly not the ahistorical Jesus presumed by the words of this text, but rather it is about the identity of God, the God of the covenant history. In that way, teaching is always open to historical judgment and comes face to face with history of the Shoah. In addition, I have argued that the debate between Jesus and Jewish leaders so exemplified by this text is a false debate and once the debate is rejected as false the text must be rejected as false. Even more, we see that historical evidence at least makes the supposed claims of the Johanine Jesus suspect and the claims of the depicted leaders believable -- that rather than lights to the world Christians possess demons. But what remains is the plan of action that can meet the debacle of religious ideologues who use Christian-like teaching as a justification for violence.

Jean Paul Sartre long ago noted that such ideologues operate on blind faith that is not susceptible to rational argument but even chooses to reject such arguments.[9] This insight lets us know that a multi-logue will not do as a direct plan of action. We can address this issue only when we act together with our Jewish colleagues (and others when appropriate) to actually denounce and combat hatred of this sort. We cannot remain silent nor can we stay on the sidelines. Amazingly, the John 8 text reveals a message that can speak to this issue. We recall that the discussion so clearly marked by the words of hatred and contempt in this text are addressed to "the Jews who believed in Jesus." What is amazing is that these very believers are the ones that Jesus labels as children of the devil. One reading, one often taken, is to think of these believers as a symbol in the narrative of the ultimate depravity

[9] An insightful discussion of this matter together with a careful dismissal of Daniel Goldhagen's cognitive argument is a helpful context for my point here and can be found in:
Richard Kamber, "Goldhagen and Sartre on Eliminationist Anti-Semitism: False Beliefs and Moral Culpability," *Holocaust and Genocide Studies*, Volume 13:2, Fall 1999. Pp. 252-271.

of Judaism. That is, even those who are inclined to believe finally reject Jesus. Isn't this at the core of the teaching of contempt? But if we see that the meaning of this text is multiple, that there is ambiguity at the heart of this narrative we might see another message. And if we note that the text links with Exodus 3, then we are led to conclude that the issue is truly one of belief but one the reverse of what I have just said. The issue is whether the people of Israel will believe that we are from God. What is hidden in this text is the truth, in part, that something in the nature of the relationship that believers have with Jesus leads them to be children of the devil. Indeed, this has been born out time and time again. If we take these to be Christians and not Jewish leaders, then the issue remains, what allows for any Christian to be believed by the people of Israel as coming from God? The question is left open for if they were from God then they would know Jesus for who he was and not for what they supposed him to be. But the issue that remains is how they will act. Will they act so as to bring freedom and hope and healing? After all, this is the intent of the Exodus narrative and not whether Moses is from God. The issue is whether release from bondage happens. Then perhaps we can talk about freedom. Then, maybe we can see that the proof is in the acting, our acting. And how long will it take until Christians can be accepted as coming from God? Is there any other way but to act together with our Jewish friends until the day when that may happen? And would this be closer to the messianic hope? This surely takes us beyond dialogue to praxis and that is the message that finally makes sense of this whole.

Chapter 10: FACING OUR TEXTS TOGETHER
Henry F. Knight

J.B. Metz has characterized the dialogical imperative of post-Shoah Christian theology in classic fashion:

> We Christians can never again go back behind Auschwitz: to go beyond Auschwitz, if we see clearly, is impossible for us of ourselves. It is possible only together with the victims of Auschwitz.[1]

That is, Christian theology must proceed in dialogue with Jewish partners, preferably those engaged in the same questions from the Jewish side of the ledger in accounting for life lived in the aftermath of the Holocaust. Whether or not the dialogue is literal or figurative, it will shape the sources consulted, the questions raised and probed, as well as the character of any intended audience of readers and listeners. Even the most solitary of musings will be undertaken as overheard by our covenantal siblings. However, more is at stake in post-Shoah hermeneutics than dialogue – even though it cannot be less than that. Our identity as Christians, is equally challenged as our dialogue forces us to come to terms not simply with a problematic past, but a biblically rooted identity too often built on contempt for our significant (signifying) covenantal other.

Emil Fackenheim has described the task of post-Shoah Jewish hermeneutics in equally daunting fashion. As a Jewish reader, he contends that the only way to read scripture faithfully after the Shoah is midrashically. That is, the questions one brings to the text and the world one expects the text to address shatter any strategy that does not provide for reading that resists conventional interpretations and easy

---

[1] J. B. Metz, *The Emergent Church: The Future of Christianity in a Postbourgeois World* (New York: Crossroad, 1987) 19, 32.

solutions to overwhelming problems. Emmanuel Levinas captures this quality in his midrashic reading of Ex. 20, "We will do then we will understand." He calls it, rather provocatively, "the temptation of temptation." When we find ourselves standing before a problematic text, the temptation is to yield the text to the problem and to disassociate ourselves from the problem by disassociating ourselves from the text as well – the temptation of temptation. Levinas proposes a stronger strategy consistent with the resistant reading of midrash. He begins with the understanding that as readers we are summoned first and foremost by the text and its witness. That is, we should not let go of the text but insist that it deal with the issue that makes it problematic. Indeed, the task is to wrestle with the text until it blesses the exegete with a meaning that can speak to the issue at hand. We wrest from the text what it may give only if it is claimed as essential to our identity at the same time we insist that there must be another way of relating the text and its conventional meaning. [2] In short, we do midrash.

Since 1993 I have been engaged with three colleagues engaged in precisely this kind of midrashic dialogue. Working self-consciously as two Christians and two Jews, we have tried to hold our concerns together: to do theology together as post-Shoah Jews and Christians and to do it midrashically, wrestling with each other's texts. Each occasion has led to unexpected insights and allegiances. In the course of a decade of working together we have learned to anticipate each other's points of view and at the same time be surprised by comments we still do not expect. We have found much common ground. At the same time, we have learned that we cannot assume that we understand the issues that separate us in the same way. Often we have aligned ourselves on topics across confessional boundaries and not infrequently found ourselves summoned by our dialogue to ask questions we hitherto had not considered. In the process of encountering our differences, however, we have learned the power and promise of mutual respect and honest debate.

By Way of the Jabbok

Our first gathering began by facing a text that has described, for me, this effort ever since: Gen. 32: 22-33. Again and again I have returned to the story of Jacob at the Jabbok to clarify what I am doing and to

---

[2] Emmanuel Levinas, "The Temptation of Temptation" in *Nine Talmudic Readings* trans. by Annette Aronowicz (Bloomington: Indiana University Press, 1990) 30-50, esp. 35, 48.

remind myself of what is at stake in this enterprise. Indeed, I have discovered that Jacob's story of estrangement and attempted reconciliation continues to provide a guiding metaphor for my own efforts in this regard. The work of post-Shoah faithfulness is always flawed; one walks this path limping. Indeed, pre-Shoah faithfulness was flawed; but the limping was overlooked and at best only myopically understood. Most recently, I presented a series of lectures outside the immediate context of our dialogue, reflecting on how a post-Shoah Christian might approach the commemoration of Holy Week following the lections of Matthew's gospel. Speaking at Atlantic School of Theology in Halifax, Nova Scotia, I posited the liturgical return to Jerusalem as occurring by way of a detour to the Jabbok, with the understanding that the faithful approach to this sacred time and place would occur limping. Indeed each moment of our journey through Holy Week, I argued, occurred while limping. However, this apparent detour by way of the Jabbok has become for me a recurring path that guides every approach I make to the sacred texts of scripture.

The story of the Jacob's night at the Jabbok is familiar. After a twenty-year exile from his estranged brother, Jacob had set out on a journey home. As he approached the encounter with Esau and prepared to cross over the river that separated them, he sent all his family, animals, and possessions ahead and camped for the night. The next morning he would face Esau and all that Esau might bring to their encounter. That night, as the story puts it, Jacob wrestled with a mysterious, unnamed figure, an *ish* or man. Together they struggled through the night with Jacob refusing to let go of his assailant until he secured a blessing and/as the assailant asking to know Jacob's identity before releasing Jacob from the figure's grip. Jacob revealed himself while the *ish*, in return, blessed him and gave him his release and a new name: Israel, for he had striven with human beings and with God and not been overcome/prevailed/survived. But Jacob emerged from that encounter limping, wounded by the wrestling or the *ish* or perhaps both. And when he departed/looking back, he moved forward naming the place *Peniel/Penuel*, meaning the face of God.

Jacob brought a mixed legacy of deceit and struggle to that night, including the history of his relationships with his father, his mother, and his brother as well as the accompanying shame and fear. Likewise he brought his relationships with his uncle and his wives. In short, Jacob brought an entire lifetime to that night. As I joined my colleagues and entered that story and its dynamics, I was facing my own mixed legacy with estranged siblings. I was bringing an historic lifetime and its accompanying shame and fear. I too was facing a history of usurpation that marked my historic relationship to Jewish brothers and sisters over the centuries. Indeed, I was facing up to it; and I was doing so in the morning shadows of a distinctively tragic night. My questions of the text opened the text at the same time they opened my own history for new exploration:

- Who was the figure that Jacob faced?
- Why was that figure unnamed in the story?
- Could the figure be more than one significant other Jacob faced in his life?
- Why did the unnamed assailant ask Jacob his name but not give one in return?
- Why after the night of struggle did Jacob name the place as he did, but not his assailant?
- Why did Jacob limp?
- What does it lead us to ponder when we remember that Jacob emerges from this night with the reconfigured identity of Israel, but that in doing so he limps thereafter?

As I worked with these questions and brought them to bear on the text and on our own post-Shoah situations, my colleagues and I wrestled with the text as Jacob wrestled with his other – facing manifold others at the river bank. Like Jacob, we held on, insisting that the text bless us by addressing (if not answering) our questions as it, in turn, asked questions of us. And like Jacob I was wounded and blessed in the process, moving from the Jabbok to the promised land beyond, walking with a limp. I cannot speak for my colleagues with regard to how they emerged from this night. However, I do know that I approached not only our next text in that first dialogue (Matthew 26: 36-46) limping, but each text in subsequent dialogues with a wounded walk.

I have approached every text since then with the full awareness of the flawed and mixed legacy I bring to it. In other words, my approach to Torah and to the New Testament is wrapped in contrition and undertaken with the full awareness of past mis-readings and supersessionary distortions. To put the matter figuratively, facing any text in its full, inquiring otherness means I face it limping. But such an approach is more than penitential even if it limps. Approaching the biblical text by way of the Jabbok also includes the other dynamics that distinguish this story.

Our first midrashic conversation took us directly into the problematic history of estranged siblings – Jacob's and Esau's as well as our own. It also led us deeper into the conflated nights of anguish to which we had committed our dialogue: the nights of each text, the nights of intense introspection vis-à-vis estranged relationships, nights of faithful anguish regarding our mixed legacies, and the twelve-year night of devastation and destruction we call the Shoah. Since then we have met annually to discuss our texts together: one from the Hebrew Scriptures, on from the Christian New Testament. Our journey has taken us from the Jabbok to Gethsemene; and thereafter from Mamre and Sodom to Galilee and Jerusalem while returning again and again to Sinai. And in my case, each journey has included a returning detour to banks of the Jabbok. Perhaps an explanation is in order.

In that first journey to the Jabbok I encountered, along with my colleagues, a text that mirrored the multi-faceted circumstances of our post-Shoah dilemma. It described a situation of estrangement between two of Abraham's descendents. That estrangement, had lingered for twenty years, half a generation's time, without healing. Indeed, the circumstances surrounding Jacob's return were life and death from his perspective. When he had last seen his brother, his life had been threatened. At issue was a stolen legacy of birthright and blessing. The younger brother had usurped the place of his elder sibling. The night before their actual encounter Jacob was met by an unknown/ unidentified "man" [*ish*] who confronted Jacob at the threshold of the boundary to be crossed the next morning. All night long the *ish* and Jacob wrestled. Just before sunrise, the other with whom Jacob wrestled demanded/asked to be let go, since neither had prevailed. Jacob refused, except upon receiving a blessing from his assailant. A dialogue of questions ensued, with the *ish* asking Jacob his name, which Jacob revealed. However, when Jacob asked the identity of the other, the *ish* replied with another question: Why do you want to know? Then Jacob was blessed, given a new name, Israel, and the *ish* departed. However, as those familiar with the story know, Jacob, survived the night wounded. His hip had been "touched" in the struggle and thereafter he would walk with a limp to accompany his new identity as Israel, one who had striven with God and human beings and prevailed. [i.e., As Israel, he walked with a limp.]

We Christians begin with a long history of usurpation with regard to our Jewish siblings. We have read our texts with a logic that usurps their place in the covenantal story by displacing them from their rightful inheritance. Furthermore, we have moved via that displacement logic to a form of triumphalism that has fed historic attitudes of contempt and disdain toward our covenantal siblings. Facing the place of this negative, yet still signifying other in our lives, brings us face-to-face with a shameful legacy that must give way to a new relationship. One enters that new relationship, as the story at the Jabbok suggests, with a newly configured relationship to the displaced other, wounded by that awareness. In the case of Jacob, his new identity of Israel is that of one who walks with a limp. He walks, but always with the sign of this struggle modifying his way of walking. Indeed, this story suggests that the larger story of Israel's walk with God and others is always one that limps. That is, it is imperfect in its embodiment. One can view that negatively, as many Christian readings of the Hebrew Scriptures have done, and see the communal story of Israel as that of a people who have failed in their fidelity to God. However, in the morning light of the Jabbok, the story of Israel's walk may be more authentically recounted as a confessional acknowledgment of the always flawed nature of walking in God's ways. Or to put the matter as Micah did, 'What does God require of us but to do justice, love steadfastly, and walk humbly (read limp) with our God?'

In this way, Jacob's/Israel's story becomes a paradigm for walking with the other/Other in our lives. We limp. As western Christians return to this story after centuries of exile from it, we can learn as Jacob did a way of proceeding that requires acknowledgment and understanding of our own flaws. And that understanding must be integrated into the re-configured identity that emerges from such a life-changing encounter. Hence, each time we encounter the other/Other, either in person or in a text, we do so with the awareness that we will limp. Or to return to the with which we began, every encounter with the biblical text in our post-Shoah context makes its journey by way of the River Jabbok.[3]

---

[3] This matter may be put another way as well: Beware of anyone who claims to bear the identity of God's people who does not limp!

Midrashic Dialogue

Limping translates into a fundamental assumption for me as I work with our texts together: Our past encounters as well as our present and future ones are and will be flawed. Therefore, dialogue is fundamental to our work, not just incidental. We do our wrestling with the text ever aware that we must listen closely to what others in the conversation have to show us about the texts and about ourselves, no matter how discomforting that might be. Likewise, my partners in the exploration have proceeded with similar assumptions. Our task is not to convince the others that our interpretations are right, since we know they are unfinished and incomplete at best. Rather our task is to venture into the world of the text together prepared to encounter ourselves and its witness in what may be re-orienting ways.

In Jacob's encounter with the *ish*, the text emphasized Jacob's tenacity in holding on to the other with whom he struggled. As the text reports, Jacob declared, "I will not let you go unless you bless me." We have insisted similarly. We will not let go of the other, whether it be a human partner in dialogue or the text or both. In fidelity to the text we take what it presents to us and wrestle with its otherness but we do not thereby relinquish the questions we bring to it, questions generated by the issues occasioned by the Shoah nor the flawed nature of our grappling. Rather, we proceed by way of a challenging and sometimes playful dialectic – walking, limping as it were, in the way of midrash.

In short, we have taken Emil Fackenheim quite seriously. Our post-Shoah return to the biblical text has occurred in the framework of midrash. We have simply added JB Metz' admonition to Christian interpreters that they must make their return in solidarity with the victims, whom they now join as partners in the interpretive enterprise. Fackenheim concluded that the return to the Jewish Bible could only occur in a midrashic framework whereby its "narrative stubbornness" would be held in tension with an "unyielding realism" that was committed to an honest encounter with human suffering. His comments express a similar sentiment echoed by Douglas John Hall, perhaps the preeminent North American Christian theologian of the last fifty years. Drawing upon what he calls the Jerusalem tradition shared by Christians and Jews, Hall argues for a truly dialectical faith that lives and thrives in the tension between honest confrontation and wrestling with human suffering and the promise that death does not have the last word in creation. Adopting language similar to Dietrich

Bonhoeffer's, he calls this "costly hope." [4] It shares with Fackenheim the tenacity of holding tight in the name of compassion to the humanity that we all share and to the God of creation who intended and still intends an abundant life for all creation. One does not let go of suffering victims in order to affirm what our theology tells us. Rather, suffering humans summon us to demand even more from our theological traditions.

Emmanuel Levinas articulates the same tenacity in his essay "The Temptation of Temptation;" however, he begins with the givenness of the biblical text by which people of faith their identities. He points out that while one does not ever let go of this source, in the name of responsibility to the other, one never ceases to challenge the text to come to terms with the other and the other's needs and concerns. Indeed, Levinas points out the creative quality that comes from this unceasing dialectic, explaining that often the text yields far more than its biblical authors may have intended, but this is the depth and richness of creation embodied in the text and the covenantal partnership in which the text is honored/served. The temptation of temptation is to collapse the tension and its accompanying ambiguity.

With these strategies and fundamental commitments guiding our way, I joined my colleagues in moving from the Jabbok to Gethsemene, the location configured in our New Testament text. We turned to Matthew's description of Jesus wrestling with his choices and accompanying anguish in the Garden of Gethsemene (Mt. 26: 36-46) as we limped along the way. In that context we wrestled with the text as we wrested meaning from the encounter. And we raised more questions as we also identified problematic paths we could no longer follow. Among them we identified reading Matthew as if it were written to show how its good news and portrait of Jesus were predicted in the Hebrew texts that were used by Matthew to tell his story. Instead, our midrashic dialogue allowed the midrashic structure of Matthew to emerge, suggesting a different way of reading. Matthew wrote from his own knowledge of the Hebrew Scriptures to convey his experiences with the figure named Jesus. It was the anchor in his knowing even when he stretched its meaning beyond the accepted boundaries of interpretation to account for the life-changing encounter he had experienced with Jesus. While this point may sound minor or heavily nuanced, its impact is significant.

---

[4] Douglas John Hall, *Confessing the Faith: Christian Theology in a North American Context* (Minneapolis: Fortress Press, 1996) 466.

As Michael Polanyi has made clear, all our knowing is rooted knowing.   As Polanyi puts it all our knowing has a *from-to* quality. All knowing, he argues, is situated.   One knows from an already known or trusted reality that orients the knowing of a focal awareness. Polanyi called these two paired aspects of our knowing the tacit and explicit or subsidiary and focal dimensions of human knowing. We know from something to something else. In the case of the Gospels, Matthew (or whomever Matthew might have been) knew from his understandings of Torah to the new experiences he was integrating with regard to Jesus. He used his knowledge of Torah to make sense of his experiences with Jesus.

Importantly, Matthew was not presuming to fully understand Jesus and then seek typological verification in the Hebrew Bible. Rather he was relying on the world he had been given by the Hebrew Bible to understand the significance and character of this one who was transforming his life.   I explained it during a dialogue with my colleagues while discussing another set of paired lections from Exodus 24 and Matthew 17:

> ...in *Matthew's* case the knowing is from the Sinai and Moses material to the figure of Jesus. Matthew knows from Sinai to Jesus and in turn reflects back upon the Sinai material. Typically, most Christians know from the Gospel portraits to the Sinai traditions, often reversing the epistemological directionality of their foundational witness.[5] Post-Shoah, this epistemological loss is significant.

> The stylistic rendering of the Jesus story we meet in *Matthe*w utilizes the larger story of the Jewish people to tell his story of Jesus. It requires a thorough knowledge of the exodus tradition, the story of Moses and the midrashic style of relating to it. What is known and cherished by Matthew and his audience is used to illumine and clarify the identity of Jesus. Allusions to existing scripture, whether explicit or implicit, are at best unclear or arbitrary unless the larger narrative context of the Torah is used by the

---

[5]Michael Polanyi's work on epistemology is helpful here. He explains that all knowing has a from-to character. We know from something to something else. The *from* dimension is known tacitly as background while the *toward* or *to* dimension is known focally and attended to in foreground.   See Michael Polanyi and Harry Prosch, *Meaning* (Chicago: University of Chicago Press, 1975) 33-42 for a concise explanation of Polanyi's distinctions.

hearer/reader in orienting and understanding Matthew's task. When we try to learn this contexting story by way of the narrative embedded in the larger one, we reverse the hermeneutic employed by Matthew. To be sure, Matthew reads the Torah back from Jesus, as a fully interactive critique. But he begins knowing Torah first. His knowing is interactive, moving from Torah to Jesus and then back. Typically, Christians have read the Matthean tradition in the reverse manner, and more often than not, failing to retain the interactive quality of midrashic knowing.[6]

After Auschwitz and as an expression of a reconfigured Christian identity, Christian readers of the Gospels must recover this forgotten dynamic if they are going to free themselves from the myopia of their displacement logic.

On this occasion we were wrestling with our texts and their relationships with what Fackenheim calls the root experiences of our traditions: for Jews, Ex. 24: 12-18 and the revelation at Sinai; for Christians, Matthew 17: 1-9 and the root confession that Jesus is the Christ. The *from-to* knowing embedded in the Matthean text is made visible in midrashic dialogue with the story of Moses receiving divine instruction on Sinai. A critical comparison of the two texts suggest that Matthew constructed his text drawing directly from the narrative of Exodus 24 and built his narrative portrait midrashically, illuminating the significance of Jesus to others who would be familiar with the scriptures he had used. He was, to use Paul's phrase, telling his story "according to the scriptures," that is midrashically. However, most Christian interpretations have overlooked this dynamic and reverse the from-to structure of Christian knowing, beginning with their experience of Jesus as the Christ and reading about the revelation at Sinai in the light of the scriptures they know. Recognizing this dynamic provides a critical wedge for reading the text of Matthew more circumspectly with regard to questions of displacement logic and triumphalistic tendencies. And, importantly, the critical leverage is supplied internally from scripture itself.

Whether or not our conversation has been marked by my avoidance of supersessionist structures is for my colleagues and other readers to determine. Nonetheless that has been an ongoing concern, operating sometimes in the foreground, at other times in the

---

[6] Henry Knight, *Confessing Christ in a Post-Holocaust World: A Midrashic Experiment* (Westport, CT: Greenwood Press, 2000) 65..

background; nonetheless, moving beyond supersessionism to another way of relating to Jewish history has been an ongoing project. Likewise the commitment to midrash and dialogue has been forthright and continues. We have faced more texts and more problematic relationships embedded in them and evidenced by them. And we have learned a great deal about each other and our respective hermeneutics in the process.

Reading Midrashically, Not Typologically

In that regard I have learned to distinguish doing midrash from reading scripture typologically. In the case of Christian hermeneutics, midrashic thinking provides a way of moving beyond the displacement logic of triumphalisitic theologizing; typology does not. According to Sandra Schwartz, typology is a way (an interpretive lens) of focusing the reading of a collection of texts in order to show their shared commitment to a uniform message or overarching meaning and truth. Typology is monolithic. She writes:

> There is little room for genuine innovation in typology, not because the canon is closed—typology promiscuously welcomes virtually all variations—but because all of these variations are reducible to one story. All events, biblical and postbiblical, all narratives, biblical and extrabiblical, are simply shadows of the real story, [for example,]the fall of man and his redemption by Christ. A procedure that looks proliferating is instead totalizing, cramming all memories into its vast interpretive maw.[7]

Midrash, on the other hand, is a way for keeping a "closed canon" open. Midrash acts as a hermeneutical wedge, resisting one meaning of a text by positing alternative readings while relying on the text itself to do the resisting. Michael Fishbane has expressed it well:

> For the truth of midrash is not the truth of historical information or textual analysis. It is the truth of the power of scriptural words to draw a reader into an authentic relationship with the mystery of the world – a world constituted by speech and the face-to-face relations which *Gesporchenheit* [genuine spokenness] demands.[8]

---

[7] Regina Schwartz, *The Curse of Cain: The Violent Legacy of Monotheism* (University of Chicago Press, 1997) 167.

[8] Michael Fishbane, *The Garments of Torah: Essays in Biblical Hermeneutics* (Bloomington, IN: Indiana University Press, 1989) 99.

In our post-Shoah context, this contrast provides a way of thinking about what Schwartz calls a form of interpretive imperialism (viz., typology) that breeds a logic of scarcity, which in turn feeds a displacing violence toward the religious other. While Schwartz does not explore the contrasting logic of midrash, it operates according to a logic of plenitude that fosters interpretive openness (hospitality?) to an abundance of meanings.

Now reading midrashically should be distinguished from recovering midrash as a missing form or genre of biblical interpretation that one restores as the "right" interpretation of a particular passage, as Bishop John Shelby Spong attempts to do. While much of Spong's work is bold and refreshing, he is nonetheless trapped in a view that looks for the text to have only one correct meaning and that the task of the interpreter is to discern the true or correct meaning of a text, which may or may not be an unending process. In Spong's case, he is not foreclosing the dialogue on the meaning of the text, but he is seeking the singularly correct meaning. In that case, when or as that meaning is determined, then the interpreter's task is to help his reader or listener relate to that proper interpretation. Midrashic reading, however, does not search for the only or single meaning of a text but seeks to open the text to its several and, at times, many possible meanings. The task is not to find what the text means and then proceed with the correctly recovered truth, which exists on its own merit, but to return to the world of the text so that its richly textured orchard of meaning can bear fruit for the gardeners tending its garden.

The contrast between midrash and typological reading clarifies what is at stake in choosing to read midrashically. Typological reading starts from and returns to the meaning or figure that guides the reader's interpretation. Midrash starts from and returns to the text and its various configurations. One interpretation does not supersede another but stands along side the other as another possible way of reading the same text. Typological reading starts and returns to the meaning or figure that guides interpretation. That is, one interpretation guides all others. On the other hand, midrashic readings is not guided by a single, monolithic interpretation but ponders the possibility of multiple interpretations and meanings. In typological reading, the meaning of the text is located outside the text and exists as an abstraction apart from it. The interpretive task therefore is to serve the relationship that exists between the recovered meaning and the truth of the text to which the text bears witness. In contrast, the interpretive anchor in midrash remains the text and its world within, in front of, and behind the text –

its narrated world. The task is to serve the text and its narrated world and the reader's relationship to them. That is, the meaning of the text does not exist independently from the text but is always an essential feature of its formative texture.

Jesus and the Law – A Case Study

In a recent dialogue my colleagues and I ventured into the testy domain of Christian attitudes regarding Jewish Law. Our task: to see if midrashic dialogue could provide a way of approaching the conflict over Jewish law between Jesus and the religious leaders in Jerusalem that did not require a return to the disdainful and supersessionary logic of past disputation. Our selected texts: Lev. 19: 1-2, 17-18 and Matthew 5: 17-20, 38-48.

Leviticus 19 recapitulates the Ten Commandments and articulates them for lived expression in the actual circumstances of Israel being a witness people set apart for that priestly purpose. Verses 1-2, like the preface to the Decalogue, summarize the intent of the sacred commands:

> The LORD spoke to Moses saying: Speak to all the congregation of the people of Israel and say to them: You shall be holy,, for I the LORD your God am holy."

Verses 17-18 provide the summary of relations toward the neighbor that Jesus references or quotes in Matthew 22:39. Then later in Lev. 19: 33-34, this admonition to treat the neighbor as oneself is explicitly linked to practicing hospitality and respect to the alien or stranger who resides in Israel's midst: "You shall love the alien as yourself, for you were aliens in the land of Egypt." (NRSV)

The Matthew text references an explicit statement in Jesus' Sermon on the Mount where Jesus expresses his commitment to the Law and the Prophets and is later intensified by his extension of its meaning to include how one relates to one's enemies and adversries. The initial reference is preceded by the so-called Beatitudes, performative words of blessing and promise, offered to confer grace and hope as they call forth the witness of God's people in troubled times and circumstances. They are followed by Jesus' declaration in verse 17 that he has "come not to abolish the Law or the prophets but to fulfull [them]."   Then Jesus expands his meaning and extends his concerns for right behavior toward the neighbor to include right attitudes – in much the same way that the commands in the Decalogue about coveting do – as well. Similarly he extends his concerns for the neighbor to include those who do not return such good will when extended to them. Indeed, he extends the love of neighbor to include good will toward one's enemies.

When Christians like me approach these passages by way of the Jabbok, we read fully aware of ways of reading them that build false dichotomies and foster disdain or contempt. Reading them otherwise than triumphalistically means resisting supersessionary postures or approaches that punctuate many conventional perspectives. For example, at the heart of Christianity's historic teaching of contempt is Christian perception of Jesus' relationship to his own tradition that would characterize that relationship as a dichotomy between Law and Gospel. Jesus brings the Gospel to those trapped in the Law. The Law is enslaving while the grace of Jesus' Gospel is not. Detouring by the Jabbok reminds Christian readers of this historic slander and abuse as they turn to Jesus' description of his relationship to the Law and the Prophets.

So we read carefully and respectfully. Even so, we cannot read these texts as if they are without conflict in their views of how to interpret God's Law as revealed in the sacred texts of Torah or the witness of the Prophets. Likewise, we find understanding the presence of this kind of conflict to be essential in finding an alternative way for reading Matthew. In fact, as we turn to Matthew, we know that Matthew's context was one of contending factions within a crisis-oriented community divided between the followers of Jesus and those we call Pharisees. And we know that Matthew's Jesus is a stylized portrait that reflects the Jewish traditions regarding Moses that Matthew was using to shed light on the Jesus who had lived and taught a generation before. That is, Matthew's Jesus, as Paul van Buren so aptly puts it,

> "is available only as he comes wrapped in Israel's scriptures... It is [therefore] misleading to say that the Church finds Jesus in the scriptures, the so-called Old Testament. What it finds is that the scriptures speak of Jesus because it was from Israel's scriptures that it first learned to speak of him." [9]

In other words, we must recover the too often obscured midrashic relationship that exists between Matthew and Torah. And in doing so, we must also read accordingly, resisting typological simplifications of the text. Instead of being guided by a promise-fulfillment theme, one may be open to all the themes present in a text,

---

[9] Paul van Buren, *According to the Scriptures*, 65.

often providing the very leverage needed to resist problematic readings generated by hidden assumptions present in typological figures. Patterns of promise and fulfillment as well as other themes pertaining to Law and Grace may indeed be present; but they arise from the text with its qualifications and fine tunings. This distinction is important.

Supersessionary logic when combined with typological reading views Jesus' relationship to the law in terms of a promise-fulfillment motif that replaces the law with Jesus, or with good news about Jesus. Namely, the law is incomplete without Jesus and is completed by him. The Law and the Prophets point toward Jesus and the reality he mediated. They foreshadow their completion in him. The promise-fulfillment motif stands outside and over against the teaching of halakhah thereby bearing witness to the triumphant victory of grace in life. Midrashic reading offers another strategy, at once able to avoid the supersessionary logic of Christian triumphalism without denying the conflict that existed between Jesus and key religious leaders in Jerusalem nor that exists between Jewish and Christian interpreters of scripture in the present. But the conflict is re-cast in fundamentally important ways.

Turning to Matthew's Jesus we meet a midrashic portrait that is itself depicting a situation of conflict between Jesus and the interpreting authorities of the synagogue not simply of his time but also of Matthew's time sometime near the turn of the first century CE. In other words, we are listening in on a complex conflict of interpretations with regard to how one reads and interprets Torah or Law. Reading post Shoah, we must resist the false dichotomy of Jesus preaching a New Law of love versus an old Law of judgment and rules. Indeed, as Matthew reports the matter, he casts Jesus great sermon in such a way as to counter any charge that Jesus is trying either to replace of abolish the law [nomos], God's expectations of God's people for their behavior and attitudes towards others and toward all creation. Indeed, Matthew's Jesus reports that Jesus said he did not intend to change even the smallest pen stroke (jot or tittle) of what has been written. It stands as it is. But Jesus did interpret and amplify the meaning he had received. After all, that is the apparent goal of the Sermon on the Mount. In similar fashion his amplified interpretation is often intensified by his parabolic discourse. The Rule and Realm of God are like…. Or the parables are linked to his interpretations of the Law and the Prophets as we see in one a companion text to those under consideration here – Matthew 22.

Still, we must ask, if Jesus was not seeking to abolish the Law, what was it that he was doing with it? According to Matthew, he was seeking to fulfill it. And of course therein lies the problem. What does Matthew mean? What would Jesus have meant? A rather simple observation may be helpful here. Any fulfillment of the Law depends directly upon how one interprets what is to be fulfilled. Was the Law predictive, foretelling things to come? If so, fulfillment would mean the coming to be of that which was foretold. [10] Many have read Matthew's reference to fulfilling the Law in just this way. Or, was fulfillment the full embodiment of the expected behavior toward others or toward the Eternal One that would have been present at any moment in time? That is, any time someone loves the neighbor as him or herself, the Law would be fulfilled. And in Jesus' radical reading, anytime someone loved not just those who were hospitable to you but those who bore hostility to you, then the Law was fulfilled in the greatest possible way. No more could be expected. Note the difference. In a predictive mode, Jesus is the object of fulfillment; in the more descriptive option, even if Jesus is the full embodiment of the Law, the object of fulfillment is the relationship with others that the Law serves. Or to use Jesus' more parabolic language, the Rule and Realm of God are manifest in human relations, lived experience.

All too easily, Christian readers will focus on Jesus' admonition to love one's enemies as a distinctive feature of Jesus' relationship to the Law that separates him from the Law. However, a midrashic approach invites our seeing Jesus reading his own tradition in precisely this way. That is, Jesus' comments that we are to love our enemies may be viewed as an expression of radical hospitality, that form of hospitality that embraces every other, even those others who resist hospitality shown toward them, indeed, who turn on it in hostility. In fact, we may claim that, this has been God's way from the

---

[10] As J. Andrew Overman asserts, "What is essential is that the fulfillment of the law is determined by one's interpretation of the law." (Overman, *Matthew's Gospel and Formative Judaism*, p. 870 His point is simple and to the point, but too often overlooked. Fulfillment of the law is dependent upon how one interprets the law. For many Christian interpreters, the law is already subservient to supersessionist logic. The law and the prophets foretell the judgment and restoration that is promised. Promise is prediction and if not prediction at least an as yet unrealized potential that awaits fulfillment. Most often, such fulfillment is singular. The promise is to be embodied once for all. When either of these two forms drives Christian interpretation of the law, supersessionism seems inevitable. But it need not be.

beginning – from the micro to the macro level. It is the wager of life we call creation whereby God has made room for otherness, every form of otherness in the gift we call creation. It is a complete act of hospitality to which we may view Jesus pointing his disciples when he concludes his comments on loving one's enemies that they are to be "perfect" (i.e., complete, whole – not flawless) as their heavenly father is "perfect." In other words, Jesus is reading the summons to be holy as God is holy (Lev. 19: 1-2) through the midrashic lens of hospitality – be holy, read hospitable, as the very host of creation is hospitable. Hospitality is the form of holiness that links Jesus with the Law and that Jesus declares that he seeks to fulfill.

As Matthew recounts it, Jesus did not come to abolish the Law or the Prophets, nor to change a single character in it. Rather, he sought to extend its logic of serving life to any and every relationship. He interpreted this as fulfilling the Law, an obligation he seemed to accept as a child of the covenant. This way of reading the notion of fulfillment is different from that of a "foretell-fulfill" logic. It is a way of honoring and serving the will and way of God that is representative, fulfilling the witness of Israel and not superseding anyone. Those places where he challenged previous interpretations of the Law's obligations were not abrogations of the Law or its claims. Rather, they were places where Jesus was guided by a different interpretation, one which was rooted in his sense of responsibility to embody the love of God for any and every child of the covenant. Furthermore, in bearing witness to that love, he demonstrated his recognition that the children of the covenant were set apart for the sake of God's inclusive rule and realm, the very blessing of creation that is promised to all.

Jesus was reading the Law radically and in a manner that conflicted with other readings of the Law, from several perspectives. But he was not reading in a way that requires his followers to dismiss the Law nor view him as superseding it. Instead one may authentically approach Jesus as reading midrashically, departing with other interpreters on matters that Jesus viewed to be essential. Jacob Neusner views the conflict similarly, contending that Jesus is departing from the Pharisaic leaders over their emphasis on individual behavior and Jesus' emphasis on the Kingdom of God. Neusner sees the disagreement focused on the future orientation of the Kingdom in conflict with the everyday, household dimensions emphasized by the Pharisees and their rabbinic descendents. Another way of approaching this conflict focuses on the parables of Jesus as describing the way of God's rule and realm not the timing of its appearance. The Pharisees had taken the purity and holiness concerns of the Temple and applied them to the everyday experiences of the household, seeing the household as a temple or house of God. Jesus similarly viewed the household as a potential place for embodying the holy, but he appears to have reversed the relationship between temple and household, emphasizing the everyday acts of hospitality that can become the sacrifices on associates with the duties of the temple. In other words, this way of reading the conflict calls for Christian readjustment as much as it might call upon Jews to regard their covenantal siblings with a new eye and ear. For Christians, they must see that the heart of the Law for Jesus was the rule and way of God that he saw every human being called upon to embody in their households and in their streets and market places. That rule and way he saw embodied in acts of hospitality toward the other.

Neusner is right to direct our attention to Jesus' parabolic expressions of God's way with humans. But he is mistaken, I believe, in insisting that we must read Jesus' parables to be focused on the future appearance of that reality at the expense of the present and the everyday. To the contrary, Jesus' parables point to those moments when the Rule and Realm of God can be encountered in a gestalt of hospitality, surprise, grace, or even judgment – all discernable in the everyday experiences of table fellowship, family gatherings, agriculture, and village commerce. Yet because of their passing/fleeting ordinariness, the promise they embody is incomplete and unfinished.

Neusner has identified an important distinction. Where one community is concerned about sanctification and reads Lev. 19 through that lens, another is more concerned about salvation and reads the Law represented by Lev. 19 through that lens. After the Shoah, we may need to look beyond these distinctions, however, to see what a concern for healing and wholeness can show us all about matters of representative life set apart to demonstrate God's ways with the world. Hospitality, each to the other, can be a threshold at which we meet, or even a doorway through which we enter a different kind of relationship.

Jesus' regard for one's enemies as strangers worthy of hospitality may be distinctive, but in holding this perspective he is neither rejecting nor betraying the Law. He is identifying a way of walking filled full with human life, a way of walking he himself embodied. But that embodiment does not require a supersessionary interpretation to be affirmed. Sadly, however, that path is the one historic Christianity followed, but it is not required by the scriptural witness. Another path remains open and applies to post-Shoah

Christianity the way it once may have been directed to the schismatic and sectarian rivalries of Jesus (and Matthew's) day. In other words, Jesus can be read to be directing his hearers/readers to regard their adversaries well, knowing that they included not simply the Roman occupiers of Galilee and Judea but the rival groups interpreting the way of halakhah in contention with him. Reading in this fashion, therefore, compels us to resist any hermeneutic that would require the displacement of those interpreting the Law otherwise.

Jesus' attitude toward the Law depends upon his understanding of Torah and how each serves the Rule and Realm of God. For Jesus, as for the contending parties in this debate, *halakhah* pertains to the daily walk with God that fulfills God's instructions/intentions for life (Torah). That conflict is not undone by these observations. But it is reframed. After Auschwitz, we must ask if Jesus' shift from "be holy" to "be perfect," (read, "be whole") or his emphasis on hospitality to the other signify a way of walking that can be both faithful and responsive to others in the aftermath of the Shoah as well as a way of Christian faithfulness that can integrate the legacy of Christian misconceptions regarding the Law and Torah?

Facing the Text, Facing Ourselves, Facing Each Other

To be sure, midrashic dialogue does not yield a single voice with regard to a text nor does it demand agreement on the meaning of the texts one might be facing with others. Nor does it mean that in the context of dialogue that there will not be conflict. Nonetheless, midrashic dialogue reconfigures the conflict so that through it those engaged in the disagreements are not seeking to win an argument but seeking instead to open the world of the text so that together we might stand before it and perhaps step more responsibly into its world of narrated meaning and grace.

We do this in multiple ways. Indeed the very notion of facing a text implies something of the richness as well as the corrective dynamics employed in our post-Shoah hermeneutics. When we face a text, we do it in dialogue facing each other. To be sure we work in solitude a great deal of the time, reading commentaries (each others' and our own) but even then we are reading and writing with an awareness of each other's presence. It is a face-to-face experience, even when it is undertaken in moments of solitude. Furthermore, when we read a text midrashically, we recognize that there are several, sometimes many, faces present in the text. The characters, named and unnamed have real, identifiable faces if we would just take the time to ponder them. For example, the other whom Jacob faced at the Jabbok could just as easily have been himself, his brother Esau, his father, his mother, or all of the above. Similarly, the enemies Jesus regard as worthy of respect could have been his adversaries in Jerusalem or Matthew's adversaries after the destruction of Jerusalem. Just as important, the adversaries we are called to love could be those with whom we contend when interpreting these very words.

To be sure, midrash proceeds by taking with absolute seriousness the otherness of the text, wrestling with it as other and not presuming to master it in the process. Very much like the story of Jacob at the Jabbok, the text becomes the other that we grasp and insist bless us in our wrestling. And in the process we face the text by facing the figures, the others in the text itself. Likewise we face the gaps and opens spaces, even the shadows in the text as we give faces to the world configured in and by the text. Most important, we face our texts by confronting them in the sense of facing up to the difficulties they all too frequently present to us; by confronting ourselves and our own history of reading them; and confronting each other in the reading that we hold precious and undertake with great passion while keeping before us the face of the other who in reading otherwise nonetheless reflects the very image of the One whom we seek to find and serve in the text.

Chapter 11 -Towards the Construction of a Post-*Shoah* Interfaith Dialogical Universal Ethic
Steven Leonard Jacobs

Introduction

I have purposely titled this paper, somewhat clumsily perhaps, "Towards the Construction of a Post-*Shoah* Interfaith Dialogical Universal Ethic" because, even prior to any examination of the texts under discussion -- *Vayikra*/Leviticus 19:13-18, Matthew 22:34-40 and 5:43-48, and Luke 10:25-37 -- this title reflects the very necessity of its component parts: *Towards the Construction*, that is to say, that *the task* before us, now more than fifty years after the horrors of 1933-1945, has, at long last, only just begun: namely the construction of a ethic which will ensure non-repetition of the past, or, even more realistically, if not non-repetition, then, at the very least, minimizing the repetition of those horrors. *Post-Shoah*, but by no means post-genocidal. The very events of Nazi destructiveness will not be repeated in their fullness either today or tomorrow, for historical events do not repeat themselves in either their exactitude or their ferocity. But they have been repeated with frightening variations in the years since 1945 with catastrophic regularity and are being repeated even as we speak. The ethical challenge before us, then, is to break these cycles of cataclysmic horrendous violence before they ultimately overwhelm us. *Interfaith,* because the profound lesson of these past ten years, at least among these four beloved brothers, friends, and colleagues, Jews and Christians, Christians and Jews, is that goodness is not confined to either community represented here; that we Jews need to realize, that, God-forbid, confronted with the nightmares of yesterday, James Moore and Henry Knight would have stood with us even at the moment of our deaths, just as Jim Moore and Hank Knight now know and understand only too well that the Christian faith they both take seriously and preciously came close to abandonment because of the obscenity of its silence during the years of the *Shoah*. *Dialogical*, because it is out of our conversations, looking directly into each other's faces, eyes and hearts that a shared tomorrow will emerge. And, lastly, *universal*, because we Jews cannot, in the years since the *Shoah*, draw our metaphoric wagons in a circle -- either here in these United States or in our beloved Israel -- and expect to protect ourselves and survive a future genocidal holocaust; and we Christians will not survive such either in a terrorist world gone mad. With these initial thoughts in mind, then, let us, even more hesitatingly perhaps than in the past, approach our texts, but let us do so with a caveat: that of Primo Levi's

> **Shemá**:
> You who live safe
> In your warm houses,
> You who find, returning in the evening,
> Hot food and friendly faces:
> Consider if this is a man,
> Who works in the mud
> Who does not know peace
> Who fights for a scrap of bread
> Who dies because of a yes or a no.
> Consider if this is a woman,
> Without hair and without name
> With no more strength to remember
> Her eyes empty and her womb cold
> Meditate that this came about:
> I commend these words to you.
> Carve them in your hearts
> At home, in the street,
> Repeat them to your children.
> Or may your house fall apart,
> May illness impede you,
> May your children turn their faces from you.
>   Primo Levi (1919-1987)

The 'Holiness Code' Rethought

Chapters 18-20 of *Vayikra*/Leviticus have been adjudged by the rabbis of the Jewish Tradition as the 'Holiness Code', for which the word *kiddusha*/holiness remains at the core, and Chapter 19 as the heart of that core. And yet, as most if not all of us already know, contained herein are not meditative discussions on the role of holiness in daily life or the centrality of ritual-ceremonial behavior in the life of ancient Israel or prescriptions on how to follow a life of prayer and liturgical affirmations. For even our predecessors wisely knew that the truest measure of holiness was not to remove oneself from one's community or one's community from the larger society. Thus, we may correctly term this understanding of holiness as *practical holiness*, lived in the context of society amongst one's fellow human beings. Its affirmative mandate is found in *Vayikra*/Leviticus 19:2, mistranslated by far too many for far too many years:

Kedoshim tiyu ki Kadosh Ani Adonai Eloheinu:
NOT: "You *shall* be holy, for I, Yahweh your God, am Holy." **BUT**
"You **MUST** be holy for I, Yahweh your God, am Holy!"

For Israel of old, for the Jewish People today, and for those who wish to stand in solidarity with the Jewish People, post-*Shoah*, *"Ayn breirah*/There is no alternative!" Holiness, as further defined below, is not an alternative possible life-style, one among many; it is the only option available to us in a world increasingly capable of destroying itself and the totality of its inhabitants.

Realistically, for one who wishes to continue affirm the viability of a Jewish or Christian *religious* life, in light of the *Shoah,* this mandate now takes on an additional dimension: To affirm the integrity of the Divine Presence demands that this God, too, re-think and re-new and re-affirm His/Her commitment to holiness: God, too, **must** be Holy because this People Israel demands holiness of God; its unmerited suffering and near total annihilation and extinction but yesterday give it an ethical claim upon a God to live up to the voice of *kiddusha*/holiness found not only in the sacred Torah but in the life of the *she'erit ha-plaitah*/the saving remnant of its survivors and their descendants.

With these thoughts in mind, then, we turn to a simple listing of those ethical mandates found in *Vayikra*/Leviticus 19:13-18:

(1) You shall not oppress your neighbor;
(2) You shall not rob your neighbor;
(3) You shall not withhold your hired servant's wages until the (following) morning;
(4) You shall not curse the deaf;
(5) You shall not put a stumbling block before the blind;
(6) You shall do no unrighteousness in judgment;
(7) You shall not respect the person of the poor, nor favor the person of the mighty (in judgment);
(8) You shall judge your neighbor in righteousness;
(9) You shall not go up and down as a tale-bearer among your people;

(10) You shall not stand idly by the blood of your neighbor;

(11) You shall not hate your brother in your heart;

(12) You shall surely rebuke your neighbor, and not bear sin because of him;

(13) You shall not take vengeance against the children of your people;

(14) You shall not bear any grudge against the children of your people;

(15) You shall love your neighbor as yourself.

Contained within this simple listing are the three universal principles by which post-*Shoah* ethics must now be governed: 19:16: "You shall not stand idly by the blood of your neighbor;" 19:17: "You shall not hate your brother in your heart;" 19:18: "You shall love your neighbor as yourself"[1]. *Neighbor,* not Israelite, not Jew, not Christian, not German, not Palestinian, not Arab; *neighbor.* Not yesterday, not today, but forever and all time.

(Parenthetically, but even more realistically, perhaps the major accomplishment of our post-*Shoah* world is *not* the requisite theological re-thinking of both Judaism and Christianity mandated by the silence, indifference, and/or complicity of too, too many so-called "religious" people and the paucity of both righteous gentiles and righteous Christians during the long dark night of Nazism's reign of absolute terror and absolute evil, but, after the International Military Tribunals of Nuremberg in 1945, the creation of both the International Criminal Tribunal for (the former) Yugoslavia and the International Criminal Tribunal for Rwanda at the end of the Twentieth Century, still functioning at the beginning of this Twenty-first Century. Hence, *Vayikra*/Leviticus 19:15: "You shall do no unrighteousness in judgment; you shall not respect the person of the poor, nor favor the person of the mighty; but in righteousness shall you judge your neighbor." These international public condemnations of genocidal behaviors, these legal and moral and ethical expressions of global outrage with their concomitant refusals to acquiesce in silence and indifference after Auschwitz are, in all honesty – despite the hesitancy

---

[1] The late Chief Rabbi of the British Empire Joseph H. Hertz's comment is particularly noteworthy: "These three Hebrew words were early recognized as the most comprehensive rule of conduct, as containing the essence of religion and *applicable in every human relation and towards all men.*" J. H. Hertz (1961), *The Pentateuch and Haftorahs* (London, UK: Soncino Press), 502. (Emphasis added.—SLJ)

of this country to affirm these tribunals -- the true first steps in the construction of this post-*Shoah* dialogical universal ethic.)

Turning Troublingly to the Book of Matthew

As I have said so often in the past during these conversations, I continue to approach these New Testament texts with trepidation but with respect for they are not mine and there remains that point of acceptance beyond which I simply cannot go. Turning first, therefore, to Matthew 22:34-40, whether in truth it was Jesus the Christ who regarded *Devarim*/Deuteronomy 6:5 as the "great and first commandment" and *Vayikra*/Leviticus 19:18 as the "second commandment," or the author or editor of this Gospel, is of lesser importance to me than their grounding in Jewish authenticity. Nor am I disturbed by their affirmation in verse 40 that upon them "depend all the law and the prophets."

Post-*Shoah*, then, the message of this first set of verses in the construction of a interfaith dialogical universal ethic is not to Jews at all but to those who profess both faith in this Christ and their self-labeling as Christians: Your very authenticity is akin to your willingness to incorporate into your very beings the understandings of both the Divine-human encounter and the human-human encounter as they have been adumbrated in the evolving Jewish Religious Tradition in the very personhood of the Jewish People. You can no longer claim legitimacy as Christians, if indeed you ever could, apart from the Jewish People. Pushed even further, your historic distancing of yourselves from both the Jewish People and the Jewish Religious Tradition must now be fully recognized, appreciated, and, ultimately, accepted, as among the primary foundational causes of 2,000 years of antisemitic hatred and activity, culminating in the horrendous epidemic we now call the *Shoah*. Not that Nazism was Christian, but the very rejection of Christianity. With open hand and open heart, then, I invite you to continue to reclaim that which is authentically Christian, namely your Jewish Heritage, as your go your own way. Here, too, becomes a second moral mandate in the construction of this ethic: solidarity with the Jewish People as both evidence and model of your sincerity to stand with all peoples who are "other," who are not like you, who do not believe as you believe, who do not pray as you pray, who do not worship as you worship, whose God or gods may not be your God or Christ.

But I remain deeply and disturbingly troubled as I turn to the second Matthean passage under consideration, that of 5:43-48, specifically verse 44 which would mandate love of my enemies and prayers for the well-being of those who have persecuted me, regardless of whether or not it is this same Christ to whom these words are attributed.

I am the child of a survivor-escapee, now deceased. One hundred fifty members of my large and extended family were murdered before my birth, including my grandparents, all my aunts and uncles except four; all my cousins except two. There is in me no love whatsoever nor compassion for those enemies of my family -- May their names be blotted out for all eternity! -- for those who perpetrated these evil deeds upon us. Am I thus not a "son of the Father who is in heaven," according to verse 45? Am I therefore outside the pale of those who must be "mature," "completely pure," "holy" or "perfect" as my "heavenly Father" is, according to verse 48?[2] Even now, more than fifty years after my own birth, the rage remains, the anger burns white hot within me as I feel ever more keenly these losses, knowing full well that what could have been for my own family, and so, so many others, will never be. No: I simply cannot accept the so-called "truth" of these verses, and publicly call upon my Christian brothers and sisters to reject them too in light of the *Shoah*. Anger and rage at those who would perpetrate Holocaust and genocide does not diminish us in God's sight nor in our own; morally and ethically, they energize us to commit ourselves once more to work ever more diligently to construct a world where these horrific acts of the past do not become the rationale for present and future behaviors.

What About Luke?

Even more disturbing than the second passage of Matthew discussed previously is this third passage, that of Luke 10:25-37, the so-called "Parable of the Good Samaritan." Assuming the "lawyer" of verse 25 is himself an Israelite, in all likelihood a Pharisee, and even granted that its statement is authentically that of the Christ, the ultimate result of its telling is, and has been for two thousand years, a denigration of Jewish religious leadership and, by extension, the Jewish People as a whole. It is we Jews who are neither merciful nor

---

[2] Along these same lines, is Simon Wiesenthal to now be publicly condemned and repudiated for the silence he informs us was his own response to the dying Nazi soldier who requested absolution of him? See both his (1976) *The Sunflower* (New York, NY: Schocken Books) and (1997) *The Sunflower: On the Possibilities and Limits of Forgiveness* (New York, NY: Schocken Books).

compassionate towards those who are not of our own people; rather, it is the representative of that people whose own temple was "rebuilt by the Romans as a reward for the aid given them by the Samaritans during the Bar Kokhba rebellion"[3], who, according to Josephus, also suffered under Pontius Pilate (*Antiquities* 18:85-89), but who, at least according to *Melachim Bet*/II Kings 17, specifically versus 34-41, practiced a form of religious hybridization merging Israelite worship with their pagan origins and thus took themselves out beyond covenant with the God of Abraham, Isaac, and Jacob, who is both merciful and compassionate. We are thus obligated today, after the *Shoah*, as Jews and Christians, to ask ourselves: What, indeed, is the purpose of such a parable?

If its purpose was to denigrate the Jewish People, then it remains successful. If its true purpose however, regardless of its authenticity on the part of the Christ, was to equate mercy and compassion as keys to inheriting eternal life, then it has been and remains unsuccessful; for by setting up what must now be viewed as a far too dramatic literary fiction, it has caused countless generations to negatively remember the *characters* themselves -- lawyer, priest, Levite, and Samaritan -- rather than the intended lesson.

But what about the lesson and its intended implications? To be sure, both mercy and compassion, both subsumed under the Hebrew term *rachmanut*, are, and always have been, Jewish values. Are we not the *B'nai rachamim shel HaRachaman*/compassionate children of the Compassionate One, according to our own Jewish Religious Tradition? Would the Christ himself, stepped as he supposedly was in the ways of Judaism, so bitterly condemn his own with a blind naivete that the generations of his own who would succeed him and bear his name would push their conclusion to its own inevitable violent end? Was he so unsophisticatedly wrapped up in the drama of his own oratory that he failed to truly and accurately perceive the implications of his story? I truly hope and pray such was not the case.

Perhaps the parable was not his at all, but, rather, that of the Lukan author, attributed to the Christ to heighten his own agenda, which was, indeed, to denigrate the Jews and hold up the superiority of an educated Greek audience of potential Christians?

Either way, regardless, after the *Shoah*, we Jews must say to our Christian brothers and sisters: Here is a text which causes us pain

---

[3] "Samaritans," (1972), *Encyclopedia Judaica* (Jerusalem, IS: Keter Publishing House), Volume 14: Red-SL, #730.

and suffering as it has done so for two thousand years. If you are in truth committed to the values of mercy and compassion, then reject the parable itself and give evidence of your commitment to these values of mercy and compassion by standing with us in our pain and our suffering.

Towards a "Universal Declaration of a Global Ethic"

In preparation for this presentation, and quite by accident, I stumbled across a new book by Leonard Swidler of Temple University, PA, and Paul Mojzes of Rosemont College, PA, entitled (2000) *The Study of Religion in a Age of Global Dialogue* (Philadelpia, PA: Temple University Press). Of particular interest and relevance are the last portions of the book: "12 Universal Declaration of a Global Ethic" (179-187); "13 A Proposed Draft: *A Universal Declaration of a Global Ethic*" (188-194); and the "Appendix: *Explanatory Remarks Concerning the 'Declaration Toward a Global Ethic'*" (197-212).

Basing itself upon the Golden Rule, whether defined positively ("*What you wish done to yourself, do to others!*") or negatively ("*What you do not wish done to yourself, do not do to others!*"), it is an attempt to building an international, interfaith, dialogical universal ethic of shared consensus in the aftermath of the genocidal tragedies, including the *Shoah,* which nearly overwhelmed the twentieth century. The document itself which highlights the text – "A Universal Declaration of a Global Ethic" – is both an answer to the *Shoah* and all other past, present, and future genocides, and well worth the investment of serious discussion and response. But there is yet more.

In his "Introduction: Ethics After Auschwitz," Editor John Roth, known to so many of us for his own moral integrity, posits seven themes which lay the foundation for the collection of remarkable essays and responses by Roth, Leonard Grob, Peter Haas, David Hirsch, David Patterson, and Didier Pollefeyt:

1. Auschwitz was not only an assault on millions of innocent human beings – Jews first and foremost among them – but also an assault on goodness itself.
2. After Auschwitz, the most difficult questions for ethicists include: *How do ordinary people come to do extraordinary evil? What, if anything, can ethics do check such evil? Or put otherwise, how did human beings who had previously lived unexceptional and inoffensive lives end up watching, condoning, or inflicting continuous acts of intense cruelty and unprecedented genocidal destruction against the aged, women,*

children, and generally helpless people who engaged in no acts of provocation and committed no crimes, as crime is defined by advanced societies?

3. After Auschwitz, the simple reaffirmation of pre-Holocaust ethics will not do anymore, because the Western religious, philosophical, and ethical traditions have shown themselves to be problematic.

4. The Holocaust is not so much the end of ethics as it is the proof that ethics can be misused and even perverted into pseudo-ethics.

5. Ethics after Auschwitz must be characterized by openness to the Other.

6. Ethics needs the support of politics, lest it be ineffectual. Politics also needs ethics, let it waste human life.

7. The ethical study of the Holocaust should not only be a particular discipline, but also it should penetrate the heart of every other discipline – from education to science, from medicine to theology, from the arts to philosophy, form politics and law to everyday life.[4]

Roth concludes his edited book with "the note....on which ethics after Auschwitz should always begin:

> If we want to know whether we are on the right or wrong track, individually or collectively, we can hold ourselves responsible by asking: Would action like mine, would policies like ours, have tended to help or harm the Holocaust's victims? For post-Holocaust ethics and the future, helping or harming those most in need measures the difference between right and wrong.[5]

As Jews and Christians, as good people of faith in the aftermath of that monstrous atrocity which almost succeeded in destroying both goodness and faith – oft-times *despite* the sacred texts we hold precious, both individually and collectively, rather than because of them – it may very well be us in our coming together after countless generations of our apartness and our distance which may yet prove the final hope of a desperate humanity before it is too late.

---

[4]   John Roth (Editor) (1999), *Ethics After the Holocaust: Perspectives, Critiques, and Responses* (St. Paul, MN: Paragon House), xiv-xv. (Emphasis added.—SLJ).

[5]   Ibid., 337.

CHAPTER 12 - TOWARD AN ETHIC OF DIALOGUE: THE PATH OF THE LOVE COMMAND LEVITICUS 19; MATTHEW 5, 19; LUKE 10
JAMES MOORE

What can we say is fair? Since this is the question that Paul Ricoeur argues is the foundation of our usual meaning of justice, it seems a reasonable question to ask of a post-Shoah dialogue between Christians and Jews.[1]   And if we say that we mean by fairness some form of the Golden Rule (Don't do to others what you would not want them to do to you), as Paul Ricoeur has also argued, then we ought to start the investigation of the question with Leviticus 19:18 or we might add and extend our exploration by turning to Matthew 19:16-30 or Matthew 5:43-48 or Luke 10:25-37. Our aim is to do jus that, but we are doing this inside the dialogue that has by now been labeled the Midrash Group. This means that we start the discussion with our usual assumptions: (1) that no theology after Auschwitz can be authentic unless it done in dialogue; (2) that no theology can be done after Auschwitz unless it is post-Shoah theology; (3) that all theology is done respecting the other, from which we have adapted the style we have called Midrashic.

The Question

The question we have posed for ourselves is whether there is an ethic after Auschwitz. Of course, the implications of this discussion extend to many of the issues we face when confronting the events of the Shoah. We also wonder who is responsible and who can be held accountable. We wonder what can be done now to make up for the past. We ask how can we prevent any future horror such as the Shoah. We hope to create a world in which people act differently.   What we

---

[1] Ricoeur, Paul. *Figuring the Sacred*. Minneapolis: Fortress Press, 1995, p. 237.

might say about an ethic after Auschwitz will also speak volumes to these other concerns that are so prominent for us. The center of the question though is what is justice.

If the golden rule becomes the focus of our search, we see certain basic parameters to our answer, which may be called, into question in a post-Shoah world, problems our dialogue cannot ignore. If there is a foundation of ethics in the notion of not doing to others what we would not want them to do to us (the most powerful expression of the command to love our neighbors as ourselves), we know that such acting has to happen inside of an agreement, a social contract, that is based on an essential trust. Within that trust we can disagree about the particulars, but we cannot possibly dispose of the foundation of trust. There is a trust that I extend by choosing to act in this way. This trust is the belief that I will hold to my principles. The second trust is in the other since my actions are defined to a great extent by the other. I trust that such acting will be reciprocated. The difficulty with Leviticus 19:18 is that expectation of reciprocation but it is obviously the foundation for any idea of justice. Our question, then, in so many ways turns us toward the expectation of reciprocation and the reality of its absence.

Leviticus 19

The Rabbis call Leviticus 19:18 the moral principle of the law.[2] But this principle seems to be understood in the context of Leviticus 19 only as we accept fully the whole set of practical principles that are the Holiness Code. That is, love of neighbor has both a specific context, that of the covenant people, and pragmatic meaning, love expressed in particular forms of respectful acts. Thus, love can only be particular and not general. Love cannot be seen as abstractly aimed at the idea of neighbor but must be aimed at the known neighbor. And this holds even if the act is restraint -- "You shall not profit by the blood of your neighbor." It is this sense of the pragmatic particularity of the moral principle that surely must be read into the two gospel stories of the young ruler or the good Samaritan. Indeed, there is little to see in these two stories that extend this meaning of the love command.

Leviticus 18-20 also presents us with a sense of the boundaries that identify the community. This sense of boundary (that some behaviors exclude people from the community) also marks the meaning

---

[2] Montefiore, C.G., and Loewe, H., ed. *A Rabbinic Anthology.* New York: Schocken, 1974, p. 172.

of the love command. This marking of boundary is much more an ethical boundary and not an ethnic boundary (see 19:34 as an extension of the love command to the alien among you). Thus, within this command to love comes a need to create ethical boundaries. Of course, the boundaries that are significant for the Holiness code are especially sexual boundaries and this makes sense if the code is intended to regulate the conduct of the community within a covenant relationship. Of course, Leviticus 19 broadens this to include slander, hate, respect for property, care for the poor and foreigner, agricultural practices, etc., but the sexual codes are the focus of the punishments of Leviticus 20 and these become the basic boundaries of ethical behavior that shape the identity of the community.

The idea of boundaries that are shaped by ethical behavior, even especially by sexual behavior takes on new meaning after the Shoah. If love of neighbor is tied to such boundaries in Leviticus, what can we say about the idea of boundaries after the Shoah? Who is it that stands outside of this command to love? Surely, we are ready to set such boundaries, but the boundaries now take on a new context. The need to focus on sexual behavior as central to the maintaining of community integrity may still remain but it is not any longer the focus for us. The focus is then what? If hatred and bigotry and disrespect for person and property and profiting by the blood of one's neighbor are listed as if they are part of the community's life even if they ought not be part of that but sexual abomination seen as deserving banishment or death, the horror of the Shoah now reverses this pattern. Isn't it likely that if boundaries are necessary to give meaning to the love command that those boundaries are now centrally focused on bigotry and hatred and slander and profiting by the blood of our neighbor? Indeed, one is inclined to say this and re-emphasize that justice requires that those, who do these things, ought to be banished.

If this makes sense in a general way, we are still troubled by two things connected with the logic of Leviticus 19. First, the command still depends on the belief that we can still establish a covenant community. That is, we can still talk about citizens and aliens in this post-Shoah world. Even if we are to set boundaries focused on behaviors, we are still troubled by this kind of understanding of the idea of neighbor. Second, the idea of boundary setting leaves us bewildered after the Shoah sense it presumes the mentality of the normal rule of law, that is, that justice is produced by rules of behavior (a way of deciding right and wrong in normal relations). Our problem is that such a view cannot adequately produce either a sense of fairness for those who have been wronged (where is a possible notion of compensation for the losses of the Shoah) nor can it really account for the implication of the Golden Rule, that is that we behave with an expectation or vision of what we hope for, the community of respect (do not do what you would not want to have done). No matter how many rules we write or agree on or anticipate we cannot give all the particulars of such a general rule of behavior. Especially in a post-Shoah world that now can expect behaviors that are unprecedented. No such rule of law could possibly provide us with what is necessary to guard against those who would act as the Nazis acted. Nor can such a rule provide us with the justification for love in the context of such brutality. This is the dilemma of the Golden Rule for us who live after Auschwitz.

A Dialogue Instead

A code is still of some value for us simply by putting before us the question of boundaries of behavior. Even so, we know that some other approach is required if our goal is justice, that is a way of acting on what is fair. We can suggest that a dialogue is an alternative to a notion of community identity, to a covenantal idea. Of course, we might claim that dialogue is our current way of stating what is the essential meaning of a covenant people. On the other hand, dialogue moves us beyond that covenant idea in that we now can create an ethic that does not create a set of rules as a boundary but rather begins with a set of assumptions that define the dialogue itself. The community remains an emerging product of a conversation and rules; such as they are would be negotiated along the way. This form of ethic is much less secure than the reciprocity of a contract but is less troubling.

The only problem with the dialogue is that this conversation needs some kind of motivation. Ricoeur, following Gewirtz and Donergan, argues that the morality of negotiation (that of the rule of love) is rooted in another ground, not the social contract but in the promise of the creator/redeemer.[3] Indeed, there is a motivation for negotiation, says Ricoeur, if this God is the God of hope, that is, that we can believe that the God who is creator is the God of Hope. The context for the rule of love the (the love command) in the religious worldview is the context of this redeemer God, what Ricoeur labels the economy of gift.[4] That is, God can command love if we agree that God

---

[3] Ricoeur, Paul. *Figuring the Sacred.* Minneapolis: Fortress Press, 1995, p. 294ff.

[4] Ibid., Ricoeur, p. 324.

is the one who "brought us out of the land of Egypt, out of bondage, into the land of promise." This is the larger context for both the command to love and the pragmatic prohibitions and commands of the Holiness Code. Even if we rebel, the economy of gift is still a motivation for dialogue.

The Loss of Foundations

However, the argument apparent in the golden rule as set into the religious context, the holiness code, that love is commanded by the God of hope is even more problematic for our post-Shoah reflection. We can remember the cry of the boy who saw the first night in the camp which "murdered my God forever."[5] Love can be commanded but the God of hope is no longer a foundation for our behavior. This is the God who brought the people not out of bondage but to the flames of Auschwitz. And if we cannot say this with the young Wiesel, we might with him say at least that God, the God who would give hope, is the one hanging on the gallows.[6] Or we might repeat with Fackenheim that there is no redeeming voice in Auschwitz.[7] This does not mean that a voice is not heard, but if we hear a redeeming voice, it is a mocking voice and we cannot say that of God, not now, not ever. Thus, we can hear authentically only the commanding voice, the command to love, if not to love God, to love neighbor (father, mother, sister, brother, child, friend, stranger).

But this is not a foundation for dialogue, for the command to love. Indeed, if this is what we have, we have lost a foundation for morality in the religious sense and are left with that of our humanity and the older Wiesel is even more inclined to doubt that as a foundation.[8] So we are left with an ethic without foundation, without a basic motivation. It is an ethic, instead, that requires a renewal with every discussion, every common task, every new issue, an ethic on the run toward hope without any real basis for hope except our awareness that hope is better than despair. This is the point where I found myself some years ago when I first wrote about the potential of dialogue, something akin to the conclusion offered to us by Roy Eckardt, that we

---

[5] Wiesel, Elie. *Night.* NY: Bantam, 1960, p. 32.

[6] Ibid. Wiesel, p. 62.

[7] Fackenheim, Emil. *God's Presence in History.* NY: Harper, 1970, p. 84ff.

[8] Wiesel, Elie. "Talking and Writing and Keeping Silent," from Roth, John and Michael Berenbaum, ed. *Holocaust.* New York: Paragon House, 1989.

can weep together.[9] That, at least, we do together, and in this is hope of sorts.

Turning to Matthew and Luke

That would hardly be acceptable though for a post-Shoah theology. How is it that we would be satisfied with crying together as a core of action? Indeed we risk much if we assume that this is what our Jewish colleagues would want from us. But, the tyranny of love is precisely what the text in Luke and Matthew suggest, that we do what we imagine the other would want. Thus I thoroughly reject the idea put forth by Alan Donergan that the negative and positive versions are logically equivalent.[10] What we can do together, at least is to talk. Talking is not enough but it is not a presumption that we already know what our colleagues want.

It is clear, though, that the gospel texts are intended as interpretations of the love command. In that sense, they also presume the context of the covenant as an essential beginning point for love. Even the story of the Samaritan who helps as an illustration offered by Jesus to define who is my neighbor, assumes that the covenant functions in some fashion for the Samaritan as well. What the gospel text does, however, is to give priority to love of the alien, or in the Matthean case, love of the outcast or poor. The two texts set up a check against the rule of the majority that requires justice for the minority group. It is so ironic that we should continue to see this given the stark inability of so many followers of this Jesus to do that, particularly during the Shoah. The ideology of the Nazis was precisely aimed to undo this ethical precept for justice. The minorities were by definition outside of justice.

Of course, this means that we need only to enforce the rule of love of neighbor as so described to reinstitute this axiom of justice. That can be done only by recognizing the dialogical character of acting in love (not merely specification of pragmatic rules and deeds and boundaries). That is, we can fully observe this axiom of love for the alien and outcast only by operating with an ethic of dialogue, by allowing all voices on the public stage. My contention has been that this principle really extends to all those who study the Shoah in

---

[9] Eckardt, A. Roy. *Long Night's Journey Into Day.* Detroit: Wayne State University, 1982, p. 139ff.

[10] Donergan, Alan. *The Theory of Morality.* Chicago: University of Chicago, 1977, p. 57-58.

whatever aspect. How can we know if we are acting in just love when we do history or study literature or engage in debates of ethics if we are not doing this in open dialogue?

Open dialogue is of course, the foundation of unifying plurality in a notion of "becoming human" or in beginning a process of speaking about our "common humanity." Paul Ricoeur argues that such notions are at the heart of being able to act justly, with justice. It is precisely the act of denying the humanity of others that so characterized the Nazis, acting on the principle of the "antiman" as Jean Amery put it.[11] So it is a principle and not merely a suggestion. The urgency of such an ethic of dialogue after the Shoah is absolute. But simply looking on the other as person does not produce an ethic. An ethic of dialogue must be filled out with specific acts. Indeed, so the story goes, the young man is encouraged to sell all that he has and the Samaritan is described as acting to bind wounds and provide for healing. There is in this interpretation a rootedness in the Torah teaching that again drives us back to the pragmatic, to doing in the day to day activities that are defined by law.

This shift from act to person and back to act suggests a dialectic between law and the motivation of the person as agent that is necessary to understand the full meaning of an ethic that produces justice, an ethic of dialogue as I have pointed us to. Paul Ricoeur again calls this a dialectic between law and conscience.[12] Among the various meanings of this dialectic we can see two that are significant for our work and for our reading of these texts. First the dialectic between law and conscience can preserve a standard of evaluation that guards against the tyranny of the love command -- to avoid both a savage vengeance that simply reacts with brute force to protect self-interest as well as the sacred sense of vengeance that is rooted in a sense of righteous indignation. But second, the dialectic also produces a level of conviction that moves us to act for justice (a strong sense of what is right or that we must act because we could do no other).

Thus, the aim is justice and not vengeance, even a righteous vengeance. But this can be tested by our sense of what needs to be done. The call of never again is made particular rather than general but retains the strong sense of conviction that would prevent us from acting. Particular situations, such as the events of brutal antisemitism witnessed in the Benjamin Smith case or even with the strong feelings

---

[11] Amery, Jean. "Torture," from Roth, John and Michael Berenbaum, ed. *Holocaust*. New York: Paragon House, 1989, p. 180.
[12] Ricoeur, 2000, p. 146ff.

so recently brought forward by the violence in Israel and the West Bank as many point to Arial Sharon or Yasser Arafat as sources of responsibility. The dialectic becomes dialogue and an ethic of dialogue and with this we gain insight into how to act even in these difficult situations.

But we have yet the most troubling of texts, love of enemies, that seems to be the demise of justice. It is a command that in abstract sounds inviting but in reality destroys all. What do we say in terms of fairness, justice concerning the former Yugoslavia or Rwanda if we hold up this as a pragmatic standard? This command fails to fit the dialectic and even undoes the dialectic. But the other side of love of enemies is the full force of the standard of protection afforded to minorities, the full acceptance of real plurality within humanity. So it must be held out as one reading of the love command that remains a principle of justice but not a law of action. Love of enemies is boundary language that challenges the false preservation of community (so obviously the problem of the churches throughout history until this day) over right action but it cannot define action in a just community.

Thus, we now need to look for an unfolding of this ethic of dialogue in terms of specific issues and actions. Above all, we have no clue whether this will actually succeed since we are only just now trying to shape a community of dialogue. Let us move forward with the task on both sides then, shaping the community and applying the ethic and let us do it with urgency.

Chapter 13: Religious Intolerance and Prejudice: What's Love Got To Do With It?
Zev Garber

The theologian Paul Tillich defined religion as a system of beliefs, rituals, symbols and myths directed toward an ultimate concern of a society. Religion has meaning in the sense of absolute interpretation of central values of a society, and it has force as sacred power which stands behind these values. In addition, a religion provides important integrative functions for its members and manages tensions within the threats from without by establishing important defensive mechanisms. Religious beliefs and practices are often couched in religious creeds and outlooks, which many scholars claim are a major force of intolerance among people today. They say that a democratic society may differ in kind and intensity from a fascist and/or theocratic society but it tolerates and in some cases promotes religious discrimination. However, I argue, religious discrimination is often a source, component, or byproduct of other social problems.[1]

Among the questions addressed to religions of the West and Occident: Is there a difference between religious intolerance and religious prejudice? Which system supports best tolerance: relativism, secularism, or universalism? Can a democratic state fulfill its mandate of allowing its citizens freedom of religion? Is tolerance inherited or learned? In short, why is it that the noblest of human experience has become for may a history of misery and evil?

---

[1] See my Editorial Viewpoint, "America Attacked and Zion Blamed - Old-New Antisemitism: Fatwa Against Israel," in *Shofar* 20.2 (Winter 2002), pp. 1-4.

The horrors of medieval religious persecution are no longer dominant but religious intolerance is still very visible. Liberal intellectuals understand the world problems of economic injustice, corruption, world hunger, racism, political repression, etc., not in religious terms. Yet is the problem in Ireland only economic? Is the Arab states' belligerency against Israel only over territory? Is warlike tension between Iraq and its neighbors and saber wrangling in post-Taliban Afghanistan purely over oil and territorial control respectfully? Is antisemitism an issue of "racism"?

In post-World War 11 years, ecumenical leaders have attempted to solve problems of religious indifference. Yet, many ecumenical leaders are associated with radical theological movements and religious traditionalists do not trust relativistic leaders. Also, many secular liberal intellectuals are themselves *intolerant.* That is to say, they are pleased consciously or unconsciously, by the continuing existence of religious intolerance for it confirms the worst opinion of religious people. Ironically, liberal intellectuals oppose the interference of church into state and secular matters, but they often condone the persecution of religious minorities. It appears that religious intolerance is here to stay. Even in the messianic period, the Talmud suggests, the message of Purim is here to stay.

We live in an era of global cynicism, frustration, and death. The early warning signs were in 1995: there was no stoppage to genocidal activity in Rwanda; religious and ethnic cleansing in Bosnia-Herzegovina; conflict within the states of the former U.S.S.R; hatred of minorities in Germany, India, Pakistan, and elsewhere; terrorist activity in Gaza and Judea-Samaria (West Bank); Tokyo, Ipil (south of Manila), Oklahoma City in the heartland of America, and other world trouble spots by criminal cartels, secretive cults, nationalistic groups, liberation movements and what have you - all inspired variously by venerated masters in the name of Supreme Truth, which cast a long dark shadow on the United Nations' "International Year of Toleration." Seven years later, in late Summer 2001, at the world racism conference in Durban, South Africa, Arab delegations succeeded in vilifying Israel -- and only Israel -- in the conference draft. A once-in-a lifetime opportunity to mount a worldwide campaign against bigotry, hatred, and racism, and to speak in behalf of the world oppressed, was severely damaged by venomous overt Israel-bashing and covert anti-Semitism - an ominous sign of the attack on America, Israel's steadfast defender, that was to follow on September 11, 2001. Enter the Grave New World.

There are differences in religious intolerance and prejudice as there are varieties in secularism, absolutism, racism, and nationalism. While the Nazi state enslaved and murdered, left and right wing dictatorships today engage in a "soft fascism," the destruction of human values at times with and a times without brute force. Christianity teaches salvation by belief in God through Jesus, whereas Judaism stresses obeying the laws of God. The Synagogue prays, in the spirit of the prophets of Israel, "Let all inhabitants of the world perceive and know that unto thee every knee must bend and every tongue give homage. Before thee, 0 Lord our God, let them bow down and worship, and unto thy glorious name let them give honor" (from the *Aleinu*).[2]

However, while the Synagogue has a doctrine of exclusive knowledge of God's truth as contained in the Torah, it does not tie to it an eschatology of exclusive salvation. The classical Church, however, does join belief and salvation. This may explain the small numbers of the Jewish People.

Sampling Love-Hate Hermeneutics

Few deny that Christian-Jewish relations turned for the better in the last third of the 2nd Century. Arguably for the Western Church this began at the start of the Second Vatican Council when Pope John XXIII deleted the phrase "perfidious Jews" from the Good Friday service thus abolishing from Catholic lectionary the age-old Christian image of the wandering Jew cursed by God. Despite theological obstacles famished by conservative bureaucrats of the Vatican hierarchy and opposition from Arab Christians and fear of anti-Christian backlash in the Muslim world, Vatican 11 issued the document *Nostra Aetate* ("In Our Times'), the first-ever Catholic document repudiating collective responsibility for the death of Jesus.

The Second Vatican Council's document on the Jews inspired many dioceses and archdioceses to implement *Nostra Aetate* and to rid the anti-Jewish bias of Christian teaching. To illustrate, consider the sentiment of the Italian Bishops to the Jewish community of Italy

---

[2] The Aleinu prayer, the proclamation of God as supreme sovereign of the universe and parent of the siblinghood of mankind, closes all services on week-days, Sabbaths, and Festivals.

(March 1998 "For its part, the Catholic Church, beginning with Second Vatican Council - and thanks to the meeting of two men of faith, Jules Isaac and John XXIII,[3] whose memory is a blessing - decisively turned in another direction (from teaching divinely sanctioned punishment of the Jews -ZG), removing every pseudotheological justification for the accusation of deicide and perfidy and also the theory of substitution with its consequent 'teaching of contempt,[4] the foundation for all antisemitism. The Church recognizes with St. Paul that the gifts of God are irrevocable and that even today Israel has a proper mission to fulfill: to witness to the absolute lordship of the Most High, before whom the heart of every person must open."

Few can rival Pope John Paul II's long papacy in ridding the Catholic Church of antisemitism. He more than any predecessor has condemned "the hatred, acts of persecution, and displays of antisemitism directed against the Jews by Christians at any time and in any place "(Yad Vashem, March 23, 2000). He has labeled the hatred of Jews as a sin against God, referred to the Jews as Christianity's "elder brother,[5] with whom God's covenant is irrevocable, and established diplomatic relations with the State of Israel (1994). The Vatican documents *We Remember: A Reflection on the Shoah (1998), Confession of Sins Against the People of Israel* (St. Peter's Basilica, March 12, 2000), *Dominus Jesus* (2000), and *The Pontifical Biblical Commission Statement on the Jewish People and Its Sacred Scriptures in the Christian Bible* (2002) are major milestones in the Church's efforts to reconcile with the Jewish People.

I leave to the historians (religious and secular) the task of setting facts in perspective to obtain truth without patronage, polemics and politics. My goal, however, is to rethink two well-known Scriptural passages or thoughts that suggest in Christian love there is contempt

---

[3] On Sunday, September 3, 2000, the Vatican beatified Pope John XXIII (1958-1963), who was admiringly called "Good Pope John," bringing him to the threshold of sainthood

[4] Term associated with Jules Isaac (I 877-1963), French authority on antisemitisrr4 who in an audience with Pope John XXIII in 1960, persuaded the Holy Father to consider the errors of the Church's teachings about the Jews. Isaac's writings on *I 'enseignement du mgpris* played a key role in the declaration of *Nostra Aetate.*

[5] Phrase introduced by Pope John XXIII.

of the Jew but in fact show commonality between Christians and Jews albeit with subtle variation. In a word, the Word of God is a manifesto for religious dialogue, tolerance and understanding. To think and act otherwise are obscene and an effrontery to the *teshuvah* (both meanings; repentance and return) of the Church to the Jewish People in our times.

Law and Grace

For centuries the Church promoted a system of degradation against the Synagogue by promulgating the inferiority of Judaism as a system of man-made self-righteous legalism and the superiority of Christianity as divinely inspired spiritual love and virtue. Take *lex talionis,* for example.

Three times the Pentateuch mentions the legislation of *lex talionis* (the law of retaliation, "eye for an eye").[6] Though the law of "measure for measure" existed in the Ancient Near East, there is little evidence that the Torah meant that this legislation should be fulfilled literally except in the case of willful murder. "Life for life" is taken literally in cases of homicidal intention, and fair compensation is deemed appropriate by the Oral Torah in the case of a pregnant woman whose unborn child's life is lost and when animal life is forfeited. Indeed, the Written Torah casts aside all doubts regarding the intent of the biblical *lex talionis* injunction: "And he that kills a beast shall make restitution for it; and he that kills a human being shall be put to death" (Lev 24:2 1).

Rejecting the literal application of *lex talionis* puts an end to the mean-spirited charge that Judaism is "strict justice." The Church teaches that the words of Jesus on the Torah ("For truly, I say to you, till heaven and earth pass away, not an iota, not a dot, will pass from the law until all is accomplished" [Matt 5:18]) are irrefutable. Accordingly, Christians citing Matt 5:38-39a ("You have heard that it was said, 'an eye for an eye an eye and a tooth for a tooth.' But I say to you, Do not resist one who is evil") to teach that Jesus cancels the Law and replaces it with non-violent Grace[7] are wrong on two accounts: 1) syntactically, the Greek text of Matt 5:39 reads *And not But* thereby

---

[6] Exod 21:23-25; Lev 24: 19-20; Deut 19: 18-21.

[7] Namely, Jesus proposes love not hate of one's enemy. See Matt 5:43-48 and Luke 6:27-28, 32-36.

removing the onus of change; and 2) Scripturally, the text in context (see Matt 5:21-26, 27-30, Jesus on murder and adultery) instructs not cancellation but affirmation of the commandments. Thus Jesus like the Sages focuses on the significance of the teaching and its cautionary warning about wrong doing in "thoughts, words and deeds."

Supersessionism

On May 1, 1987, during the beatification ceremony for Sister Teresa Benedicta of the Cross (Edith Stein),[8] who was murdered in Auschwitz on 9 August 1942, Pope John Paul 11 proclaimed that "salvation is from the Jews," and made reference to the words of Jesus to the Samaritan woman at a place tradition calls Jacob's well:

> Jesus said to her, "Believe me, woman, the hour is coming when you will worship the Father neither on this mountain nor in Jerusalem. You worship what you do not know; we worship what we know, for salvation is from the Jews. But the hour is coming, and is now here, when the true worshippers will worship the Father in spirit and truth, for the Father seeks such as these to worship him. God is spirit and those who worship him must worship in spirit and truth." The woman said to him, "I know that Messiah is coming" (who is called Christ). "When he comes, he will proclaim all things to us." Jesus said to her, "I am he, the one who is speaking to you."[9]

Knowingly or not, elements of *Veritas Israel* are inserted in the Pope's homily: earthly Jerusalem is replaced and Jesus refers to himself as the true Messiah. Further, by beatifying Edith Stein as a true worshipper of God in spirit and in truth contra Judaism's *Lebensphilosophie* of worldly realism and spirituality, the Catholic Church is signaling supersessionist Christology: a Christ-like sacrifice for the salvation of her people, her Church, and the entire world.[10]

---

[8] 'Blessed Edith Stein was canonized on October II, 1998, corresponding with the seventh day of Succot ("Tabernacles") in the "Season of Our Joy" 5759.

[9] John 4:21- 26.

[10] Catholic devotional literature teaches that Stein died as a daughter of Israel for the glorification of the most holy name of God in imitation of Christ's passion and to expiate for the human sins which caused the Shoah.

Indeed, Blessed Edith Stein's own words on the way to Auschwitz suggest this: "I am quite content now. One can only understand the science of the Cross if one feels the Cross in one's own life."[11]

How to reconcile the Vatican's teaching on Blessed Edith Stein as part of redemptive suffering and the charge of supersessionism? We suggest, with all deference, that the Catholic Church and the Jewish People can agree that the courage and passion of Edith Stein should help Christians learn the lessons of Shoah, but they necessarily differ in their theology of redemption. For the Church, it is the Easter faith, spirit over matter, that enables victory to be proclaimed over Golgotha and Auschwitz. For the Synagogue, it is the covenantal oath at Sinai, uniting spirit and matter and resulting in everyday acts of holiness, that permits Zion to triumph over Auschwitz.[12]

Commandment Numerology

Classical Judaism teaches that the Torah instructs 613 Commandments *(TaRYaG Mitzvot),* which is derived by the numerological device of *gimatriyyah* from the Deuteronomic verse *Torah tsivah lanu Mosheh morashah khillat ya'akov,* "Moses charged us with the Teaching, a possession for the assembly of Jacob" (Deut 33:4). The numerical value of "Torah" is 611, to which the first two commanclments of the Decalogue (sovereignty, unity, spirituality of the Lord God) are added because they are not from the mouth of Moses *(mi-pi Mosheh)* but revealed by God directly to the Children of Israel.[13] Similarly, there are 365 negative prohibitions corresponding to the days of the solar year, with the understanding that daily we must remember and avoid the evil path, and 248 positive mandates corresponding in number to the limbs of the human body, suggesting that one serves God with every part of one's being.[14]

---

[11] Quoted in the Vocation Newsletter of the Cannelite Sisters of the Most Sacred Heart of Los Angeles, Winter/Spring, 1999.

[12] Our thoughts on Edith Stein are quoted in the *Advisory on the Implicationsfor Catholic-Jewish Relations of the Canonization ofst. Edith Stein* by William Cardinal Keeler (September, 1998).

[13] Exod 20: 4-6 and Deut 5: 6-10. Others say that the different explanation for the Sabbath commandment (Exod 20:8-11 and Deut 5: 12-15) spoken in One Voice directly to the people is the reason.

[14] *Mak.* 23b

From verses of Torah, the Sages understood that the yoke of the *TaRYaG Mitzvot is* required only of Jews.[15] Non-Jews, who are seen as the "Children of Noah," are bounded by minimal moral duties known as the Seven Noachide Laws read from and into Gen 9: establishment of courts of justice; the prohibition of blasphemy; of idolatry; of incest; of bloodshed; of robbery; of eating flesh cut from an animal.[16] Primitive Christianity appears to agree. To live in the context of Mosaic law was expected of Jewish believers but not Gentile believers, who were conjoined to live a type of Noachide life in Christ not troubled by circumcision and other Jewish utterances.[17] On the strength of practicing monotheism, Judaism recognizes Christians and Muslims (and others) as Noachides.

In rabbinic homiletics devoted to ethical and moral teaching, fanciful numerology is found. To extol the miracle of the Exodus, for example, different Sages augmented the Ten Plagues to forty or fifty blows in Egypt and two hundred and forty or fifty blows, which the Egyptians suffered at the Sea.[18] Similarly the Rabbis reduced God's Commandments to extol His Teaching in a simple and dignified manner. Third-century Rabbi Simlai collated various biblical verses associated with Moses, David, Isaiah, Micah, Amos and Habakuk to show how the 613 Commandments were progressively reduced to eleven, to six, to three, to one: "Seek you Me and live" (Amos) or "The righteous shall live by his faith" (Habakuk).[19] Second-century martyred Rabbis Ben Azzai and Akiba quoted respectfully, the verses, "This is the book of the generation of Adam" (Gen 5:1) and "You shall love your neighbor as yourself" (Lev 19:18) as the greatest of the Torah.[20] And the first-century crucified Rabbi Jesus expounded

---

[15] About 200 function today. Many commandments related to Temple (ritual purity, priesthood, sacrifice),
Land (agriculture, monarchy, slavery), People (aspects of civil and criminal law)are no longer operative.

[16] Sanh. 56-60

[17] Acts 13-20 and Galatians (all).

[18] MidrashimonExod 14:31, *seemek. R.* Sim.onExod 14:30; *Exod, Rab.V.14, Y-XIH.9;Midr. Tehillim on* 78:49. *Avot* 5.4 records another tradition; "Ten miracles were wrought for our fathers in Egypt and ten at the Sea."

[19] *Mak.* 23b-24a.

[20] *Gen. Rab.* YXIV.7.

principle that "Hear 0 Israel" (Deut 6:4) and "Love your neighbor" (Lev 19:18) are the great commandment.[21]

Rabbi Jesus, Rabbi Hillel, and Rabbi Akiba [22]

There is a line of basic continuity between the beliefs and attitudes of Jesus and the Pharisees, between the reasons which led Jesus into conflict with the religious establishment of his day, and those which led his followers into conflict with the Synagogue.

Two of the basic issues were the role of the Torah and the authority of Jesus. Rabbinic Judaism could never accept the Second Testament Christology since the Godman of the "hypostatic union" is foreign to the Torah's teaching on absolute monotheism. As the promised Messiah,[23] Jesus did not meet the conditions, which the prophetic Rabbinic tradition associated with the coming of the Messiah. For example, there was no harmony, freedom, peace and amity in Jerusalem and enmity and struggle abounded elsewhere in the Land. This denies the validity of the Christian claim that Jesus fulfilled the Torah and that in his Second Coming the tranquility of the Messianic Age will be realized. As Rabbi Jesus, he taught the divine authority of the Torah and the prophets,[24] and respect for its presenters and preservers,[25] but claimed that his authority was equally divine and that it stood above the authority of the Torah. I agree with others who see this testimony as the major point of contention between Jesus and the religious authorities that ultimately led to the severance of the Jesus party from the Synagogue. However, I maintain, that the quarrel began in the words of Jesus on the road to and from the Torah.

For example, the distinction between the positive articulation of the Golden Rule as given by Jesus, "Whatever you wish that men do to you, do so to them,"[26] and its negative form as given by Hillel, "What

---

[21] Matt 22:3 7-39; Mark 12:29-3 1; Luke 10:27.

[22] This section is adapted and elaborated from my "Torah and Testimony: Making Sense of Disputation in
Dialogue, " SIDIC, vol.24.3-24.1, pp. 40-41.

[23] Cf, among others, Matt 26:62-64; Mark 14:60-62; Luke 22:60-70.

[24] Cf. Matt 5:17-20.

[25] Matt 23: 1-3a

[26] Cf Matt 7:12 and Luke 6:3 1.

is hateful to you, do not to your fellow creature."27[27] Jesus' ethic is seen in Christianity as altruistic and denies the individual moral value and dwarfs the self for the sake of the other. Hillel's moral code and dictum, "If I am not for myself, who will be for me? And if I am only for myself, what am I? And, if not now, when?" are understood within Judaism as a pedagogical directive to find the proper balance between self-interest and self-sacrifice. Hillel's teaching represents abstract justice, which attaches moral value to the individual as such without prejudice to self or other.

Hillel's luminary message, namely, no person has the right to ruin another person's life for the sake of one's own life, and one has no right to ruin one's own life for the sake of another since self and other have the same value before the heavenly throne of 'justice, was re-echoed in the teaching of Rabbi Akiba. Akiba declared that "Love your neighbor as yourself"[28] implied that the scales of justice must be in a state of equilibrium with no favorable leaning either toward self or neighbor. Self-love must not be a measuring rod to slant the scale on the side of self-advantage and concern for the other must not tip the scale of justice in his/her behalf.[29]

Rabbis Hillel and Akiba stand in contrast to Rabbi Jesus, whom Christians believe as God incarnate is above the authority of the Dual Torah. The disparity of self and other in the ancestral faith of Jesus is abolished in the new faith in Jesus: "There is neither Jew nor Greek, slave nor free, male nor female, for you are all one in Christ Jesus.[30]

---

[27] *Shab. 3* la. The origin of the Golden Rule is Lev 19:18. Evidence of the Golden Rule as an essence of the moral life is found in Jewish tradition long before the period of Hillel and Jesus. E.g., the books of Ben Sira and Tobit (both second century B.C.E.) expound: "Honor thy neighbor as thyself' (Ben Sira) and "What is displeasing to thyself, that do not do unto any other" (Tobit). Similarly, *Testament of the Twelve Patriarchs* (first century B.C.E.), warns: "A man should not do to his neighbor what a man does not secure for himself

[28] Lev 19:18

[29] Cf the Baraitha in *B. Mes.* 62a, which pits the view of the altruistic Ben P'tura against R. Akiba, and *Pesah.* 25b where a man asks Raba (280-352) what he should do if an official threatened to kill him unless he would kill another man.

[30] Gal 3:28. Also, lcor 12:13; Col 3:1 1.

This may well explain the words of Jesus on retaliation,[31] on love of one's enemies,[32] and on forgiveness at the crucifixion.[33]

The difference between the Synagogue and the Church, on the purpose of Torah and the person of Jesus, acquired new intensity after the passing of the Jewish Jesus and the success of Pauline Christianity.

Much Ado About the Love Commandment (Leviticus 19:18)

Judaism and Christianity share an immense spiritual foundation based in great part on the commandment to love the Lord your God and neighbor. For centuries, the Synagogue and the Church, with their respective methods of tradition and interpretation, have attempted to teach constructively this teaching. Tragically, specific forms of anti-Judaism and anti-Semitism, couched in "replacement theology" and mean-spirited deeds in Christendom, have precipitated a millennia-old conflict between the Church and the Jewish People. Succinctly put, Christian militant and triumphant equated to the nullity of Judaism. Nonetheless, the challenge of enlightenment, emancipation, modernity, and especially the uncontested use of Christian teaching for the Shoah, arrested the Church's Jew hatred.

Since Second Vatican Council, the Roman Catholic Church has progressively issued official documents condemning religious supersessionism and antisemitism. Most recently, the statement from the nearly 200-page *The Pontifical Biblical Commission Statement on the Jewish People and its Sacred Scriptures in the Christian Bible (2002)*. Among the themes acknowledged are that the Jewish reading (rabbinic) of Hebrew Scriptures is analogous to the Christian reading (Second Testament), which developed in parallel fashion; Jewish messianic expectation is not in vain though different than the Christian expectation; it is wrong to view biblical prophecies fulfilled in the life of Jesus, whose message is "new and original"; Second Testament polemical texts deal with the life of the people then and are not meant to applied to all Jews of all times and places merely because they are Jews. Clearly, the Vatican admits that God's call of the Children of Israel, the Jews, is definitive and irrevocable. But the Vatican also avows the Pauline claim that the biblical covenant-

---

[31] Matt 5:38-42; Luke 6:29-30.

[32] Matt 5: 43-48; Luke 6:27-28, 32-36.

[33] Luke 23:34.

promise has been extended to baptized gentiles through the sacrificial death and resurrection of Jesus of Nazareth.

I wholeheartedly support this official shift in Roman Catholic thinking today.   Out is the old "old covenant/new covenant" theological reflection and in is the "double covenant." I assert that the hallowed hermeneutics of the Church and Synagogue, are living paths to the reign of God. I uphold that individually and together, Christian and Jew can penetrate their suspicion of one another. It is a sign of reconciliation and genuine *teshuvah* when the Church acknowledges its participatory role in the history of theological anti-Semitism and its "firm resolve to build a new future in which there will be no more anti-Judaism among Christians."[34] In turn, Jews must see the Body of Christ as a professing and confessing Church and respect and support its bold moves to a common future with the Jewish People.[35]

There are differences among religions and empathetic understanding and dialogue are proven keys to reducing religious prejudice and intolerance. But what to do with religious extremists who revise sacred scriptures and tradition for their own ideological claim and gain (e.g., religious superiority, nationalism)? Constant vigil from without and self-policing from within are a start to contain this exceedingly bad stain imposed on humanity. If clergy and leaders of organized religion do not teach religion with tolerance then it is the business of responsible intellectuals, teachers and thinkers to make this happen. One must declare zero tolerance for prejudicial extremist ideology which masquerades as truth in the name of religion. At all costs optimism must prevail. Think of the alternative.[36]

Finally, a last word, which I construe as the first thought, about the Love Commandment. How does one "love" an enemy, murderer, terrorist, who despises you? I read Hebrew Scriptures with Jewish eyes. Lev 19:18 does not say, "Love your neighbor as yourself," but "Love your neighbor for s/he is like you." For me, this means, one must know the Self, senses this in the Other, before one can *respect*

---

[34] We Remember: A Reflection on the Shoah (1998), penultimate paragraph.

[35] A Jewish reassessment of Christians and Christianity is found in *Dabru Emet* (2000; "Speak Truth"), a
document signed by more than 150 Jewish scholars, teachers and rabbis across the spectrum of Jewish denominationalism in America.

[36] See further my comments in the "Book Symposium" *in Religious Education* 97.2 (Spring 2002), pp. 184-197.

the Other thereby circumscribing the view that it is natural to man to love. Seen thusly, the biblical mandate of the unity of the human race demonstrated by the love of neighbor are fulfilled. *E Unum Pluribus.*

Chapter 14 - COMING TO TERMS WITH AMALEK
Facing the Limits of Hospitality
Henry F. Knight

Religion and Violence

Religion and violence build a terrifying alliance when they work in partnership with each other. Since September 11, that image has haunted our thoughts about either entity. Some deny the linkage. Some see only the linkage. Since September 11, we have heard our own leaders declare that what happened in our nation on that day had nothing to do with Islam. What happened was a sheer act of terror, erroneously linked to a distorted view of Islam. At stake: to avoid labeling that religion *in toto* as a religion of violence. The motives have been understandable, whether they have been solely political or a mix of political wisdom and spiritual grace. On the other hand, some wise souls have been warning us not to overlook the religious nature of what happened. While it would be wrong to cast a totalizing glance at the religion of Islam as violent, it would be equally wrong, as well as unwise, to fail to see that what happened was indeed motivated by religious sensibilities and understood to have divine sanction. As Andrew Sullivan reminded his readers in his Oct. 7 essay for the NY Times Sunday magazine "this was a religious war." [1] But, as Sullivan points out, the religious sensibilities at work are not found only in Islam. They are the sensibilities of revolutionary fundamentalism. Or what in a later editorial for the New York Times Thomas Friedman called "religious totalitarianism." [2] What Sullivan and Friedman each have grasped is that there is a form of fundamentalism that is so single-mindedly fanatic that it denies any other faith claim legitimacy except

---

[1] Andrew Sullivan, "This Really Is A Religious War," *The New York Times Magazine,* Oct. 7, 2001.
[2] Thomas Friedman, "The Real War," *The New York Times,* Nov. 27, 2001.

its own.   Friedman explains, quoting Rabbi David Hartman, "the opposite of religious totalitarianism is an ideology of pluralism – an ideology that embraces religious diversity and the idea that my faith can be nurtured without claiming exclusive truth.   America is the Mecca of that ideology, and that is what bin Laden hates and that is why America had to be destroyed." [3]

Sullivan, in his article, called attention to the violence located not simply in Islamic tradition but in Jewish and Christian tradition as well.   None of the three great Abrahamic traditions are exempt from this problem.   Sullivan's point was to challenge public debate to recognize the religious dimensions of violence without failing to see how embedded it has been among Christianity and Judaism as he called attention to the violence undertaken in the name of Islam.   Regina Schwartz, in her unsettling book, *The Curse of Cain*, has sought to do the same thing, but pre-dating the September 11 tragedy and linking the problem to matters of identity when one's identity is built on a logic of scarcity requiring that one identity negate the claims of others because they each contend for the same ground of divine confirmation.   Indeed, for several gatherings, our midrashic dialogue has wrestled with this issue, probing the ways in which violence is embedded in our texts and searching for ways to re-conceive our relationship to those texts and to the identities they configure.   Today we look at one of the most troubling of biblical references, the figure of Amalek and the related texts that call for Amalek's complete destruction.

A Disturbing Encounter

Who is Amalek?   In the biblical texts, scripture describes Amalek as a marauding, nomadic figure, a tribe of the Sinai peninsula who attacks the people of Israel from the rear as they make their way through the wilderness following their liberation from Egypt. Furthermore, the testimony of Exodus 17 specifies that Israel was particularly vulnerable at the time they were attacked.   Joshua, under the direction of Moses standing above him on a prominent hill top, leads the battle against Amalek, winning when Moses' arms are raised holding his staff and losing when in fatigue Moses lowers his arms. Eventually, with the help of Aaron and Hur, Moses keeps the staff aloft and the Israelites are victorious with God declaring, "Write this as a reminder in a book and recite it in the hearing of Joshua: I will utterly blot out the remembrance of Amalek from under heaven." (Ex. 17: 14)

---

[3] *Ibid.*

According to Gen. 36: 12, Amalek the grandson of Esau by way of a liaison between Esau's son, Eliphaz, and a concubine named Timna. In other words, while he is of Abraham's lineage, the connection is tainted. On the Sabbath before Purim, the Torah portion, *Zakhor*, Deuteronomy 25: 17-19, is read, admonishing Jews to remember what happened when Amalek attacked them in the wilderness on their journey of liberation and to blot out the name of Amalek while doing so. In that regard, I Samuel 15: 1-34 is read as the Haftarah. Behind each of these readings, of course, is Ex. 17: 8-16, which describes the ambush in the wilderness. The texts tell the story of egregious violence perpetrated by the Amalekites and commands the Israelites to remember what happened in the wilderness, to forget the name of Amalek, and then to destroy Amalek's descendents completely when they are encountered later in the time of King Saul. Furthermore, these texts are read just before Purim because Haman, the oppressor of the Israelites who sought their destruction at the time of Esther is seen to be a descendent of Agag, the King of the Amalekites with whom King Saul was confronted by the prophet/judge Samuel for having disobeyed the divine commandment to destroy all the Amalekites by sparing their king.

The violence in the passages is unsettling. In each of them, utter destruction is bearing down on the children of Israel, and in each case God sides with them in their battle to survive and destroy their attackers. However, the utter visciousness of the violence is disclosed in the scene from I Samuel, where Samuel confronts Saul with the divine expectation that every Amalekite was to be slain – "Now go and attack Amalek, and utterly destroy all that they have; do not spare them, but kill both man and woman, child and infant, ox and sheep, camel and donkey.' " (I Sam. 15: 3) What else is this but genocide, divinely sanctioned genocide at that?

After Auschwitz, we cannot gloss over this. However, Jewish scholars did not gloss over it before Auschwitz without showing their discomfort with the violence in the text. My colleague Zev Garber in 1992 recalled the resistance of Kabbalistic theology in his chapter on Amalek in his book, *Shoah: The Paradigmatic Genocide*. He writes: "The moral imperative of the *Zachor* commandment is for each individual to join together to eliminate evil, not by destroying the sinners, but by eliminating sins." Garber cites Psalm 104: 35, midrashically: "May sinners disappear from the earth, and the wicked be no more," reading "not *hattaim* (sinners) [with the doubled/dageshed tet] but *hataim* [without the doubled tet] (sinful acts). [4] Wiesel makes a similar point in his essay "Myth and History," saying, "The law commands any living Jew who meets a living Amalekite to kill that Amalekite. The law is the law, but at the same time our sages adopt all measure to prevent us from identifying an Amalekite.   So he has become myth." [5]

Amalek Returns

To say Amalek is myth is not to say that Amalek is not historical, however. Indeed, Amalek has returned in the guise of others displaying his hatred for Jews and what they represented. That is the ongoing significance of Purim. Amalek returned to confront Israel in the identity of Haman and once more Israel prevailed.   So Israel remembers at the same time Israel blots out the name of Amalek née Haman. Sadly, however, the cycle did not end with Haman. Haman has given way to Antiochus. Antiochus has given way to Titus; and he to Hadrian; then to Torquemada, Chmielnitzki, and eventually to Hitler. As Gunther Plaut points out in his commentary on *Torah*, "Amalek has appeared and reappeared in many guises. [6]

Indeed, Amalek, the mythic enemy of Israel has found a human face again and again in history.   Amalek, however mythic, is also very real.   And with the pogroms of the second millennium, followed by the Shoah's definitive exclamation point at the end of it, we find ourselves pondering an inexplicable dilemma.   A figurative reading of the Amalek story is not strong enough. Over and over again, Jews find themselves ambushed by those who hate them for no other reason than that they are Jews. Who they are, a people set apart by God for covenant, stirs up such animosity that they are attacked with genocidal ferocity.   At the same time, as a people victimized by genocide, how dare they accept a divine mandate to do the same? For in coming to terms with the literal truth that Amalek returns, the literal command to destroy Amalek returns as well. How do they read their scriptural mandate to remember Amalek, knowing how very real

---

[4] Zev Garber, *Shoah: The Paradigmatic Genocide* (Lanham, Md.: University Press of America, 1994) 132.
[5] Elie Wiesel, "Myth and History" in *Against Silence: The Voice and Vision of Elie Wiesel*, ed., Irving Abrahamson (New York: Holocaust Library, 1985) I, 362
[6] W. Gunther Plaut, *The Torah: A Modern Commentary* (New York: Union of American Hebrew Congregations, 1981) 514.

Amalek is without becoming the figure that they themselves fear when that memory retains a mandate to destroy Amalek utterly?

Perhaps there is a clue in Amalek's return. In each biblical record of battling Amalek, there is a report involving the extensiveness of what is at stake: In Exodus 17, God declares to Moses that God will utterly blot out any memory of Amalek. In Deuteronomy 25, God declares that when the time comes that Israel is free from all her enemies that God will blot out the memory of Amalek completely. Then in I Samuel, the text reports that Saul had utterly destroyed all the Amalekites except for Agag, their king. Samuel confronts Saul over his failure to destroy their king and then slays Agag himself. Complete destruction is accomplished. Then in II Samuel, an Amalekite, one who had taken the life of King Saul after he had fallen on his spear, reports of the kings demise to David and hands him the crown that Amalekite took from Saul. Not surprisingly, David has the Amalekite killed for taking the life of the Lord's anointed. Then centuries later, when Haman acts with genocidal intent toward the people of Israel, the text cites that he is descended from Agag. The point: the biblical record continues to report that the Amalekites had been defeated, destroyed. Even declaring a complete destruction in I Samuel after the killing of king Agag by Samuel. But again and again the Amalekites return. Is the biblical record oblivious to this flawed description or is this recurrence after their presumed destruction significant? Of course, until the Samuel passage there is only an implication of total defeat and a remnant of Amalekites can be presumed. But after the Samuel passage the incongruity is unavoidable.

Surely the incongruity would not have been missed by those compiling the scriptures, or overlooked by later scholars. Just as surely we should not miss it. When we think that Amalek has been defeated and removed from the historical flow of events, he returns, unexpected, to claim his place in the story of Israel. The biblical authors, like the Rabbinic sages, we might argue, were more concerned about ideological lines, not blood lines. That may be true, but I cannot help thinking they wanted the incongruity to show nonetheless: whenever it appears that Amalek has been removed from history and banished to realm of myth only, he reappears, ambushing Israel once again. When we read the command to remember, perhaps it is this we must remember more than anything else. Amalek will return and we must be prepared for that.

Facing Amalek

Facing Amalek is dangerous work. One the one hand, Amalek is real and a threat. He is particularly a threat when the people are fatigued from their struggle to make their way from exile and slavery to freedom and promised land. But that fatigue, no matter how prominent it might be, is never a final cause – even when the fatigue is spiritual, as Wiesel points out in his reading of the Exodus 17 text. He explains,

> Just before Amalek attacked Israel, you read a description of the moral atmosphere, of the moral climate among the wandering Jews. Suddenly they began doubting themselves, their spirit, their destiny, and the sentence which expresses this in the text is *Hayesh Adoshem b'kinbeynu*? They suddenly began wondering one to the other, "Is God really with me?" That was the moment of weakness. And because of that weakness Amalek attacked.[7]

Note well, the cause is instrumental, explaining why Amalek attacked when he did – not why he sought to attack the Israelites in the first place. Amalek simply strikes when Amalek has the greatest advantage. As Rashi says, Amalek just happens.

But even though Amalek is real, recognizing Amalek is difficult. Amalek strikes from behind. Amalek strikes by ambush, when and where the people are vulnerable. Providing a face to the mythic name is therefore difficult – until Amalek strikes.

However, providing a contemporary name for Amalek in disguise is dangerous for another reason. When that is done, one identifies an other as the irreconcilable enemy of Israel and of God. That other, whether an individual or a people, is cast beyond the boundaries of mutual, moral regard. That other no longer count within one's moral universe of concern. That is what happened to Jews as victims of antisemitism in western Europe. They were cast outside Christendom's universe of moral concern. They became Christendom's Amalek. From the perspective of our time we must not fail to see that the demonization of the other that occurs when one is identified as Amalek. After identifying someone or some group as Amalek, the particular identity of that other is lost. Hereafter one relates to a cipher, not to a human being. After Auschwitz that is an abomination that can no longer be tolerated.

---

[7] Wiesel, "Myth and History" in *Against Silence*, 138.

As strong as these cautions are, the story of Amalek reminds us that while we may have good, strong moral and spiritual reasons to resist identifying anyone with Amalek, Amalek exists nonetheless. He returns no matter how we might try to get rid of him. He has not been eradicated from history. God's people, representing the way of generous hospitality to others remain vulnerable to attack by those who live without covenantal regard for others. Amalek exists in every generation.

The message is strong and disturbing. Amalek cannot be eradicated completely even when he is pursued relentlessly. It is in the structure of creation that Amalek can and will return. Indeed, Amalek is aligned with the primal chaos present from the beginning of creation, for Amalek opposes the movement of liberation and the abundant unfolding of life. Amalek, in relation to others, is the un-doer of creation. That is, the very hospitality that makes room for our freedom makes room for that other who cannot accept hospitality's welcome. Of course, Amalek will destroy himself, but he will destroy every other as well if he is allowed. Therefore Amalek must be resisted. Israel and any who would join in Israel's cause must stay on guard. Amalek works by work in ambush. Amalek obstructs god's people and her journey toward freedom and any people's movement of life to fulfill life, to flourish. Amalek is like a cancer in this regard. Amalek returns, again and again. Remember that. Be on guard. But do not let Amalek win by allowing Amalek to be in control. Do not honor Amalek nor allow Amalek to define the terms of resistance. Blot out Amalek's name and significance thoroughly each time Amalek returns. But do not become Amalek in the process, lest Amalek win.

Perhaps this is a variation of Fackenheims's 614th commandment: " Do not give Hitler (read Amalek) a posthumous victory." Remember, but remember in a way that retains the identity of being God's people, do not become Amalek when remembering Amalek. Perhaps we can draw the implication further. Amalek is real and must be remembered because Amalek will return and ambush his victims from the rear when they are weak and where they are vulnerable. At the same time, one must beware of identifying anyone with Amalek, lest in doing so they become the other denying one they fear. Instead, we must all learn to ask if someone or some group *could* be Amalek but without drawing the final conclusion. If we are not careful in this regard we may discover to our regret that Amalek has taken on the image of our own reflection. This must be the limit beyond which we dare not go.

Facing Amalek In Our Time

Who then is Amalek? Amalek is the other who opposes Israel and any of us who identify with Israel so viciously, so completely, so utterly that he/she opposes not just us/Israel but he opposes God and God's intentions for life and all creation. Amalek is that other whom my hospitality will never be able to make welcome in the world because Amalek's identity and place in the world requires that any other be eliminated. Amalek is that other whom hospitality cannot welcome because Amalek's identity denies the validity of hospitality even when it welcomes Amalek.

When we face the other in our post-Shoah, violence-riddled world, we are called to move beyond tribal, cultural, and religious parochialisms. Indeed, we are led there in a shared Exodus from the confining regions of oppression and bigotry. We follow Israel as Israel bears witness to the liberating intention for every people. As we make our way, we will be ambushed from behind when we are most vulnerable. However, our vulnerability, like Israel's, is not the cause of the ambush. The ambush happens because Amalek exists. Indeed, Amalek is the embodiment of that chaotic force that resists the generous and hospitable ordering of the universe as creation.

In a post-Shoah world, we cannot escape Amalek's presence. We are mandated to remember that for the sake of our Jewish friends as well as for our own. But how? How shall we remember? How should we remember? Furthermore, we are still called forward with all of God's people, in the movement of redemption and liberation toward the promised land. Likewise, we must ask how? How shall we move forward? Especially as we ponder the stalking presence of Amalek in the shadows behind us. We will be ambushed, yet we must wage a struggle for survival, not only for ourselves but for every other engaged in the movement of liberation toward the promise of a full and free life. How shall we engage Amalek when the ambush occurs? How shall we defeat him, now, millennia later. How?

We must also come to terms with another telling fact of life. Every attempt to eradicate this *other destroying other* has failed. Even though in each telling of Israel's story, it appears that Amalek has been destroyed, another generation finds itself ambushed by this returning figure? Why? Amalek returns, even when Israel has done everything within human power to eradicate him. How does anyone defeat such an enemy?

We may state the other side of this insight as a limit. We cannot finally identify Amalek until he has perished. The story of

Amalek is a story of memory, Jewish memory, for the sake of the future and the present. We can fear someone is Amalek, we can beware of Amalek in any circumstance, but we cannot know until afterwards, for Amalek is the one who is irreconcilable. As long as that person or group is alive, he or she or they may surprise us yet again by showing us that they are not Amalek but one who seeks to return in penitence from exile – not in chaos against life. In other words, Amalek is named as an act of memory in order to be alert in the present. To do otherwise risks becoming the one who is named.

While we may fear that another can or may be Amalek in our time, we must learn to differentiate types and levels of evil, remembering that when we identify someone as Amalek we mythologize the one we so identify. The mythic dimensions of that act demonize the other, removing the particularities of his or her identity from our view. We begin to relate to Amalek, not to the one who stands before us, or who may literally stalk us. When we do that, we reduce another human being to a cipher and participate in the undoing of creation.

Not all tragic actions are full embodiments of the evil Amalek represents. Not every evil can be identified as an expression of the nihilism we associate with Amalek. But refraining from the mythic language of Amalek does not mean we embrace, endorse, or even understand why someone has acted how they have. Nor does it mean we cannot recognize the act they perpetrate to be evil. But we also know that when Amalek is identified as a living other, that other ceases to retain his or her humanity as a child of God, before whom we share our moral accountability. More importantly, we know what can happen when others are identified with Amalek. Religious fanatics can burst into sanctuaries of prayer and slaughter persons in them without remorse if they believe they are attacking such a figure. This is true regardless of whether the figure is named Amalek or Satan. We may even cite Baruch Goldstein murderous deed in Hebron as well as the actions aimed at the World Trade Center. As heinous as they are, each event is still understandable as a fanatical action undertaken by perpetrators who believe themselves to be acting under divine sanction. We may call the attack on the World Trade Center an atrocity, as Michael Bernebaum claims we should, to distinguish it from Goldstein's angry deed. But neither is not a nihilistic act. Rather, they are understandable if those who perpetrated them thought they were attacking a figure like Amalek who had to be utterly destroyed. Nevertheless, we must be careful of slipping into a mythic identification that can dehumanize all parties and perpetuate the survival of Amalek in new disguise.

Christians need look no further than their own historic misuse of this kind of mythic identification preserved in scripture. Whenever we deal with the presence of violence in our own identity and our relationship to Jewish siblings, we come face to face with scriptural contempt in the accusatory treatment of Jews in the Gospels. In the case of Matthew 27: 25, following the crowd's request to release Barabbas, Matthew states, "Then the people as a whole answered, "His blood be on us and on our children!" Matthew appears to have turned midrashically to 2 Samuel 1: 16, and adopted David's statement condemning the Amalekite who killed king Saul for taking the life of God's anointed: "Your blood be on your head for you have taken the life of the Lord's anointed." In other words, with his midrashic use of this passage, accusing other Jews of being Amalek, he has set up the demonizing logic that flows from this passage in subsequent generations. In the hands of later Christians, this language will lead to actions that draw forth telling fears from Jewish quarters that the Church had become Amalek in their time. Only penitential action and changed attitudes lie between that fear and its confirmation in actuality.

While the issue s are much more complex, I hope that his analysis underscores not only the problem of demonization, but also show how mythologizing a very difficult conflict only makes the conflict worse, more intractable, setting two groups at odds with each other, each one accusing the other of being opposed to their mutual existence. When this happens each group is driven by these mythic dynamics into accusing the other of being their ultimate fear personified.

The Limits of Hospitality

What does this reading have to do with Matthew and Luke's texts we have also placed before you this morning? To be honest, almost nothing, except that they are part of the biblical framework of hospitality that I rely on to read my world post-Shoah. They guide not just this encounter but every encounter I have. Perhaps that is as it should be. They frame my encounter but they do not prevent me from coming to terms with the other, in this case a very disturbing other, who stands before me.

But they also recognize that the way of hospitality is dangerous. In other words, there are limits to hospitality. There is no way to avoid conflict about this. But the conflict may not fall where we think. That is, it too, will ambush us from behind.

In both Christian and Jewish traditions there is a strong mandate to see in the face of every other the image of God. In that spirit we are called to embody hospitality to the other. As Emmanuel Levinas has reminded us, the face of the other is our summons to ethical action, our *ayecha* to which we are summoned to reply *hineni*, here I am. But in the face of modern violence, particularly understanding its religious expressions in revolutionary forms of fundamentalism, we must not forget that Amalek ambushes all of us from behind, even, perhaps especially, the religious fundamentalist. When that happens, Amalek grows in strength, feeding off religious passion that Amalek uses for the destruction of life as a cancer feeds off its otherwise life-giving host. Hospitality is vulnerable to this as well.

When we are truly practicing hospitality we are welcoming others into our households and other domains. As we do, we expand our world, our life space and take responsibility for those who have entered into our domain. We serve them as our guests and as their hosts take responsibility for their safety and welfare. Consequently we cannot place them in harm's way, exposing them to the wrath and violence of Amalek even if we might wish to risk being open to one we might suspect is Amalek. This is Samuel's strong word for Saul, that we must hear even as we resist Samuel's support of genocide. Saul was king and therefore responsible for the welfare of an entire people not just himself. When we are hosts, we are responsible for others, not just ourselves.

Many of us who face Amalek from the Christian side will wonder what we do with Jesus' language about turning the other cheek and loving our enemies as we do ourselves. Is not Amalek the personification of the enemy? Are we not called to embrace Amalek according to the dynamic of agapeic love? That is what we have been taught as the way of Christ. But we can only offer ourselves in sacrificial relationship to others. We cannot offer others on our behalf. Here Jesus' words about hospitality are especially instructive. As he admonishes his disciples at the beginning of Matthew 10 to go out in search of hospitality in the surrounding cities and to announce its healing and life giving significance where it is encountered and embodied, he also warns his disciples about the dangers of hostility that does not welcome them. Move on; do not tarry in those places. Be wise as serpents, gentle as doves. Know the difference and act accordingly. Then, as he concludes his comments he warns his followers that hospitality will generate its own conflict, though it most probably will surface in the familiar domains of household and family, between parents and children, between siblings. His additional caution is focused interpersonally. In other words, Jesus recognizes the limits of hospitality as well as its promise and its risk. When we practice hospitality and welcome others into our domain, we promise to provide them protection and care, serving them responsibly as they dwell with us as our guests. We cannot offer them to Amalek when he attacks our households when more life is at stake than just our own. Yet even there we must be honest about the face of Amalek. For Amalek does not want our shelter; rather Amalek seeks to destroy it.

This caution about Amalek is focused within a broader range of social interactions. Its scope is social and cultural as well as tribal and in our time religious. There are limits to hospitality at the micro and macro levels. Beware. Be alert. We wise as serpents; gentle as doves. Remember. But remember as well, we have undertaken, as Jews and Christians, a larger journey, moving from exile to the promised land; from bondage to liberation; from survival to covenantal wholeness. As long as we have not arrived, Amalek is a threat. As long as Amalek is a threat, we have not arrived.

Summary

What then does it mean for us to remember Amalek? Is it enough to know the story? Clearly not. The plain meaning of the text, whether we encounter it in Exodus 17, Deuteronomy 25, I Samuel 15 or in other allusions to the Amalekites elsewhere in scripture, is unsettling. It tells of an utterly destructive enemy as well as a summons to destroy that enemy. However, when we allow the plain meaning of the text to include all the encounters with Amalek, the text, as often happens, provides doorways for increased understanding and opportunities for important critical leverage. Such is the case with these texts as we encounter the mythic dimensions of Amalek along with the historical reality of Amalek's returning presence in the story of Israel.

The biblical along with the mythic identifications it opens up, invite the probing analysis of *derash*, explaining implications hidden in what the text says and doesn't say. As well, we draw from the wrestlings of others who over the years have encountered this text, preserving, as it were, its *remez*. But the secret of how to live with even this more inclusive text does not come without the uneasy sense that we are not to live with these texts comfortably. Consequently, we find ourselves wrestling with the same question we posed at the beginning, How do we, Christian or Jew, live with the returning presence of Amalek and honor as well the summons to live hospitably with every other? Our response must be, "Carefully."

No one lives outside the possibility of reconciliation except if he or she who keeps himself there. And that can be known only after they have succeeded, not before. But what they succeed in doing is destroying their own place in the domain of life, not the domain of life itself, which they seek to reduce to something less than what it is. However, in our gratitude that no one dwells beyond the possibility of reconciliation, we cannot forget that some, in the freedom they have to return, have the same freedom to oppose the hospitality and generosity that makes that return possible.   Creation is always exposed to this risk.

Those of us who live out of this perilous promise cannot forget the dangers represented by Amalek.   Neither can we overlook the conflict we may introduce in our most intimate groups when we insist on living within a commitment to hospitality toward the other that refrains from closing the circle of hospitality prematurely by relating to the other as a cipher, not a person – even if later that same individual may prove to be Amalek him or herself. But we cannot know that until memory gives us that perspective. However, we can place ourselves in the dilemma and choose to live with it, holding fast to the memory of Amalek at the same time we resist both his obvious and more insidious attempts to redefine our world.

Finally, however, we must face the fact that these remarks are general and the reality of Amalek is always very particular and very real. People are attacked, taken hostage, killed. Amalek strikes the vulnerable when we least expect. Furthermore, as a Christian I must recognize that I can speak of Amalek opposing *us* only as I identify with Israel, for Amalek is Israel's enemy first, simply because Israel exists. But I cannot leave the matter there, since Amalek can ambush from within as well as from behind. Amalek is not just Israel's problem, but my own in this regard. Still, I am learning how to come to terms with this figure from But that only complicates the matter as I attend to Israelites who do take the step of identifying Amalek with living persons and groups who contend with Israel.

Chapter 15 - The Genocidal Mind
Steven Leonard Jacobs

Amalek, Jihad, and Holy War

The age of innocence and naiveté is over; the age of vulnerability has now begun. And we are not talking about children born, almost growing up and dying in Israel, in Ireland, in the Sudan, in Afghanistan, in Bosnia or in Rwanda, children too old before their time. We are talking about American *adults* – Jews, Christians, Muslims, secularists, what have you – whose lives after September 11, 2001, have been irrevocably altered. The simplest of examples: I have traveled by air in October and November, and now, again, in March, as have many if not all of you. The decibel level of conversation on board has markedly decreased; almost everyone now reads the safety instructions when directed to do so; and the sigh of relief upon landing safely is palpable. The Arabic word *jihad* – all too easily translated as "holy war" – has entered our vocabulary, and is now used in all manner of discourse, not only events relating to 9/11 or the presidential-led "war on terrorism." And the United States' penchant for simplistic solutions to complex problems results in tarring the entire Arab-American community with the poisonous brush of terrorists and terrorism, and Islam as a monolithic and violence-prone and anti-Western expression of the Divine-human encounter; falsely identifying the current Middle East crises and setbacks as the *sole* rationale behind the horrendous events in New York City, Washington, DC, and Somerset, PA; and even spills over onto our college and university campuses where our historic commitment to the safe, free and open exchange of ideas is no longer, safe, free or open, and where faculty who question racial profiling of Arab-Americans and our military tactics in Afghanistan find their employment and tenure status subject to disproportionately intense review. All of which bespeaks an America afraid, groping somewhat blindly towards tomorrow, and reminiscent, sadly, of the tensions which existed in our country not only during the Viet Nam War but the oil crises of the 1970s, when in

Cincinnati, OH, where I was in graduate school, more than one automobile had on its bumper, "Burn Jews, Not Oil!"

Perhaps this feeling of enormous vulnerability now is not too terribly different from that of ancient Israel upon its initial trek from the hell and enslavement of Egypt into its four-decade wandering towards the freedom of its home in the Promised Land. Both the Exodus and the Deuternomic texts inform us of Israel's – and God's – response to the cowardly attack upon Israel's stragglers – its women and children, its aged and wounded – by Amalek at Rephidim, and Israel's successful defeat of their hated enemy under Joshua's leadership at the visual inspiration of Moses' upraised hands. More powerful, however, than the military victory itself is God's instruction to Moses:

> (17:14) Write this as a memorial in the book, and rehearse it in Joshua's hearing; for I will surely wipe out the remembrance of Amalek from under the heavens...(16) ...the Lord will have war with Amalek from generation to generation. (The NET Bible [Dallas, TX: Biblical Studies Press] 1998.)

Were this Exodus text not strong enough, Moses, at least according to the Jewish and Christian traditions of authorship, replays the injunction in Deuteronomy:

> (25:19)   ...you must wipe out the memory of the Amalekites from under heaven – do not forget!
> (The NET Bible [Dallas, TX: Biblical Studies Press] 1998.)

Commenting upon the first passage, and referencing the second, William H. C. Propp, in *The Anchor Bible,* writes:

> The battle with Amalek may be regarded as Israel's prototypical "Holy War" (cf. Deut 25:17-19; I Samuel 15) – that is, a military action sanctioned by Yahweh, prosecuted in a state of ritual purity, involving total extermination of the foe and dedication of their property to God, whether by destruction or by donation to the Temple...Among the story's morals may be that successful Holy War requires both sensible military strategy and divine favor (cf. Joshua 8).
> (William H. C. Propp, *Exodus 1-18: A New Translation with Introduction and Commentary* [New York, NY: Doubleday] 1999, 621.)

Commenting upon the Deuteronomic passage, Samuel Abramsky writes in the *Encyclopedia Judaica*:

> This implies that Israel is commanded to wage a holy war of extermination against Amalek (Deut. 25-12-19), for in the early days "the wars of Israel" and the "wars of the Lord" were synonymous expressions (cf., e.g., Judg 5:23).
> (*Encyclopedia Judaica* – CD-ROM Edition © Judaica Multimedia [Israel] Ltd.)

What is this: In a text held as sacred by both Jews and Christians, and continually affirmed and re-affirmed as contemporarily relevant, precedent for the waging of Holy War – *Jihad*? – against one's enemies to the point of extermination and sanctioned by the Divine? Can we today simply dismiss such passages as historical anachronisms bearing no relationship to our lives today? Not so, argues W. Gunther Plaut in *The Torah: A Modern Commentary*:

> The ancient Amalek has appeared and reappeared in Jewish history in many forms and guises: he wore the signet ring of the king as Haman; the royal crown as Antiochus; the general's uniform as Titus; the emperor's toga as Hadrian; the priestly robe as Torquemada; the Cossack's boots as Chmielnitzki; or the brown shirt as Hitler. All of them had in common their hatred of Jews and Judaism, and they all failed in their objective to crush the faith and the people of God.
> (W. Gunther Plaut, *The Torah: A Modern Commentary* [New York, NY: Union of American Hebrew Congregations, 1981] 514.)

No so argues Gary Rosenblatt's recent (February 8, 2002) column in *The Jewish Week* of New York:

> Today, alas, there appears to be no shortage of Amaleks in the world, from Saddam Hussein, who has pledged to wipe out Israel with weapons of mass destruction, to Osama bin Laden, who blames Israel for the evils of the world, to Yasir Arafat, whose campaign for Palestinian statehood, after decades of terrorism, includes ensuring that there is no Jewish state in the Mideast.

Thus, Amalek, whoever he was historically – and scholarly knowledge of the Biblical Amalek, the Amalekites, their king Agag, and the Agagites (including Haman himself in the Book of Esther) is by no means conclusive – remains the eternally contemporary enemy of Israel and the Jewish People, worthy of extermination by whatever means possible and viewed as an act of Divine favor. Could a Jewish People, therefore, not conclude in our post-*Shoah* world that the Nazis still alive today *and their descendants* – children and grandchildren – are Amalek? Could a Jewish People, given our 2000-year essentially negative history of Jewish-Christian encounter not conclude, therefore, that the early founders of Christianity *and their descendants* are Amalek? Could an Orthodox rightist Jewish community, not only those living in Israel at this moment but others as well, therefore, not conclude that *all* Arabs and *all* Palestinians are, therefore, Amalek in his present physical reincarnation? Could Christians not conclude that all those who *reject* the Christ as the one and only begotten Son of a God, given to humanity in love and murdered by it, are Amalek? Could Muslims living in the sanctified *Dar al-Islam* (the world of Islam) not conclude that those who are part of the unsanctified *Dar al-Harb* (the world of war) are Amalek?

Most disturbing, Jewishly, however, is the recent article by Reuven Firestone, Professor of Medieval Judaism and Islam at Hebrew Union College in Los Angeles, CA, and author of, among other books, *Jihad: The Origin of Holy War in Islam* (New York, NY: Oxford University Press, 1999), and, recently, *Children of Abraham: An Introduction to Judaism for Muslims* (Hoboken, NJ: Ktav Publishing, 2001). Entitled "Our Own House Needs Order," he writes:

> "Holy war" with all its connotations of mindless excess, fervent, and wild fanaticism, is not a Christian monopoly; the sooner Jews and Muslims acknowledge this fact, the better…Before dismissing the appalling behavior of our Muslim cousins engaged in holy war, let us put our own house in order. Holy war has been revived among Israel the people and within Israel the state. Why is *milhemet mitzvah/hovah* obligatory war? Because God-the-Commander (*haMetzaveh*) requires it…holy war has been revived in contemporary Israel, especially among ultranationalist Orthodox settlers in Judea and Samaria (the West Bank) and their many supporters. The war – and it may now be accurately called a war between Israel and the Palestinians – is defined by many religiously observant settlers and their supporters as a divine obligation to

reclaim the whole of the Land of Israel as either a prelude to or as actually part of the messianic awakening. Many in this camp cite *ad nauseum* the now famous statement of Nahmanides in his gloss on Maimonides' *Book of Commandments* (Positive Commandment 4), who teaches that the conquest and settlement of the Land of Israel lies in the category of obligatory war (*milhemet mitzvah*). "It is a positive commandment for all generations obligating every individual, even during the period of exile"...As Jewish holy war has entered religious and political discourse in relation to the Israel-Palestine conflict, so has the increase of Jewish atrocities in the name of a higher cause. It reached its peak in the mid-1980s to mid-1990s with the maiming and murder of Muslim non-combatants by the Jewish Underground, the massacre of Muslims in prayer by Barukh Goldstein, and Yigal Amir's assassination Prime Minister Yitzhak Rabin. Holy war ideas continue to inform the behavior of many religious settlers to this day, though there has been a concerted effort by both the Israel government and the settle movement to refrain from committing such blatant atrocities...We must neutralize if not eradicate the ugly and gravely dangerous revival of holy war within Judaism. The first step is to acknowledge its existence. The next is to engage in public discussion within our own community, especially among the spectrum of religious leaders, to mitigate the inherently self-destructive and ultimately immoral efforts to define our fighting with the Palestinians as a holy war.
(Reuven Firestone, "Our Own House Needs Order," www.shma.com/dec01/firestone.htm)

And the public debate rages on within the Jewish community. Witness, for example, the recently *New York Times Magazine* article by Jonathan Rosen "The Uncomfortable question of Anti-Semitism" (November 4, 2001), wherein he writes "I have awakened to anti-Semitism," and "Israel has somehow become an obstacle to war and an obstacle to peace simultaneously," and, more importantly,

...European anti-Semitism, which made the Holocaust possible, is still shaping the way Jews are perceived; Arab anti-Israel propaganda has joined hands with it and found a home in the embattled Muslim world...people who threaten evil intend evil.
(www.nytimes.com)

and the (*Wall Street Journal,* February 5, 2002) critically-negative and seemingly controversial response to Mr. Rosen's piece by Hillel Halkin, "The Return of Anti-Semitism: To be against Israel is to be against Jews:"

> ...one cannot be against Israel or Zionism, as opposed to this or that Israel policy or Zionist position, without being anti-Semitic. Israel is the state of the Jews. Zionism is the belief that the Jews should have a state. To defame Israel is to defame the Jews. To wish it never existed, or would cease to exist, is to wish to destroy the Jews...The new anti-Israelism is nothing but the old anti-Semitism in disguise...the moral undermining of Israel is anti-Semitism's primary goal. (www.wsj.com)[1]

Before addressing possible ways out of this nightmare of hostilely-competing visions of reality – Jewish, anti-Jewish; Christian, anti-Christian; Muslim, anti-Muslim; American, anti-American – we need add to our discussion of Hebrew Biblical texts two New Testament texts which are themselves emblematic of a Christian *weltanschauung,* world-view or perspective, alive and well for far too many in our midst, those of Matthew 10:34-39 and Luke 12:49-53.

Rejection of the Christ = Enemy of God!
It is my understanding that the coming or appearance of this Christ was that this loving Gift of a Divine Parent to redeem an unredeemed world was presented in peace, and only humanity's (read "Jews") rejection of him ultimately led to the warlike divisiveness of

---

[1]   Relevant to this entire discussion, therefore, is the rise of modern fundamentalism not only in Israel and Judaism, but both Christianity and Islam as well. See, for example, Karen Armstrong (2000) *The Battle for God* (New York, NY: Alfred A. Knopf); Karen Armstrong (2001) *Holy War: The Crusades and Their Impact on Today's World* (New York, NY: Random House); Paul Fregosi (1998), *Jihad in the West: Muslim Conquests from the 7th to the 21st Centuries* (Amherst, NY: Prometheus Books); Samuel P. Huntington (1996) *The Clash of Civilizations: Remaking the World Order* (New York, NY: Simon and Schuster); Bruce B. Lawrence (1989) *Defenders of God: The Fundamentalist Revolt Against the Modern Age* (New York, NY: I. B. Tauris); Ian S. Lustick (1988) *For the Land and the Lord: Jewish Fundamentalism in Israel* (New York, NY: Council on Foreign Relations); Laurence J. Silberstein (Ed.) (1993) *Jewish Fundamentalism in Comparative Perspective: Religion, Ideology, and the Crisis of Modernity* (New York, NY: New York University Press); Ehud Sprinzak (1991) *The Ascendance of Israel's Radical Right* (New York, NY: Oxford University Press).

our world today between the accepters of this Christ and the rejecters of this same Christ. Not so terribly different than the aforementioned division of the world, from a Muslim perspective, between the *Dar al-Islam* and the *Dar al-Harb*. Nor a Jewish perspective as referenced in Professor Firestone's article. Thus, properly understood, these two passages are not to be taken as an activist stance on the part of the Christ, but, rather, a description of the reality which will ensue once his messiahship is known and accepted by some (read "Gentiles and some Jews") and rejected by others (again, read "Jews"):

Matthew 10:34-39 .

"Do not think I have not come to bring peace but a sword. For I have come to set a man against his father, a daughter against her mother, and a daughter-in-law against her mother-in-law, and a man's enemies will be a member of his household. Whosoever loves father or mother more than me is not worthy of me, and whoever loves son or daughter more than me is not worthy of me. And whoever does not take up his cross and follow me is not worthy of me. Whoever finds his life will lose it, and whoever loses his life for me will find it." (The NET Bible [Dallas, TX: Biblical Studies Press) 1998.)

Luke 12:49-53

"I have come to bring fire on the earth – and how I wish it were already kindled! I have a baptism to undergo, and how distressed I am until it is finished! Do you think I have come to bring peace to earth? No, I tell you, but rather division. For from now on there will be five in one household divided, three against two and two against three. They will be divided, father against son and son against father, mother against daughter and daughter against mother, mother-in-law against her daughter-in-law and daughter-in-law against mother-in-law." (The NET Bible [Dallas, TX: Biblical Studies Press] 1998.)

Lest we Jews become too complacent in our reading of these two passages, and the two thousand-year-old enmity between Jews and Christians which flowed, in part, from a consistent classical commentary understanding of the Christ's words as activist rather than descriptive[2], consider the following two examples from our own Biblical and Talmudic literatures. Both are consistent with a rabbinic reading of what has been known in our Jewish Religious Tradition as the "birth pains of the messiah," the time *before* his actual appearance.[3]

The first is from the seventh chapter of the prophet Micah, verses one toseven, which Christians have seen as indicative of Jesus' initial travails among his fellow Jews, and Jews have understood as the initial problematic reception of the as yet-unnamed messiah:

> Woe is me! For I am like the last of the summer fruits, like the grape gleanings of the vintage; there is no cluster to eat, no ripe fruit which my soul desires. The good man has perished from the earth; and there is no one upright among men; they all lie in wait for blood; each man hunts his brother with a net. The hands are upon that which evil, the prince asks, and the judge asks for payment; and the great man utters the evil desire of his soul; thus they weave the web. The best of them is like a brier; the most upright is shaper than a thorn hedge; the day of your watchmen and your punishment comes; now shall their confusion come. Do not trust your friend; do not put your confidence in a guide; guard the doors of your mouth from her who lies in your bosom. *For the son dishonors the father, the daughter rises up against her mother, the daughter-in-law against her mother-in-law; a man's enemies are the men of his own house.* Therefore I will look to the Lord; I will wait for the God of my salvation; my God will hear me. Rejoice not against me, O my enemy; when I fall, I shall arise; when I sit in darkness, the Lord shall be a light to me.
> (*Bible Scholar* CD-ROM, Monsey, NY: Torah Educational Software)

The second example is from the Babylonian Talmud, Tractate Sanhedrin 97a:

---

[2] See, for example, the writings of Adam Clarke, Albert Barnes, Matthew Henry, among others, all which declare in commenting upon these passages the enmity which will exist between the followers of the Christ and the Jews who are, themselves, primarily culpable and responsible for his death.

[3] "Rabbinic writings also declare that suffering will herald the messianic age." W. F. Albright and C. S. Mann (1977), *Matthew: Introduction, Translation, and Notes* (Garden City, NY: Doubleday & Company), 132.

> It has been taught: R. Nehorai said, "In the generation
> when Messiah comes, young men will insult the old, and
> old men will stand before the young [to give them honor];
> daughters will rise up against their mothers, and daughters-
> in-law against their mothers-in-law. The people will be
> dog-faced, and a son will not be abashed in his father's
> presence."

Thus, Jews and Christians understood only too well that the
appearance of the messiah – either first visit or return visit – would be a
time of chaotic readjustment and social dislocation of the religious
community wherein he would reside.   Internally, the divisiveness
would result – as it did historically within the Jewish communities of
the past, for example, the tragic journey of Shabbtai Tzvi and his
followers in the early Middle Ages – between those who would line up
on the side of the messiah and those who would stand opposed. The
calamity, however, between Jews and Christians has been the Christian
reading of Jesus words as an activist agenda for his followers against
those who stood opposed to his and their messianic claims, rather than
a description of what, sadly, in all likelihood would happen and how
such pain could be alleviated. The contemporary tragedy of both the
Muslim versus non-Muslim and fundamentalist Jewish versus non-
fundamentalist Jewish and non-Jewish worlds has been their own
consistent bi-polarity, that is, their view of the world as "us versus
them," the enemy versus the family or friend of the family. How to
break this closed circle of paranoiac thinking amongst Jews, Christians,
and Muslims thus becomes the agenda for this twenty-first century,
even more imperative after September 11, 2001, than it was before.

"Covenants of Dialogue:" An Idea Whose Time Has Come
At the conclusion of his article "Amalek Today: Dealing With
Our Enemies," Gary Rosenblatt writes tantalizingly that "the struggle
to maintain humanity in the face of murderous foes remains." Other
than his comment that "Israel's army has a strict moral code, including
trying and disciplining offenders, in contrast to those who praise
suicide bombers as soldiers and martyrs and have no compunctions
about attacking women and children," he offers no positive suggestions
or additional thoughts. He is, however, correct: to maintain one's own
humanity in the face of the enemy – examples of which abound
throughout the time of the *Shoah* – is most assuredly in accord with the
ideals of all three religious traditions. To affirm the humanity of the
other in one's own presence, as an equal partner in the Divine-human

encounter, is far more difficult, examples of which are far more
sporadic throughout our history of interactions than our consistent
denigrations of the other and worse. Thus, I re-present an idea I first
expressed in my (1994) book *Rethinking Jewish Faith: The Child of a
Survivor Responds* (Albany, NY: State University of New York Press),
that of "covenants of dialogue:"

> If we are now to enter into religiously sensitive and
> renewable covenants, they must be with each other as
> individuals, as communities, as nation-states. Humanity
> having now actualized and demonstrated the potential to
> destroy larger and larger groups, we Jews (and I would add
> "we Christians and we Muslims") having now been the
> recipients of such destruction, together, we must guard
> against repetition by our continual willingness to engage in
> dialogue, despite our differences, even with those whose
> value systems we fundamentally reject. Historically and
> contemporarily, Russians and Americans, Jews and
> Christians, Jews and Jews, Jews and Arabs, Jews and
> Palestinians, Jews and Germans[4], Christians and Christians,
> Christians and Arabs, must, in fact, enter into "covenants of
> dialogue" to ensure the survival of all people on our planet.
> We *must* commit ourselves to searching out those who can
> best bring about such covenants of dialogue between
> seemingly disparate groups. Appeals to God will not make
> such dialogues possible, nor will appeals to historical
> relationships or nonrelationships. Only direct appeals to
> each other will. Our very survival depends on it. Notions
> of politics or "one-ups-person-ship" have no place
> whatsoever in such calls to "covenants of dialogue."
> Such dialogues, therefore and initially, require any number
> of difficult commitments, foremost among which is a
> radical rethinking of the whole notion of the "other." True,
> honest, and open dialogue among opposites now demands
> an intellectual, emotional, and spiritual integrity and
> respect more so than ever before. Group representatives
> must now meet as true equals with no so-called hidden
> agendas whatsoever. The purpose of all such "covenants of
> dialogue" is the mutual sharing of information and the
> setting forth of common agendas and agreements. Respect
> for differences in attitudes, perspectives, and orientations,

---

[4] Following the *fact* that, during the darkest days of the *Shoah,* representatives
of the organized worldwide Jewish community met with Nazi representatives in
an ultimately fruitless effort to save Jewish life, but they met nonetheless.

to problem solving must be affirmed no matter how difficult they at first appear.[5] (23-24; 27)

I, for one, see no alternative other than to continue this cycle of horrendous murderous deaths, distrust of the other, however defined, and a long dark night of violence as a prelude to global destruction.

---

[5] I have long, envisioned, for example, the creation of an Institute for Interreligious Understanding and Dialogue, associated with a college or university, that, through conferences and scholarly publications, would explore the difficulties and inherent tensions in all such dialogues.

Chapter 16 - The Genocidal Mind at the Heart of Our Religions
James Moore

The events of September 11th and the aftermath since then have made our task imperative. What good is our reflection together on texts if we do not face the urgencies of the present, the possibilities for violence that seem to recur year after year and find a home nearly everywhere on the globe. Even while addressing the key theme of violence and religion at this Scholars' Conference, we are also struck by the way that religion in the strangest ways has resurfaced as an essential factor for even the daily lives of people. Naturally, there are those for whom religion became an important source of strength and resolve in the face of threat. Yet, it is the sense that religion has power to provoke violence that has so captured our imagination. With that has come the clear and loud voices who wish to deny that "religions" are essentially about violence.

It is this loud denial that comes for many reasons, both internally religious and externally political, that strikes me mostly because of the way that the things that are said echo so much the reverberations of reflections about Christianity and the Shoah. Both of these phenomena are central to what has been the refrain on Christianity after the Shoah. Religion does have the power to provoke violence even if only and mostly in league with other political powers that aptly manipulate religious sentiment toward violence. And so many also want to argue that "Christianity" at its heart is something else altogether, a religion of mercy and love. The faces of violence are too clear in our vision, however. We cannot be easily fooled and hear once again the voice of Irving Greenberg who wonders emphatically whether Christianity is now so tainted that it would be next to impossible to reclaim its credibility, a thought he has recently restated even more strongly than in his classic essay of years ago.[1]

And so, with my colleagues, I go in search of the face of violence rooted at the core of our religious tradition and its sources, perhaps ideas too easily at times pushed aside or given a far too glib reinterpretation. This search is what takes us this year to the fate of Amalek and then with that to a difficult text from the Christian gospels, the words of Jesus proclaiming that he brings not peace but a sword. I am indebted to Zev Garber for his words written a few years ago on Amalek[2] which have provided many a striking discussion for my students in the Shoah class and some opportunity to reflect on these matters long before the events of September 11th. The shadowy figure of Amalek emerges over time as a symbol of the one completely beyond redemption, the evil one par excellence, the Judas, if you will, of the Hebrew scriptures. It is this assumption based on the texts of Exodus and Numbers that lead the narrators of Israel's history to call for the complete annihilation of the Amalekites in the name of God, a command that brought King Saul to ruin for his lack of obedience even though it was still carried forward by the Priest, prophet, man of God, Samuel, only to drive home the point that it has the full sanction of the divine. This is the tale we pursue with twists and turns that are surely surprising and disturbing. To this task we now turn.

Amalek

My aim as always is to show the midrashic interplay between texts. The root story of Amalek is the story of Exodus 17, the story of the battle between Amalek and Joshua which ends strangely with the curse, which is repeated in Deuteronomy 25. It is in Deuteronomy that we see clearly that the curse arises because Amalek "attacked you on the way, when you were faint and weary, and struck down all who lagged behind you..." (25:17) It is this reading of the narrative, that Amalek's attack was devious, coming from behind and against the weakest of the Israelites, whoever might be lagging behind, that becomes the basis for the general view of Amalek that he is certainly evil (he did not fear the LORD) and deserves utter annihilation. Of

[1] Greenberg, Irving, in Frymer-Kensky, Tikva, David Novak, Peter Ochs, David Fox Sandmel, and Michael A. Signer, ed. *Christianity in Jewish Terms (Radical Traditions)* New York: Westview Press, 2000.
[2] . Garber, Zev. *Shoah: The Paradigmatic Genocide.* Lanham, MD: University Press of America, 1994.

course, it is this eternal curse that haunts Saul in I Samuel 15, only to result in Saul's failure. It is this same image of the curse that extends to the tradition of Haman, the one who deceitfully plots against Queen Esther and is finally exposed and destroyed.

The structure of this narrative cycle is clear enough with the various components becoming within the Jewish tradition of thought and then later within some Christian thought a pattern for understanding theodicy, God's relation to evil. Still, the extreme evil of Amalek does not seem to be sufficient cause for the violence of God's command as later Rabbinic interpretation has it. (Montefiore and Rowe, 1974) The rabbis did not like the imputation of such violence to God. Thus they tended to make the narrative a metaphor of evil and God's command a symbol of the basic need to root out evil in our lives and communities. The actual genocidal command is modified in the later reading to be transformed into a form of self-examination. Such is the content of some rabbinic appeals to the symbol of Amalek, for example, in the post-September 11th American public reflection. Not so with some Christian websites in which the symbol of Amalek is directly applied to the actual threat of terrorism and some can talk of "Christian war." (for example the website christiananswers.net)

If the tendency in Midrash is to modify the violence of the narrative cycle, the problem certainly remains as we interpret the latter story involving Saul and Samuel. There can be no mistake that this narrative piece calls for the actual annihilation of the Amalekites, including the old, the women, the children. This is clearly a genocidal command. The rabbis tend to historicize this narrative by suggesting that the command was necessary as the subsequent generations of children would be so captured by the evil of their elders that they would be lost to God's redemption nevertheless. It is still difficult for the Rabbis to generalize on this command as, for them, God's intent cannot be genocide for every group seen as Israel's enemy.[3] Thus, the midrashic approach to material when applied to this text leads to a conclusion that God's intent must be for the redemption of all but the particular reading of this intent at a particular time in Israel's history led the leaders of the past to apply violence in the name of redemption. Later such an understanding of redemption would be rejected.

What is puzzling in this entire saga is that despite the Rabbinic rejection of violence in the name of redemption, the story of Amalek is

---

[3]Montefiore, C.G. and H. Loewe, ed. *A Rabbinic Anthology.* New York: Schocken Books, 1974.

reified in Israel's liturgical story. At least the cycle of remembering Israel's story includes a re-application of the symbol of evil (the Amalek symbol) in the figure of Haman. This symbol is then placed within a liturgical event in which the memory of animosity is retold year after year in the celebration of Purim. This reenactment of the symbol of evil seems rather innocuous since the event of Purim is cast as a lark with children playing out the scenes in comical response while the figure of Haman becomes something of an evil clown. Strangely this joyous celebration of redemption apparently so casts the evil symbol in frivolity that the whole meaning of animosity (thus, the genocidal command) is tempered into a morality play. But is it?

Social Speciation

I would take the cue here and pause for a moment in this midrashic reading to borrow an analysis that was developed jointly by Erik Erickson and his son Kai.[4] Erickson offered an interpretive tool for understanding the ages long practice of cultures in which the most probable enemy, likely the most likely competitor for power in a region, is set apart as a separate species, as if. The other becomes not us and with that not fully human. The harsh sense of not belonging to the group so characteristic of the ancient world (banishment would surely mean vulnerability, even death, as with the figure Cain in Genesis 4) actually would mean that the other as not us becomes the other as enemy and, thus, subject to attack. The act of speciation (Erickson labeled this pseudo-speciation since the act of so labeling another human group as such separated humans who were "naturally" part of the same species) allows for treating the other as not human or sub-human.

The argument is really two-fold. First Erickson wants to indicate that humans, through a social necessity, are historically inclined to do this (perhaps even as a response to mere survival) and secondly that this practice is widespread, both temporally and spatially. The son, Kai Erickson, in an effort to focus attention on the social mechanisms of this process, asked rather whether this should be called social speciation. And what sort of social mechanisms could become ways to accomplish this form of speciation? Surely one powerful form would be to incorporate the matter into the religious story of the people

---

[4] Strozier, Charles B. and Michael Flynn, ed. *Genocide, War, and Human Survival* (Lanham, MD: Rowman & Littlefield , 1996.)

and then to ritualize the memory. Even with the later Rabbinic abhorrence at the genocidal implications of the Amalek image, the practice of social speciation had already been integrated into Israel's memory. It has been ritualized, even if we argue in this comical farce of Purim.

A Shoah Midrash

Even with the re-reading of the Amalek cycle of texts in the later Rabbinic material, the presence of this symbol of genocide in the Torah narrative is alarming. The question becomes, as we have asked in this group so often, whether this narrative can be read as such "in the presence of the one million burning children." [5] This is a text that surely qualifies as one that cannot be read with the same intent as it has in the past since it so configures the process of racial speciation that was the rule that marked so many for death in the Shoah. It is even more alarming that it is the configuration of a narrative that sets the pattern for the farcical liturgy of Purim for which the participation of children is so obviously intended. And is there an effort to re-think this story in the light of the Shoah? Actually, my memory informs me that many synagogues do replay this narrative with post-Shoah themes.

But as we are thinking about this point, we are confronted immediately by the very morality play that was later to be rejected by the Rabbis. Indeed, even as we are worried about the ritualizing of genocide in the stories of Purim, we are also clearly led to the doorstep of another reading. Indeed, can we not say that in the Nazi machine, in the Shoah itself, we have met the very figure of Amalek. Would we now change our mind about the linking a genocidal approach to the divine command, that the memory of these Nazi perpetrators be wiped out, obliterated completely? If there is a divine cammand that comes from Auschwitz as Emil Fackenheim posed, and if this is more than mere survival of the people as Fackenheim argued, then would it not be the replay of Amalek in the just cause of bringing the Nazis to their end. [6]

Indeed, this notion comes close to the heart of the meaning of "never again." If we mean by the pledge that we are to fight and to put to an end every possible genocide, don't we mean to say that we are to

---

[5] Greenberg, Irving. In John K. Roth and Michael Berenbaum, ed. *Holocaust : Religious and Philosophical Implications.* (New York: Paragon House, 1989)
[6] Fackenheim, Emil. *God's Presence in History.* New York: Harper Collins, 1972.

rid the world of evil? Is this not the very argument that has been thrust before us as "the American" thing to do in the aftermath of September 11th? It seems a copy of the same argument and the pillars of the religions are even in a memory play of the prophet Samuel called to justify this "holy war." I doubt that we would have such arguments so successfully presented to us by political, community and religious leaders if it were not for our memory of Auschwitz. Even so, we may reject this ploy but still see that the Shoah has radically changed our point of view. Does the Shoah justify in a way seemingly utterly justifiable the use of violence to destroy the evil enemy?

I doubt that we can accept such an argument in the name of our sacred texts. Justice cannot be reduced to vigilantism and the desire to confront evil with justice is not the same as the genocidal mind that seeks to obliterate all of the other from the face of the earth. And we must be cautious in employing such arguments since the need to face up to evil is too important as a modern question for us to be drawn into the rhetoric of politicized holy wars and allow the religious establishment to be used once again for such ends. As much as we remember the atrocities of the perpetrators, we also remember that we hope for another way, not the way of revenge that only seeks to continue the evil practice itself of social speciation.

Thus, we have to be careful about the image of the evil one so embedded in our stories. As a Christian, I know the horrid theological twists that can be offered in so labeling the Jews.[7] So we cannot tolerate such a model of thinking. We need to challenge the image of Amalek and this narrative for it cannot be a religious word said in our post-Shoah world. Now let me say one more thing since the implication is so troubling. We do not really know who the Amalekites were. It is so convenient to argue that this is a mystery tribe of people. It is so easy to universalize the image because of this. Nevertheless, we know that the apparent referent is to a group who inhabited the territory between the Sinai and the Arabian peninsula. That is, they seem to inhabit a territory identical to the land of the Ishmaelites. Now is it so coincidental that the ancestors of the modern Arabic peoples were associated in this narrative with the symbol of Amalek? We are led to question the actual story itself if this is indeed the etymology. It is even more troubling that such a symbol can survive into our time.

---

[7]   Moore, James. *Christian Theology after the Shoah.* (Lanham, MD: University Press of America, 1993.)

The Christian Narratives

My search does not indicate any obvious connection between the stories of Amalek and any of the narratives of the Christian texts. The model of the deceiver who attacks by surprise seems reminiscent of the story of Judas and such an examination could be quite fruitful. On the other hand, the narrative about Judas in its various versions in the Christian gospels is by no means so clear as I have argued in previous materials. And there is not clear evidence that Christians made a connection between Amalek and Judas. Thus, my Midrashic reading takes another turn, not to find obvious links but to uncover the Midrashic intent of the Christian narratives, particularly in the way this is recorded as a teaching of Jesus.

I am, therefore, drawn to another set of texts that seem to be a reflection on the tradition of theodicy that is reflected in the Amalek cycle. Jesus is recorded in both Matthew and Luke talking about what he is bringing to the earth with his teaching. The comparison of these two texts is instructive in itself. In Luke (12:51-53), the words of Jesus are clear. He brings division and this division is not only general (insiders and outsiders as I noted in another paper a couple of years ago) but in the family – literally fathers against sons and daughters against mothers, etc. The text in Luke is followed by a reference to an apocalyptic vision in which the images appear to be those applied to the "day of the Lord." Thus, the commentators tend to take this text and apply the images not to the present effect of Jesus' teaching but rather to the end times, to the judgment. The text is, thus, modified in its intensity since the actual divisions brought seem only apparent, according to this reading, at the end of time.

If this is the case, then the model presented here might be a modification of the sort of theodicy represented by texts like that of Amalek. The aim here seems to be cautious even as it is inflammatory since the end result would be that we cannot act to sort out the divisions now since the signs only become clear with the coming of the end days. Applied generally to a morality, the result might be quite contrary to the opening phrase of this section in which Jesus argues, according to this text, that he does not bring peace. But, there is no apparent command here (except to be a follower), no divine sanction for action since the divisions apparently emerge spontaneously as a result of a response to the person and teaching of Jesus.

The Matthean text (10:34-36) is, however, different. Though repeating the form of Luke's version, Matthew adds that Jesus brings not peace but a sword. Obviously, this alteration of the narrative can also be tempered and universalized. It can also be attached to the end of time except that the Matthean context does not follow with apocalyptic images and is rather directly put into the context of the actual decision to follow the lead of Jesus. Thus, the addition of the word sword makes a real difference in meaning since for this Jesus the result is in the present and is linked directly with Jesus, so much for the often voiced claim that the God of the Christian texts is a God of peace and the God of the Hebrew texts is a God of just violence. Such stereotypes abound and are simply not supported by the actual texts.

Now two disclaimers can be offered at the outset. First, we have all tried vigilantly to recast Jesus as the Jewish teacher and thus we cannot allow ourselves to lose sight of that goal and take these words outside of the Jewish context in which this Jesus appears to be a dramatic voice for reform. That he speaks in such harsh terms does not make him completely unique in this context. Of course, we have no idea just what words can actually be attributed to this Jesus, which is our second caution. Especially in a case as this, we are alerted to the likelihood that both the author of Luke and the author of Matthew have adjusted whatever memory of Jesus' teaching is recorded in these texts in order to address a particular contemporary concern in the church or in the wider community. In fact, Matthew's image might well reflect an awareness of threats of violence already emerging and most commentators on this gospel narrative have shown that the audience was likely already a divided church or set of churches. [8] Thus, the actual situation may well mark divisions, but not so much in families per se but in the churches. Such a reading would also change our reading of this text as a Midrash.

On the other hand, I am not so convinced by efforts to retrieve meaning in texts since we are in fact left with the narratives we have and these are the narratives that have influenced the teaching of the churches through the ages. And we have in this Matthean text a significant new element added to the sort of theodicy that we find in the Amalek cycle. Matthew's Jesus makes the deceiver out to be an insider (indeed, the Rabbis already recognized that early Christians were making the effort to identify Amalek as a Jew).[9] The immediate implication of this move is that the insider becomes the most evil one,

---

[8] Kingsbury, Jack Dean. *Matthew : structure, christology, kingdom.* (London: SPCK, 1968.)
[9] Ibid. Montefiore and Rowe.

the one set on destroying God's people and God's purposes. The implication here is similar to the abominable texts in John 8.

A Shoah Midrash Once More

The full implication of the Matthean extension of a theodicy of genocide plays itself out as a motif behind much of what we see as a religious justification of killing the other. The move to see the evil one as the one inside, the betrayer, adds fuel to the already combustible narrative. The image of the fifth column, the betrayal from the trusted one (the family member) is precisely the scenario of the Nazi narrative about the Jews after the First World War. Is it so surprising that theologians lent their support to this line of thinking? It is surprising only if we do not recognize the long tradition that lurks within the texts of the Christian religious tradition. Add to this sense of betrayal the charge of Deicide, and the justification for elimination of the Jew is made complete.

Thus, we are not able to tolerate letting this text stand either, and we are not so impressed with the possibilities of either making the whole a metaphor of the judgment or universalizing the idea as any betrayal. Surely a similar set of myths allowed the Hutu majority to justify murder of their Tutsi neighbors while the clergy stood by and at times directly participated.[10]   The point is that this line of thinking, so characteristic of Christianity in its history, is at the heart of the genocidal mind and fully unleashes genocidal actions in the name of a righteous God.

Thus, I am now at the point of extending our Midrash. We have tried to carry out the task of doing a midrashic reading of our texts over the last decade with special attention to reading our texts post-Shoah. Now we know as we have always known I imagine that violence is not peripheral to religion nor is it simply a poor interpretation and/or implementation of our traditions. The potential for genocide is at the center of the claim to truth that has motivated the Christian witness and mission from the first century on. Thus, we cannot move forward toward our promise, our pledge, of never again without disowning this claim, openly refusing to let protection of the church's future be our aim. We need to find another way.

---

[10] Gourevitch, Philip. *We Wish to Inform You That Tomorrow We Will be Killed With Our Families: Stories from Rwanda.* (New York: Picador USA, 1999.)

The Way Forward

Of course, the church will survive and our voices pointing to the violence within our traditions will hardly be heard in the din of those calling for retribution and talking about an axis of evil. But we must try to point to another way. Above all we have argued from the outset for a truly midrashic approach that refuses to claim any interpretation as "the truth." The fact is that we know of the ambiguity in our texts and we know of the plurality of possible meanings. But now we must claim this principle as a rule for us, that no text from our traditions that sustains the exclusive claim to having the right answer, knowing the truth can be accepted as a legitimate expression of our Christian identity. Thus, we will strive vigorously for accepting disagreement not as a measure of betrayal or heresy in whatever way we might see this expressed but rather as a healthy expression of our being human, our being Christians and Jews in this world.

Of course, we reject the theodicy of genocide and even those attempts to re-interpret the ideas for the ritualizing of violence in these narratives have already had their effect despite our interpretations. Instead, we must eliminate this effort to label the other as evil and rather see that matters of justice are matters not of labels applied to peoples but rather of accountability for our individual actions. It is this religiously supported form of social speciation that is clearly at the heart of the genocidal mind and this we must diligently expose and reject.

Of course, the way forward for us is to cross the boundaries that we have so falsely created through our myths and meet each other as we have tried to model in these dialogues, face to face. Dialogue is the way or as we see the larger implications of this genocidal theodicy, a multilogue, that draws us together in our plurality. And so we will say, you may have seen that we have come to bring the sword and division, but I tell you that from this day forward we come to bring peace. And I say it again, shalom.

Chapter 17 - Deconstructing Theodicy and Amalekut: A Personal Apologia
Zev Garber

I. Theodicy

In the theistic theology of Jews and Christians, God is seen as all powerful, all-wise, completely benevolent. all-caring, and all-love. But evil exists in His world created from nothingness and how to reconcile the goodness of God in spite of the presence of evil?

Three centuries before the Christian era, the Greek pagan philosopher Epicurus stated the problem of theodicy (from the two Greek words, god and justice) in terms that gods cannot or will not prevent evil. If the gods cannot prevent evil, they are not omnipotent. If the gods will not prevent evil, then they are not omnibenevolent. And if the gods are not limited in either power or benevolence, why is there evil in the world?

In a popular college text, *Exploring the Philosophy of Religion*[1], editor, David Stewart suggests that thereare two types of evil in the world: natural and moral. Natural evil refers to those elements of nature which -cause pain and suffering to human beings, such as natural disaster, disease and death. Moral evil is suffering brought about by human perversity, and history testifies that human beings are capable of causing great physical and psychological pain to their fellows, which makes natural evil pale in comparison.

Stewart further points out that these two kinds of evil challenge important theistic teachings on the nature of God's management of the world. Natural evil raises questions about the order of nature and moral evil raises questions about human nature. In both cases, the

---

[1] David Stewart, ed., *Exploring the Philosophy of Religion* (New Jersey: Prentice Hall. 1988), pp. 254-261.

question for the Jew and Christian is why God allows a world such as ours to exist.

> Why does the natural order produce human suffering? Could God have created the world in such a way that it would not produce events that cause human suffering? If so, why did God not? The question posed by moral evil is why God allows us to inflict misery and suffering on others. Could God have created free beings who nonethelessa,ouid not produce misery and suffering for their fellow human beings? (cited in D. Stewart, *loc. cit.*, p. 246)

The fundamental evil of human nature permeates the novels of Fyodor Dostoevsky (*The Brothers Karamazov*, *Crime and Punishment*, and others). who asks why does God let children suffer? Rabbi Milton Steinberg in his classic, *Basic Judaism*[2], posits if God is why is the world not better? Why is it so marred and weighted down with disorder and suffering that it seems at times not the handiwork of a God of goodness but the contrivance of a fiend? Also, radical Christian theologian, A. Roy Eckardt, sensing the silence of God during the Shoah, questions if God is alive and not dead, then how can He live with Himself knowing that millions of Jews, including 1.5 million children, were murdered so cruelly in Hitler's inferno.

The attempts to answer the question of theodicy, in rabbinic terms. why the good suffer and the wicked prosper, match the moral and metaphysical nuances of the question itself. In the end, modernist Rabbi Steinberg comments, evil is inscrutable, an enigma. beyond unraveling, to which the answer, if any, is known to God Himself. This is the purport of the rabbinic epigram: "It is not in our power to explain the tranquility of the wicked or the suffering of the upright."

The traditionalist Jew, however, goes one epoch backward and thus one step further. For him, the question of theodicy is the question of anthropodicy (evil by man):

> The Rock, His work is perfect.
> For all His ways are justice.
> A God of faithfulness and without iniquity, just and right is He.
> Is corruption His? No His children's is the blemish;

---

[2] Milton Steinberg, *Basic Judaism* (New York: Harcourt, Brace and tiaid, 1947), pp. 53-57.

A generation crooked and Perverse.
Do you requite the Lord,
O foolish people and unwise?
Is He not thy father that has gotten thee?
Has He not made thee. and established thee?
(Deut 32:4.6)

Free will and man's ability to discern right from wrong are implicit in the doctrine of anthropodicy. Without this Power, man cannot be responsible for his actions and the fabric of society will dissolve into chaos and anarchy.[3]

In Jewish theology, strict traditionalists believe that the dire effects of antisemitism and Shoah are caused by Israel's own backsliding:

> And the Lord said unto Moses: You are soon to lie with your fathers. This people will thereupon go astray after alien gods in their midst, in the land which they are about to enter; they will forsake Me and break My covenant which I made with them. Then My anger will flare up against them. and I will abandon them and hide My countenance from them, They shall be ready prey; and many evils and troubles shall befall them. And they shall say on that day, . 'Surely it is because our God is not in our midst that these evils have befallen us.
>
> (Deut 31:16-17)

The antidote to "the lure of strange nations and trust in them"(Targun, Onqelos for "go(ing) astray after alien gods in their midst") is strict adherence to the Torah, teshuvah-returning to its teachings, leaming and passing on its moral Precepts (Deut 3 1: I 9). For the righteous who follow rhe Torah way, the Deuteronomist proclaims:

> The secret things belong unto the Lord our God;
> but the things that are revealed belong unto us
> and our children (these words are dotted) forever.
> that we may do all the words of this Torah.
> (Deut 29:28)

---

[3] See Deut 30:15-20; and especially, verses 15 and 19.

In discerning a suitable hermeneutic for the *puncta extraordinaria,* we *suggest, why* do the righteous suffer? Do we parse the verse and connect "revealed things," with God, there suggesting that He alone knows why mortality suffers?; or are the overt acts' doing Torah, which are not capable in preventing suffering by the righteous? On this verse biblical exegesis and homiletical eisegesis and *form* a circle – a theodicy circle.

II- Jewish Theodicy

In recent years, a number of thinkers and politicians has suggested a variant to classical theodicy: *Jewish* theodicy. In their view, the problem of evil for Jews is group oriented; the paramount effect of antisemitism, the Shoah, and threats to the sovereignty of Israel. Inthistheodicy, Jews are always innocent victims Of hatred and violence.

John Murray Cuddihy- Professor *of Sociology* at Hunter college of the, City University of New York, comments that religious and secular Jews alike see themselves as a small, weak, good group dispersed among a large, strong, bad group (the nations), which consistently and persistently victimizes them. Further, the Jewish People considers itself blameless and sinned against *by* other groups, itself not sinning against them.[4]

Thus, many liberation theologians[5] maintain that the Zionist action in Palestine created a stateless people, who in turn, blame the

---

[4] John Murray Cuddiiy, "'The Elephant and the Angels, Or, The Uncivil Irritatingness of Jewish Theodicy," in *Uncivil Religion: Interreligious Hostility in America,* edited by Robert N. Bellah and Frederick E. Greenspahn (New York: Crossroads, 1987), pp. 23-37.

[5] Exempli gratia. Rosemary Radford Reuther and Hertnan J. Reuther. *The Wrath of Jonah* (Harper and Row, 1989) and Marc Ellis, *Beyond Innocence and Redemption: Confronting the Holocaust and Israeli Power - Creating a Moral Future for the Jewish People* (Harper and Row. 1990). R. Reuther and Ellis strongly advocate Arab and Palestinian views in academic symposiums highly critical of Zionist respectability and Israeli responsibility. Case in point. Liberation Theologies Group section of the AAR Annual Meeting (November 19.1989) in Anaheim. CA, and Symposium on "The Role of America Religious Leaders in the Middle East Peace Process," held at

Jews and the Israelis, and how does Jewish theodicy respond? They blame the victims, the Palestinians, and see nothing hypocritical or irrational in this.

Similarly, Black antisemitism is wrong but Jewish racism is equally repugnant. Also, Jews have an obligation to understand Christian categories of forgiveness (Waldheim affair Auschwitz Convent) and theology of suffering (New York Cardinal John O'Connor's conviction that the Jewish suffering in the Shoah is seen as"gift to humanity) before reacting to them with denunciations in the media. In short, Jewish theodicy is preventing many Jews *from* seeing their own faults and wrongly perceiving the Jews as blameless and benevolent as God *Himself* is supposed to be in the dilemma of classical theodicy.

Are the proponents of Jewish theodicy fair in their assessment of Jewish group behavior? We think not, and let us explain.

Jewish Racism. An enforced negativism against black people is not the problem; it never has been. Afro-Americans have never suffered at the hands of Jews. Individuals, yes; but en masse, the issue is not Jewish racism: The issue is what it has always been, racism and the oppression, of black people by a racist system; a system which Jews did not create and are themselves a perennial victim.

For example. the accusation heard at the NAACP Los Angeles Convention (Summer 1990). that Jewish racism limits the Afro-American in the film industry, is unfounded.

True. Jews built the "dream factory" and are well positioned behind the scenes. It was, however, in response to antisemitism in WASP America that immigrant Jews built an empire of their own. Likewise in the areas of banking, insurance, hospitals, higher education, private clubs, etc. Second class Jewish "greeners" came to America and proved that they are as able and capable as first class blue blooded aristocracy. Further, on the silver screen, proper Jewish types are minted as frequently as the buffalo nickel.

Some black leaders on the Mideast and Black-Jewish relations appear self-righteous and arrogant. From Bishop Tutu to

---

Marquette University in Wisconsin (November 7. 1990). On the latter symposium, see American-Arab Affain. Fall 1990. pp. 53-103.

Jesse Jackson, we hear that Jews must show more sensitivity and be prepared for more consultation before taking positions contrary to the best interests of the Afro-American community.

But American Jewish Black writer and educator, Jules Lester (previously an accuser of Jewish racism and now a victim of black antisemitism[6]) writes:

> While I understand that such a statement (Jewish racism) comes from years of anger at active Jewish opposition to affirmative action, and how deeply Blacks were hurt by this opposition to what was in our "best interests," Black leadership still seems to be ignorant of the fact that Jews have been hurt by Black indifference to the fate of Israel.
>
> *(Jerusalem Post,* November 6,1979)

Ethnocentric insensitivity knows no discrimination; it lives in everybody's neighborhood and traverses everyone's group line.

Christian Reconciliation. Jewish leadership welcomes the attempts of rapproachment made by the Church to the Jewish people. Recent announcements from the Vatican and the World Council of Churches Protestant) condemn antisemitism from any source, person, and place; recognize the biblical source for Jewish attachment to Eretz Israel (but not necessarily the style of Israel); and confirm the "inextricable connection" between Israel and the Shoah.

These are among the first fruits of a fruitful dialogue between Jewish and Christian communities of faith. However, Christian protagonists of Jewish theodicy must understand that many Jews feel that these official announcements are from Christians "at their best."

Hear the perspective from respected Protestant theologian, Robert McAfee Brown, writing in *Christianity and Crisis* (October 23, 1989):

> But Christians are not usually "at their best,"and so to Jews the cross almost immediately became a symbol not of divine love but of the very human hatred it was meant to overthrow. Ample historical evidence over two millennia

---

[6] As told in his autobiography. *Lov~g: Becoming a Jew* (New York: Henry Holt and Company, 1988).

confirms the tragic accuracy of their perception. Very early in its history, the Christian church, in the name of the one who died on the cross, took the cross and made it a symbol, in Christian hands, not of love but of conquest and terror - a symbol in the name of which Christians felt mandated to force "conversions" from Jews, subject them to ghettoization, bloody pogroms, and outright murder. With that record, Christians should not be surprised when the presence of a cross suggests to others, and particularly to Jews, a deity who is at least in complicity with human evil if not the direct inspirer of it.

The jury is out while Jewry waits and sees if the Church can match deeds with creeds, e.g.. move the cross from the Carmelite convent at Auschwitz; officially recognize the State of Israel and Jerusalem, its capital; and excommunicate Nazi murderers, alive and dead.

Jewish 'self-centeredness' is the right way when Christian divines advise Jews to practice a theology of forgiveness, and to forget the perpetrators of the Shoah.

For example, A.C.J. Phillips, Chaplain of St. John's College, Oxford, commented on the Jewish advocacy against Bitberg Sunday thus: "In remembering the Holocaust, Jews hope to prevent its recurrence: by declining to forgive, I fear that they unwittingly invite it."[7] This statement, typical of counsel from many Christian friends, occupies the moral high ground of which Jews are accused, and put frankly, it is obscene.

Palestinianism. The Israeli-Palestinian conflict is not only an issue of economics, politics and militarism. It is an ideological one as well. Jews have every right to question the tendency among Arab intellectuals, who accept unequivocally the adverse teachings against the Jews (Christian "teaching of contempt" literature: czarist *Protocols of Zion*; Hitler's *Mein Kampf*, etc.), and then proceed to fabricate evidence in the *Qur'an* and *Shari'a* to support them.

---

[7] Cited in Alice L. Eckardt and A. Roy Eckardt, *Long Night's Journey into Day* (Detroit: Wayne State University Press, 1988), p. 173.

This misanthropy, deicide, blood libel and other deep-rooted prejudicial fears and accusations are read into the *Qur'an*, the Tradition and the Commentaries by revisionist historians, theologians and politicians.

Anti-Jewish sentiments in Islam may be traced scripturally to Koranic injunctions which see the Jews as a people who do eveil, and politically to the Pact of Omar issued in the seventh century, which recognizes freedom of religion of Jews, in exchange for high taxation and a host of discrminatory laws. These include a halt in synagogue building and the wearing of distinctive dress to ostracize Jews from Islamic society. Yet the measures against the Jews were less extreme than in medieval Christian Europe because Judaism was portrayed as unimportant and Jews, who lacked political and military power, offered no threat to the Islamic state.

Historically, Jews were not forced to convert to Islam, nor is there any record of state-sponsored slavery and genocide of the Jews. Consequently, Jews felt more at ease under the Crescent than the Cross. Signficantly, Jewish tribes aided Mohammed, assisted the Moslems in their wars against Christians, particularly in Egypt, Tunisia and Spain during the High Middle Ages (900-1200 CE). Unfortunately, humanism and tolerance were replaced by regidity and religiosity from the thirteenth century on, and Jews were prohibited from many trades and guilds, forced into hated professions, e.g., moneylending, and placed in mellahs, created ostensibly to protect Jews, but in reality self-contained ghettos which restricted them from social contact with Moslems.

In due time, Judaism became a despised faith, and Jews suffered from public humiliation. Norman A. Stillman reports in his history and source book, *The Jews of Arab Lands* (Jewish Publication Society of America, 1980), that in some communities Jews had to walk barefoot and in others they were required to wear metal rings around their necks so that they could be isolated at the public bathhouse. Turning inward to Jewish spiritual and messianic tendencies provided some relief, and when western secularism penetrated the Arab world in the nineteenth century, many Jews gladly followed its beacon of light. Arab Jews educated in western mores, languages, education, and mindsets were tolerated but seen as a third column in the reawakening of Arab values and nationalism beginning in the nineteenth century. The successful rise of modern-day political Zionism, advocating freedom, equality, independence and sovereignty of the Jewish people in its historic homeland of Eretz Israel, confronted the geographical dominance of pan-Arabism in all countries from the Mediterranean to the Indian Ocean.

The rise of the Jewish state in 1948 and the succession of Israeli victories in Arab-Israeli wars, including the Six Day War of 1967 which resulted in the establishment of Israeli/Jewish/Zionist authority over a significant Arab population, exacerbated Arab stereotype of the Jew. How So? The Jew is seen as greedy, cunning, cowardly -- the trait goes back to *Qur'an* -- and lacking in the basic Allah-given virtues of self-respect and self-defense. Then how to explain Israeli victories?

In his important work, *Semites and Anti-Semites: An Inquiry into Conflict and Prejudice*, Professor Bernard Lewis opines that the Arab views the Jews as "the sons of Satan. exercising demonic powers, engaged in a conspiracy against mankind extending through the millennia and across the world ... The struggle against such an adversary gives cosmic stature to those who engage in it, and lends some dignity even to these who suffer a defeat, which. they firmly believe, can only be temporary."[8]   Shades indeed of vitriolic pagan, Christian and Nazi antisemitism.

In summation, we may say that the conflict of nationalisms is the contributing factor to today's animosity and strife between Israeli and Palestinian, and by extension, Jew and Moslem. The 1989-90 ballots for Allah in Algeria, Tunisia, Kuwait, Jordan, Egypt, and Iran have brought fundamentalists to the streets shouting,"Oh, Jews! The army of Mohammed will return!" But Islamic antisemitism ascribes to the Jews a quality of' world-historical cosmic evil which zealously precipitates ugly fratricidal features. Consider, too, the platforms of two vying factions of the Palestine National Movement, PLO and Hamas, expressing the eradication of the Jewish state by armed Palestinian struggle.[9]

---

[8] Bernard Lewis, *Semites and Anti-Semites* (New York: W.W. Norton, 1986), P. I 9 1.

[9] *The Covenant of the Islamic Resistance Movement* (Hamas) proclaims in part:
Our struggle against the Jews is very sad and very serious.
It needs all sincere efforts. The Islarmc Resistance Movement is but one squadron that should be supported... It strives to raise the, banner of Allah

The Israeli/Jew after Auschwitz reacts in brash, non-conforming terms because he knows well the long night's journey into hell. To defend oneself, honor and homeland when attacked is not wrong. It is the right thing to do. Are Palestinians choosing differently in their much publicized campaign of Intifada? 'Jewish theodicy' like the Shoah is not a problem. It is the mindset of genteel Gentile critics who cannot accept fully Jews as Jews.

If this fact cannot be faced, then there is little else to be said. It is this which Jewish people understand. If there are caring and empathetic criticism of the Jews, let the voices be heard. All we hear is silence, accusation, indifference and hypocrisy.

If that is all there is going to be, then Bilaam's words are starkly true. Israel "is a people that dwells apart, and not to be reckoned among nations" (Num 23:9).

The Jews may not be blameless but they are certainly not guilty. Jews are not like most people: Good, yes but evil, no.

III. Genocide: Commandment 604

The Sabbath before Purim, designated as Shabbat Zachor, confronts the traditional Jew, who is committed to living within the

---

over every inch of Palestine... it is one of the links in the chain of the struggle against the Zionist invaders...
The Prophet, Allah bless him and grant him salvation, has said:
The Day Of Judgement will not come about until Moslems fight the Jews (killing the Jews), when the Jew will hide behind stones and trees. The stones and trees will say, ..there is a Jew behind me, come and kill him"...
There is no solution for the Palestine question except through Jihad.
Initiatives, proposals and international conferences are all a waste of time and vain endeavors. Palestine is an Islamic land.
PLO Covenant Against Israel. Article 21, reads:
> The Palestinian Arab people, in expressing itself through the armed Palestinian revolution, rejects every solution that is a substitute for a complete liberation of Palestine, and rejects all plans that aim at the settlement of the Palestine issue or its internationalization.

In their mutual desire to liberate the --Islamic Homeland," PLO and Hamas are credited with at least two-thirds of the violent Palestinian deaths in the territories since the start of the Intifada. Among the victims, moderate Palestinians in favor of a peaceful resolution of the Israeli-Palestinian conflict.

bonds of Halachah (Jewish law), a system of divinely inspired biblical commandments, as well as rabbinic decrees and derivations, with a paradoxical dilemma. On the one hand, as a survivor of a state-sponsored policy of genocide, he is a strong supporter of the United Nations Genocide Convention. Also, moral and ethical concern for other families of man is demanded by the repeated biblical injunction: "Remember, you were slaves in the Land of Egypt" (Lev 19.34, and elsewhere).

On the other hand, this same Jew is confronted with an explicit Mitzvah the 604th - to commit genocide:

> Remember what Amalek did unto these by the way as you came forth out of Egypt: how he met you by the way, and smote the hindmost of you, all that were enfeebled in thy rear, when you were faint and weary-. and he feared not God. Therefore, it shall be, when the Lord your God had given you rest from all your enemies round about, in the land which the Lord your God gives you for an inheritance to possess it, that you shall blot out the remembrance of Amalek from under heaven; you shall not forget. (Deut 25:17-19)

Other tribes have warred against Israel - Edomites, Moabites, Ammonites, Egyptians, and others - but none have been totally rejected or stigmatized by divine decree for eternal genocide and damnation .

Could it be because Amalek "feared not God" and could not be like others, who after a period of moral regeneration are accepted into the Household of Israel?   Contrast Deuteronomy 25:19 and Deuteronomy 23:8-9.

In rabbinic literature, Amalek is shown as a paradigm of absolute wickedness and evil, destroyer and rejecter of all that God and man leave wrought.[10]   Thus. the Halachic Jew, were he to be confronted with a *bona fide* descendant of Amalek, would be duty - bound to kill him/her forthwith without the necessity or requirement to obtain a mandate from any rabbinical court.

---

[10] Cf. Pesikta Rabbati 12:47; Pesikta de R. Kahana 27; Exodus Rabbah 26:2.3; Numbers Rabbah 13:3; Sifrei, Numbers 84, Lamentations Rabbah 3: 64,66; Mehilta, Amalek, etc.

How does one balance Abraham's agonizing plea over the fate of Sodom and Gomorrah, "Shall not the Judge of all the earth do justly?" (Gen 18:25) and the divine injunction of the descendants of Abraham "to do righteousness and justice" *(loc. cit.,* verse 19), with this imperative:

> Write this for a memorial in the book. and rehearse it in the ears of Joshua: for I will utterly blot out the remembrance of Amalek from under heaven. And Moses built an altar, and called the name of it A-nai-nisi. And he said: "The hand upon the throne of the Lord: the Lord will have war with Amalek from generation to generation." (Exod 17:14-16)

Any attempt at understanding this warrant for genocide against the Amalekites and their descendants must start with knowledge of the biblical texts, in conjunction with known historical data.

The Bible records the collective life of the Amalekites from the days of the Exodus (mid-thirteenth century BCE) till the time of King Saul (1020-1005). The tribe inhabited the Sinai peninsula in the region of Kadesh (Gen 14:2) as far to the south as Shur (I Sam 15:7; 27:18), from which they made raids on the settled population of southern Palestine (Num 13:29; 14:25,43; 1 Sam 27:8 ff.).

The Israelites first met with the Amalekites in the region near Sinai when Amalek naturally tried to prevent the entrance of a new tribe into the region (cf. Exod 17:8-16). The battle which pursued left a powerful impression on Moses: "Then the Lord said to Moses, 'Inscribe this in a document as a reminder, and read it aloud to Joshua: I will utterly blot out the memory of Amalek from under the heaven'" (Exod 17:14).

Deut 25:17-19 (cited above) suggest that Amalek made other attacks on Israel, including "from the rear." On the southern border of Palestine, the Amalekites also helped at a later time to prevent Israel's entrance from Kadesh (Num 13:22.14:25).

During the period of the Judges (1200- 1000), Amalekites aided the Moabites in raiding Israel (Judg 3:13), and at a later time, they aided the Midianites to do the same thing (Judg 6:3.33.7:12). This enmity kept alive the old hostility which continued in the days of Saul (see I Sam 15; the haftorah *of parshat Zakhor, which* talks of the command to exterminate all Amalekites) and David (I Sam 27:8).

We read of the last of the Amalekites in I Chr. 4:42 ff. There a strange story is reported that 500 Simeonites attacked and smote a remnant of the Amalekites in Edom. Finally, Ps 83:8 refers to the Amalekites as aiding Israel's enemies; but this is probably a poetical imitation of ancient conditions.

In Summation, the biblical material on Amalek notes:

. The hatred between the Israelites and the Amalekites is an expression of clan warfare and feudal conflict over territory.

. Amalek engaged in a war of killing non-combatants, and this has forfeited all claims of mercy ("smote all that were enfeebled in your rear, when you were faint and weary"; Deut 25:18).

. Amalek shared with other enemies of the Israelites in battles, against the Jewish people. This is compatible to conventional warfare among belligerents, and when completed, it is normally forgotten and forgiven. However, the Jew is obligated to "remember," to "blot out," and "not to forget," since the unique evil of Amalek is his war against the Covenant, against Judaism ("he feared not God"; Deut 25:18).

The biblical record sees Amalek as the traditional enemy for primarily political-military-survival reasons. But how to explain the existential, *theological* input after the disappearance of Amalek as a recognizable entity?

Why the need to mold the Jewish character by means of genocide?; to wit, "The Lord will be at war with Amalek throughout the ages" (Exod 17:16).

IV. Amalekut: Seeds of Amalek

The Mitzvah of Genocide cannot be easily dismissed.

The Book of Esther, which is read twice on Purim day, claims that Haman is a direct descendant of Agag (Esth 3: 1), the Amalekite king (I Sam 15:8), who from his authoritative position to the emperor of Persia and Media, attempted to eliminate all Jews.

His protagonist is Mordechai, the Jew, who, according to rabbinic tradition, is a descendant of Kish the Benjaminite (Esth 2:5). Kish is identified as the father of Saul, the first king of Israel. Biblical tradition maintains that Saul's downfall came about as a direct result

of his failure to eradicate Amalek as commanded by divine decree
through Samuel (I Sam 15).

1 Sam 15:33 suggests that the Prophet Samuel "hewed Agag
(=Amalek) in pieces before the Lord," His action is existentially
imitated whenever and wherever Jews celebrate Purim.

How so? Each time Haman 's name is read in the Synagogue
on Purim, noisemakers, foot-stomping, and jeering uterably 'blot out'
his name in the observance of the Mitzvah of 'remembering, what
Amalek did and not 'forgetting.'

The biblical record on Amaick defends the genocide
commandment by suggesting that this People "smote the hindmost of
you, all that were enfeebled in your rear, when you were faint and
weary; and he feared not God" (Deut 25: 1 8). Thus, Amalek is a
robber and outlaw tribe, which attacks a tired and defenseless people,
and does not accept basic standards of morality and humanity .

Two biblical characters, Agag and Haman, represent the same
characteristics. In contradiction to the Mitzvah, "And you shall love
the stranger," stressed 36 times in Scripture, and the principle that
"every man be put to death for his own sin" (Deut 24:16). Amalek
represents evil in potential, if not in actuality.

He is to be eradicated in keeping with the often repeated
Deuteronomic admonition: "And you shall eradicate the evil from the
midst of you" (Deut 13, 17. 19, 22, and 24).

With recourse to biblical texts only, we read of the end of the
Amalekite Reich: "... the sons of Simeon, 500 men ... smote the
remnants of the Amalekites" (I Chr 4:42,43).

Rabbinic texts and commentaries abound with Amalekite
references. But do we know how to read such texts?

In a paper presented before the National Association of
Professors ot' Hebrew, meeting in Boston on December 6, 1987, we
observed:

> Jews in pre-modem eras did not look backwards with the aim of
> discovering facts. They sought rather to derive paradigms from
> the sacred events of the past by which they could then interpret
> and respond to contemporary events. Paradigmatic and not

pragmatic concern was the issue and emphasis. Jews dabbled in historiosophy (a philosophy of history) and not historiography.[11]

Rabbinic illusions to Amalek are not transmission of historical data but of the Bible, and "historical facts" are not interesting as such, only as applications of the biblical texts. Present events for the Rabbis and Commentators (traditional.) get their meaning when put into the biblical mindset: God now speaks through texts.

Furthermore, biblical Amalekite passages illustrate well the strong hermeneutical concern to be felt in the Rabbis' comments on Amalek in general. The rabbinic interpretations are colored by the milieu in which they are used and for which they are intended.

Let us Illustrate.

Gen 36:8 states that Esau (brother of Jacob) is Edom, and "Timna was concubine to Eliphaz. Esau's son; and she bore to Eliphaz, Amalek" (C;en 36:12). Amalek was the illegitimate grandson of Esau.

The blessing of Isaac to his son, Esau, is that he will live by the sword (Gen 27:40), and the Torah records, "Esau hated Jacob because of the blessing wherewith his father blessed him *(loc. cit., verses 27-29)*. And Esau said in his heart: 'Let the days of mourning for my father be at hand; then will I slay my brother Jacob'" (Gen 27:4 1).

The medieval commentator, Nahmanides (1194-1270), understands the fear of Moses and his charge to Joshua to fight with Amalek (Exod 17:9), because the latter lives by the sword. Nahmanides teaches that the first and last wars against Israel come from this people.

First? Note the biblical verse, "Amalek was the first of the nations" (Num 24:20).

---

[11] Zev Garber, "Interpretation and the Passover Haggadah: An Invitation to Post-Biblical Historiosophy," *BHHE*, vol. 2.2 (Spring 1988), P. 27, The paper is reprinted in Duane L. Christensen. ed., *Experiencing the Exodus from Egypt* (Oakland: Bibal Press, 1988),pp.51-60.

Last? The descendants of Edom - Amalek, viz., Rome and Christendom. The latter was particularly meaningful to Nahmanides, since he lived during height of the medieval Church's absolutist "teaching of contempt" and persecution of the Jewish people. Totalitarian ideology, political and economic antisemitism, and Christian anti-Judaism combined in the 20th century, and helped bring about the Great Catastrophe, the Shoah, in the lands of Christendom!

God speaks through texts. In destruction there is the seed of creation. Edom-Amalek in the classic rabbinic mentality become a synonym for treachery, violence, oppression, and injustice, which one day would be obliterated.

"But his end should come to destruction" (Num 24:20), said of biblical Amalek, and applied in talmudic-midrashic historiosophy to foreparent Edom and to posterity Rome.

Thus by associating in the rabbinic mind (Amalek-) Edom and Rome, a hope theology was born that was intended to ease the Jewish catastrophe of the first and second centuries by suggesting that a day of vengeance against the enemy was coming, and that the day of victory was at hand.

After the fall of Rome, medieval commentators read into Edom-Amalek their contemporary sources of evil, such as, Christendom and the Great Exile. Again. the teaching of Nahmanides: Edom and associates would be discomfited and Israel will be saved from exile. "And saviors shall march up to Mount Zion to wreak judgment on Mount Esau (=Edom-Amalek); and dominion shall be the Lord's" (Obad 1:21)

Now whatever Moses and Joshua did with Amalek at first (Exod 17), Nahmanides comments, Elijah and Messiah ben Joseph will do with their descendants. This was why Moses strained himself in this matter (Exod 17:9,12).

The Amalek Zachor commandment is not just academic, but a verbal remembrance. It is not only recalled on Shabbat *Zakhor;* it is promulgated as obligatory Jewish law (see *Orach Hayim* 685:7). Its importance is to mold the Jewish character.

Tradition sees Amalek in metaphorical, metahistorical, and metaphysical categories:

. The Jews are to destroy the descendants of Amalek when those descendants follow in the Edom-Amalekite path of purposeless cruelty. Amalek represents cruelty and criminality for their own sake. And so do daily acts of terrorism, thousand years later.

. Amalek "did not fear God" (Deut 25:18). The crime of Amalek was an act of defiance, predicated on the denial of God's existence. The assumption that morality is neither universal nor important, and that chance and survival for their own sake dominate the universe. Amalek's perversity, therefore, derives from his nihilistic theological posture. And so does Nazism and other forms of extreme technological dehumanization current today.

. Amalek represents unredeemed evil; and Kabbalistic theology places its onus on the shoulders of man. The moral imperative of the Zakhor commandment is for each individual to join together to eliminate evil, not by destroying the sinners, but by eliminating sins. "May sinners disappear from the earth, and the wicked be no more" (Ps 104:35). Read not *hattaim* (sinners) but *hataim* (sinful acts). This supports the rabbinic Halachic thought that teaches the rehabilitation of sinners. Condemn drugs, promiscuity, AIDS, for example, but show compassion to the victim, and certainly support sincere repentance.

In addition, we may add, the "Seeds of Amalek," dwell *within* the Jewish peoplehood.

In the Song of Deborah, we note:

"Out of Ephraim came they whose root is in Amalek; After you, Benjamin, among thy peoples" (Judg 5:14).

So rendered, the phrase can mean a) some of the Ephraimites (=Joseph tribes of Israel) dwelt among the Amalekites; or b) some of the Amalekites were absorbed in Ephraim.

Rashi (1040-1105) and others translate "against" instead of "in," and explain: From Ephraim, the root (viz., Joshua. a scion of the tribe, see Num 13:8) fought against Amalek (Exod 17:10.13), and after him Benjamin (viz., Saul the Benjaminite: see. I Sam 15) will also fight against him.

But over involvement today with external powers to be the war against Amalek" as a result of the Shoah and Arab terrorism an is Amalekite-inspired red herring.   This is *Amalekut,* which semi-paralyzes and deflects the Jew from going about his/her business, ie., the redemption of the Jewish people from the "Seeds of Amalek" by doing what is right and nurturing a climate which would encourage others to do the same.

Because the Children of Israel strove with Moses and "tried the Lord. saying, 'Is the Lord among us or not?' Then came Amalek and fought..," (Exod 17:7b-ga).

V. A Final Note on Amalekphobia

Many types of Amalekut exist in the Jewish world today.   For example, extreme right-wing Zionists and anti-Zionist traditionalists' statements on the current Israeli-Palestinian impasse.   However divergent their views, the former speaks of the expulsion of the Arabs from the Jewish state and the latter insists on Jewish national contrition and dismantling the (secular) Jewish state, they both claim to speak in the name of God and Jewry.   Equally shortsighted and sinister is the oft-repeated slogan, "Saddam Hussein is worse than Hitler -given prominence and notoriety by President George Bush - articulated in and out of the classroom during Operation Desert Storm (1991).

Many said that Iraq's declared policy of P.O.W. treatment, homicide and ecocide is equivalent to the ultimate sin of Nazi Germany: Evil acts done for thoroughly evil purposes, with no foreseeable nor farseeable redeeming value.

But Hussein is not Hitler and the Iraqis are not Nazis.   There is historical inaccuracy when we equalize the Shoah with any human disaster we wish to condemn.   For all its moral odiousness, calling victims of conventional warfare (or non-conventional warfare) another Holocaust, betrays an effort to compromise the uniqueness of the Nazi brutality.

Likewise, it is thoroughly unsound and wrong headed to see Saddam Hussein as a modern-day Amalek and the current Middle East crisis as a prelude to a final Armageddon (Rev 16:16), for this carries the divine obligation to obliterate every man, woman, child of the Amalek/Iraq nation in the case of the former and million of innocence in the case of the latter. After Auschwitz, this is an unbearable notion and morally repugnant.

If the crimes of Hussein and his Baath regime are to be seen as horrendous, they are in this respect: Nuremberg-like war crimes: Rape. looting. murder of civilians. hostage-taking of thousands of reluctant 'guests'; unprovoked Scud missile attacks on Israeli and Saudi civilian centers; humiliating abuse of P.O.W.s; the threat and possible use of chemical-biological weapons; and the continual "war of aggression" fed by politics of hate and destruction against the Kurdish nation and others.

There is no need to add metaphorical allegations and biblical allusions to Iraq's dark record. Or contribute exaggerated atrocities regarding her Occupation of Kuwait and her performance in the Gulf War (e.g., the number of Kuwaiti hostages taken back to Iraq is less than 3000 and not the reported 40,000).

To paraphrase Yehudah Bauer on the dangers of Shoah distortions. False-history (also, false analogy) establishes false consciousness and creates false myths. What is needed in the fight against old world orders and establishing new world orders is truth not Amalekphobia.

And truth making is the stuff of scholarship, free from government intervention, ecclesiastical bias, and academic deconstruction.

INDEX

Contributing Authors

James Moore, editor of this volume, is a professor in the Department of Theology at Valparaiso University and the Director for Inter-faith Programs for the Zygon Center for Religion and Science. He is author of *Sexuality and Marriage* (Augsburg Publishing, 1987), *Christian Theology after the Shoah* (UPA, 1993) and *Toward a Dialogical Community* (UPA, 2004). He has authored numerous articles on Jewish-Christian relations, Holocaust education, and post-Shoah theology and is a member of the advisory boards for the Studies in the Shoah series at UPA, the Center for Holocaust, Genocide and Human Rights and the Wyman Institute.

Zev Garber is professor of Philosophy and Jewish Studies at the Los Angeles Valley College. He is the author of *Shoah: The Paradigmatic Genocide* (UPA, 1994), editor of several volumes on Jewish-Christian relations and teaching Judaism and the Shoah. He is also author of numerous articles in Jewish Studies and Shoah studies and regularly contributes commentary to among other places the newsletters of the National Association of Professors of Hebrew. He is chief editor of the journal *Shofar* and is the managing editor of the Studies in the Shoah series at UPA.

Steven Leonard Jacobs holds the Aaron Aronov Chair of Judaic Studies in the Department of Religious Studies at The University of Alabama, Tuscaloosa, AL, where he is also an Associate Professor of Religious Studies. Among his many books are *SHIROT BIALIK: A NEW AN ANNOTATED TRANSLATION OF CHAIM NACHMAN BIALIK'S EPIC POEMS* (1987); *CONTEMPORARY CHRISTIAN and CONTEMPORARY JEWISH RELIGIOUS RESPONSES TO THE SHOAH* (1993); *RETHINKING JEWISH FAITH: THE CHILD OF A SURVIVOR RESPONDS* (1994); *THE HOLOCAUST NOW: CONTEMPORARY CHRISTIAN AND JEWISH THOUGHT* (1996); *RAPHAEL LEMKIN'S THOUGHTS ON NAZI GENOCIDE: NOT GUILTY?* (1993); *PIONEERS OF GENOCIDE STUDIES* (2002)co-edited with Samuel Totten. He also served as Associate Editor of the *ENCYCLOPEDIA OF GENOCIDE* (1999), and is, today, the Secretary-Treasurer of the International Association of Genocide Scholars.

Henry Knight is currently University Chaplain and Associate Professor of Religion at The University of Tulsa in Tulsa, Oklahoma where he teaches courses on Christian Theology, the Holocaust, and Jewish-Christian Relations. He is co-chair of the biennial Pastora Goldner Holocaust Symposium and an active participant the Annual Scholars' Conference on the Holocaust and the Churches. He is the author of *Confessing Christ in a Post-Holocaust World: A Midrashic Experiment* (Westport, CT: Greenwood Press, 2000) and co-editor with Marcia Sachs Littell of *The Uses and Abuses of Knowledge*, vol. XVII, Studies in the Shoah (University Press of America, 1997); his articles have been published in *The Journal of Ecumenical Studies*, *Quarterly Review*, *Shofar*, and *Encounter*.